IMPROVING YOUR CHILD'S BEHAVIOR CHEMISTRY

Books by Lendon H. Smith, M.D.

THE CHILDREN'S DOCTOR
THE ENCYCLOPEDIA OF BABY AND CHILD CARE
NEW WIVES' TALES
IMPROVING YOUR CHILD'S BEHAVIOR CHEMISTRY

IMPROVING YOUR CHILD'S BEHAVIOR CHEMISTRY

LENDON H. SMITH, M.D.

PRENTICE-HALL, INC., *Englewood Cliffs, New Jersey*

**IMPROVING YOUR CHILD'S
BEHAVIOR CHEMISTRY
Lendon H. Smith, M.D.**

Printed in the United States of America

Prentice-Hall International, Inc., London
Prentice-Hall of Australia, Pty. Ltd., Sydney
Prentice-Hall of Canada, Ltd., Toronto
Prentice-Hall of India Private Ltd., New Delhi
Prentice-Hall of Japan, Inc., Tokyo

10 9 8 7 6 5 4 3 2 1

Library of Congress Cataloging in Publication Data
Smith, Lendon H.

    Improving your child's behavior chemistry.

    Bibliography: p.
    Includes index.
    1. Hyperactive children. 2. Deviant behavior.
3. Brain chemistry. 4. Stress—Physiological aspects.
I. Title.
RJ506.H9S64   618.9′28′58   76-4085
ISBN 0-13-453449-2

PREFACE

This is a pioneering book, a daring book. Dr. Smith does not pretend to know all the answers, but he certainly asks the right questions. For too many years, understanding and treatment of confused, unhappy, unsuccessful, and often violent children has been slowed down by all too many specialists seeking the answers for unsatisfactory behavior somewhere in the environment. It was the person's mother, or his whole family, or even his entire neighborhood that was to blame.

Dr. Smith seeks his solutions closer to home. His title tells his story—*Improving Your Child's Behavior Chemistry*. Not mother, but the child's own physical functioning may be the source of the difficulties which make him unacceptable to himself and to those around him. Smith insists—correctly I believe—that *the successful functioning of any individual depends upon the full nourishment of the brain*.

Though he covers a very wide scope of behavior problems (from preschool hyperactivity and bedwetting through adult alcoholism and drug addiction), his main focus is on the young person in trouble.

There is a new feeling in the air that we must turn from purely

environmental toward more biological explanations of unsatisfactory behavior, that an unsuspected allergic or other unfavor-
able reaction to artificial coloring or flavoring in food and drink
may be at the basis of such hyperactivity and other deviant behavior. Smith supports this general notion and then takes the
next step. He points out that it is not enough to label. We must
ask *why* the body in trouble responds as it does.

Though he offers a marvelously scholarly explanation of the
chemistry of behavior, he by no means stops with theory. Many
of you will recognize in the anecdotal and case materials that he
presents your own all-too-troubled girl, or more likely, boy. If he
is a preschooler, he won't eat (at least not what you think he
should); won't sleep (at least not when you want him to); he is
rude and sassy; he tears up the house and is never still. If he is
older, your problems may be worse: he lies, cheats, steals, sets
fires, and then moves on to neighborhood delinquency and active violence. All along the way he is unable to understand why
what he does is wrong.

Smith emphasizes that early recognition is the key. "We have
the medical, nutritional, educational, and counseling skills now,
but they are not being applied early enough or fully enough." In
fact, he states specifically, "The whole purpose of this book is to
identify those at risk and to help change the course of their
personal history early, before 'bad' behavior becomes fixed as a
way of life.

"The doctor must learn, or teach parents, to recognize the
first slip in the body's interaction with the environment
—internal or external. If the adrenal glands are the key organs
in the constant daily battles with stress, then we should be able to
discover which people will be at greater risk for stress in childhood and adulthood by the frequency and severity of allergic
and infectious problems of the first few years.

"This book presents a grouping of problems and situations
that can mean the red warning flag is up. Some require acceptance and patience; others, medical supervision or an educational re-evaluation or psychological counseling.

"Main emphasis is given to the fact that in cases of hyperactivity or actual violence, the cerebral cortex's ability to make a valid
decision compatible with the human response breaks down if the
cortex receives too many stimuli, if the stimuli are too intense or

too painful, or if the cortex is not properly nourished. *We must protect the cortex.* It is our only hope of a comfortable existence."

And, Dr. Smith points out, it is conceivable that when the cortex slips, the animal, emotional, limbic brain may take over, and the input from the environment may elicit only mean, impulsive, aggressive responses.

In the terrible child the cortex cannot do what we want it to do because of too many incoming stimuli (approachers), or perception distortions (sight and hearing dysfunctions), short circuits (epilepsy or epileptic equivalents), not enough nutrients (low blood sugar, calcium, B6, or poorly functioning enzyme systems). "It's as if the stimulus that enters the nervous system pathway (see a match) goes right up to the response area in the motor cortex (light a fire). It does not check with the area that stores the information that some actions are not socially acceptable."

Smith inquires: "Is there a gene for violence? Or does a fluctuating blood sugar level make some people so mean that they don't care what they say or do?" His discussion of the mechanisms at work as the basis for violence is creative and helpful. And there is a forthright, lively, and helpful discussion of causes and cures for the Jekyll-Hyde dangerous super-violent predelinquent teen-age boy who terrorizes so many families.

Many readers will enjoy and find helpful the practical tables included: among them one for identifying true hyperactivity, one for checking genetic traits which might indicate a genetic basis for hyperactivity, one which checks pregnancy data as a clue to possible damage to the fetus.

Smith clearly believes that much malfunctioning in human behavior has a clearly genetic background. In fact, a statement which will endear him to many is that "I suppose my problem is that I've got an idea about genetic influences on human behavior and I'll go to ridiculous lengths to make each situation fit the mold."

He admits that "genetic weakness" or "constitutional inadequacy" may be a weak explanation in the light of present-day knowledge of cellular biology, and that such an explanation may discourage hope of improvement. But, he asks, "How about a genetic weakness that allows enzyme systems to malfunction, permitting environmental forces to gain entrance to the body?

Everyone has a different threshold for stress, whether it is sight, sound, pain, bacteria, or pollution."

He tells us that if we can accept the concept that we are all chemically different and that our genes are responsible for the enzymes that make the chemicals that operate our bodies, then we should be able to accept the premise that we are able to alter our responses to stress by fortifying the enzyme systems that are responsive to stress.

He feels that "In a way it is unfortunate that antibiotics, tranquilizers, cortisone, and antihistamines all came into widespread use at about the same time, in the early 1950's, just as we were beginning to understand what cheap, safe, benefits could be derived if the doctor would listen to the patient telling him what the patient's body was telling the patient. The doctor treats the *end product* of the body's imbalance because he gets quick results. But if he would move up the chemical chain a couple of links, he could be more permanently helpful and produce fewer side effects on the way."

There is much beautiful humor. Thus the author suggests that it is very important to compliment your child, even if the best thing you can say to him is "I like the way your right arm is attached to your right shoulder," or "Your nose is exactly between your eyes."

Throughout this book the use of medication is strongly and convincingly defended: "The rationale of medication is based on the theory that these hyperactive children have a chemical lack of norepinephrine (a stimulant) in their limbic systems. Proper medication can be as specific as penicillin for a strep throat or insulin for a diabetic."

Dr. Smith is a pediatrician after Dr. Gesell's own heart. As long ago as the early 1940's, Arnold Gesell steadfastly maintained that "Development as well as disease lies in the province of clinical pediatrics." Smith accepts this dictum and goes it one better. As this book shows, he concerns himself not only with development, but delves into the seemingly mysterious *causes* of deviant behavior.

I recommend that any parent, educator, psychologist, or pediatrician concerned wtih the many deviant children who trouble us today, read and then re-read this valuable book.

Louise Bates Ames, Ph.D.
Co-Director, Gesell Institute

CONTENTS

IMPROVING YOUR CHILD'S BEHAVIOR CHEMISTRY

PART ONE

THE BASIC SYNDROME

1 · The Problem

Pediatrics was established as an official branch of medicine fifty or so years ago, when it became obvious that infants and children had to be treated differently than adults. The tremendous loss of life from infections, injuries, and birth trauma demanded some specialists in child care. My father was one. Pediatricians were put down as "kid doctors," but they have persevered and are now given credit for the improved survival rate and lower morbidity rate of infants: We began to have a better self-image, even though our work is usually nondramatic hand holding.

I have the feeling that parents bring their children in for the reassurance that they are doing the best job possible. Most parents who bring their children in to see the doctor want to be reassured that everything is all right. They can tolerate a few colds a year; an occasional attack of the flu; some infrequent fevers, headaches, crabbiness, loss of appetite, restless nights; and a few cuts, scabby knees, or even a broken bone every five to ten years. Pinworms are a must for most children once a year or so; anemia, ear infections, bronchitis, and snotty noses are all a part of growing up. A few allergies are expected.

Health-care books are helping parents make their own diagnoses and suggest some home remedies. The new generation of parents would like to be more involved in the medical decision making. Most everyone is aware that adequate growth; appearance of the eardrums; size of tonsils; swollen glands; heart sounds and murmurs; enlarged liver, spleen, kidneys; normal genitalia; presence of hernia; dislocated hips; turned-in feet;

femoral pulse; blood pressure; blood and urine anomalies all require the doctor's special skills and instruments.

Most doctors enter medicine because they want to be helpful. We love a clear-cut case of ammoniacal diaper rash or a strep throat or pneumonia because we know how to be helpful therapists. But we feel guilty or at least depressed when faced with a colicky baby who does not respond to a change to soybean milk. We assume that if the standard remedy does not effect a cure, the parents have fouled up the treatment in some way or did not give us all the facts of the case so we could make the proper diagnosis in the first place. We might become hostile or at least grumpy and indicate by word or body English that we do not want them back. The doctor needs to win.

All of us were taught that each infant came into the world with equal potential of fulfilling his genetic endowment, and if he did not achieve this, his parents, his environment, and/or his society was to blame. Most of us have been impressed, however, with the differences in children's behavior and temperament despite common parentage.

If a nineteenth-century child turned out to be a drunken bum or a criminal, it was suggested that he was the result of "bad seed." This theory sounds neat and tidy, but why *do* we have misfits, criminals, and evil people?

Ever since Freud and psychotherapy the emphasis has been on environmental influences as the chief determinants of psychopathology. This fit nicely with the idealism of democracy; everyone is born with equal potential, and with a little motivation, anyone can be President. But to anyone with more than one child—or to anyone who is minimally aware—it is obvious that we are *not* born equal. Of course personality is multifactoral, which makes the human a fascinating mixture of heredity and environment. Admittedly different children with different attributes are treated or reacted to in a family in different ways, and hence basic traits may be reinforced and perhaps exaggerated. But still one child in a family may be a wild, flighty pest and the very next sibling a shy, withdrawn recluse.

The sex drive tricks us into continuing the race, but fertility does not guarantee adequate parenting skills. The number of abortions and adopted or foster children suggests a not-too-efficient system. Obviously there are some disinterested, non-nurturing parents whose children are mere boarders while they grow. How might they flourish if they could be reared in an accepting home?

Even if couples about to embark on the uncharted waters of parenthood could promise to love and accept whatever they produced, I'd doubt the benefits. If a growing child has a choice, obviously it would be best for him to avoid neurotic and antisocial parents. Yet such parents often have children who grow up to be normally functioning adults.

Most of the children a pediatrician sees are products of the loving union of couples who desire to fulfill their lives with children. But despite this salubrious background, some of these children grow up to become neurotic or antisocial. How can we, as parents and caretakers, determine when that first slippage occurs? Is it reversible if we recognize it early enough?

As the birth rate declines and measles disappears, I have noted a shift in my practice load. I see a higher percentage of children who don't conform either at home, with their peers, or at school. The great bulk of literature aimed at parents suggests that difficult-to-rear children are the reward of bad parenting, so guilt and depression motivate the office visit. Parents tell us about night wakefulness, irritability, nonconformity, inability to fall asleep, school phobia, unprovoked attacks of aggression, temper tantrums uncontrolled by isolation, headaches, stomachaches, and a few hundred other non-life-threatening symptoms:

"She had a one-year-old birthday party with ice cream and cake. Three one-year-olds were here. Their mothers are not strict disciplinarians, but they were very well behaved. My daughter was a monster— she put her face down in the cake and squished ice cream as if kneading dough, then threw it on the floor. What's the matter with us? The bedlam gave me a headache, and she was irritable for twenty-four hours and slept fitfully. It wasn't worth it."

"Sixteen months old he was cruising about the house touching, pulling, tasting, and banging. I tried not to say 'no,' but I had to occasionally. He fell on the floor and screamed as if I had stabbed him. But when I left the room so he wouldn't have an audience, he kept it up for an hour!"

"He is now two and a whirling dervish. I can't leave him for a minute. I hide the medicines and drain cleaners, but he can climb up to any shelf. He just thinks my efforts to save his life are a game. The police found him in his nightie crossing a boulevard three blocks away from our house one morning at 6 A.M. He can get through any barriers I erect. He found a screwdriver and removed the taillights of our car."

"We took her to an isolated beach where we thought she could run and play and we wouldn't have to say 'no.' She was furious with a man a half mile up the beach wading in the ocean. She jumped up and down screaming, 'My bath! My bath!' I can't get her to shut up. She just jabbers on, oblivious to our mood or interests. If I don't pay attention, she will grab my chin and turn my head. When she was little I couldn't get her to talk, and now I can't find the 'off' button. I finally scream 'Shut up!' She looks hurt, pouts for a while, and starts all over again. I don't want to hurt her feelings, but enough is enough. She has to learn to control herself."

"He is eighteen months old and has about five words, but the one he uses most is *no*, I suppose because he hears little else. I try to reward him for socially acceptable acts, but I can't find any. He kicks off his shoes as soon as I get them on. He puts his toys in the toilet. I cannot cuddle him or read him a story without him leaping out of my arms at some slight distraction. He is constantly 'clearing' the coffee table. He has all the backs of the books pulled off. He chews the buttons off his clothes. The nurse and I had to lie on top of him so our doctor could get a look into his ears. He sits and rocks and sucks his thumb, holding a dirty piece of blanket (he won't let me wash it) on his ear. When he has a hand free he clutches his bottom; he seems to need to check out all the holes in his body. He'll even shove one finger or some fuzz up his nose when he has a free moment. He has never slept well through the night; I have stopped going in to comfort him unless he is sick, as I am afraid he will think he is supposed to call out for me. But now, since I don't go in to him, he has begun to come out and find me. I feel trapped."

Is there a common bond that unites all these difficult-to-rear children? Is this some learned attention-getting device? Do these attacks signify epilepsy, worms, anemia, gas, allergy, autism, or something else entirely? Is it always the parents' fault? If naive, neurotic, hostile, or inadequate parenting produces these odd-

ball children, why aren't all the children in a family equally afflicted? Were they all not wanted? Or does God provide some
sinners so the nice people can make favorable comparisons? Do
we have to have these losers around so the winners know who
they are?

The pediatrician has a few standard responses; his advice may
be dictated by his own problems. If his own parents were tough
and he prides himself on self-control, he may say, "You've got to
get control; don't let him get away with this." If the doctor is
interested, he may search around in the mother's psyche, leaving
little kernels of guilt: "You should have fed him every four
hours when he was a baby; by your permissiveness, you've allowed him to take over the entire household."

Why did that active fetus kick the mother out of bed during
the pregnancy? Why did the four-month-old climb out of his
crib? Why don't all four-month-old babies climb out? As medical
students, we had no course in odd behavior. Peculiar antics, we
were told, represented some neurotic, environmentally insti-
gated defense against anxiety. We knew that floppy children,
hyperactive pests, and maladroit nonathletes could be the result
of prematurity, oxygen-lack insults, traumatic deliveries, head
injuries, or meningitis. But if there was no history of such insults
to the nervous system and the child was difficult or different, we
just assumed a distorted family life. Your doctor, who is supposed to accept you, has been taught that if someone has too
many allergies or aches and pains that are not due to anything
he can feel or see under a microscope, then that person is a crock
or a neuropsychiatric cripple, and should be scorned or told to
shape up, "You've brought it all on yourself." If the doctor is
pushed for time and is turned off because the mother seems
depressed or hostile, he might give her the old line, "It's only a
phase, give him some time."

Is it a phase that he will outgrow? Or is it just the doctor's easy
way out because he does not know what the hell is going on?
Why do so many children turn out so badly? Why does a cute,
bright, happy little baby grow up to be a delinquent? Religion
claims if we turn to God, the problem will be solved. Psychiatrists
say childhood experiences determine our adult personalities.
Behaviorists believe we learn to be bad because someone impor-

tant has paid attention to our bad behavior. Social scientists may feel we are stuck within our customs and mores.

Maybe they are *all* correct, because there is a pattern in all this. I believe we are now in a position to recognize those infants who have a problem, who are close to having a problem, or who might have a problem in adolescence or adulthood. We can now identify those children who are more at risk for stress, sickness, nervousness, hyperactivity, enuresis, allergy, dyslexia, alcoholism, obesity, and other problems traditionally assumed to be psychologically or environmentally produced. Even though our knowledge is limited, we now have enough information about behavior, metabolism, and brain chemicals to be able to predict which infants and children are liable to develop adult psychopathology.

Assuming that we are unable to prevent conception amongst unfit adults, and aware that even the best of parents may be saddled with a difficult-to-rear child, perhaps at the present we had better not change the rules of the mating game, but concentrate on recognizing those infants and children most likely to run the risk of developing into problem people.

Early recognition is the key. We have the medical, nutritional, educational, and counseling skills now, but they are not being applied early enough or fully enough to prevent fixed psychoses, emotion-draining neuroses, alcoholism, depression, drug addiction and—as a byproduct—moroseness and plain dissatisfaction with life.

This book describes a number of problems that get in the way of a child's development into a useful adult, worthwhile to self as well as to the community. I believe that recognizing the child who has or will have a problem is important; it must be done a long time before he gets to feeling cheated.

The following chapters are a grouping of problems and situations that can mean the red warning flag is up. Some require acceptance and patience, others require medical supervision or an educational reevaluation. Medical management, nutritional readjustments, psychological counseling, and environmental manipulation may all have to be tried.

Don't just stand there feeling guilty! Do something!

2 · The Neurochemistry of Stress

This book is basically the result of a recent detective story into what makes children—and adults—go "tilt." The origins of antisocial behavior, peculiar thoughts, and odd feelings are multifactoral; several stressful, emotional and nutritional events may have to be operating simultaneously to produce these deviations. So to really help you understand why things go wrong, I have to start by telling you what medicine has known all along.

Nerve cells conduct impulses. Consciousness is the summation of the rhythmical firing of the billions of neurons in the nervous system. In response to incoming stimuli, the neurons respond at a faster or slower rate.

Way back, eons ago in the primordial ooze, the organisms that survived were those which somehow developed a rudimentary form of such neurological communication. In this way the front end could tell the back end that it should follow. It probably was useful in preventing the mouth from eating its tail. Survival depended on its ability to recognize the difference between self and nonself, to approach nourishment and to avoid nonfood and enemy. Receptors for smell and taste (and later sight and sound) were connected to areas of its simple brain. Reflexly triggered motor functions turned the body toward or away from its environment.

In experiments with animals, areas have been mapped out for pleasure and displeasure which correspond to that prehistoric approach-and-avoid behavior. Stimulating electrodes can be positioned into these areas. These wired animals can then be taught to push a button that makes them appear to "feel good;" science has found the "fun place" in the limbic system. The animals will spend hours pushing their buttons. They act as if they are on the verge of an orgasm, but don't quite achieve it.

The electrodes can be moved to other areas and again arranged for self-stimulation. But when the animal pushes the button now, he is apparently overwhelmed with some unpleasant sensation, and never pushes it again. He has tapped his unpleasure area.

Like the simplest of living organisms, humans spend their lives either avoiding or approaching the environment. All of our lives we are searching for sights, sounds, tastes, smells, and thoughts that give us pleasure, and we attempt to avoid the "unpleasure" events.

This yes or no, on or off, left or right, come and go is easily noted in the single-celled organism. But because of the complicated mixture of nerve connections and chemicals, the human is able to modify his involvement with the world. He can qualify his response with "maybe" or "later," or a "yes" today but a "no" tomorrow. We want to feel good, but short of that, we might be content to at least feel comfortable.

God, Mother Nature, and/or evolution placed the neocortex on top of the old animal brain to serve the human condition.

The cortex is the thinking or cognitive department of the brain. Memory, comprehension, perception of the environment, integrative functions (using memory of previous events to analyze new situations), and motor function are rooted here.

If these functions are not disturbed, then the cortex is adequate. As an infant grows, he incorporates memories about his environment into his cortex. His parents smile and show love when he does certain things; gravity works; a full stomach is pleasurable; some things are sharp, some are soft and comfy.

The reduction of tension when food assuages hunger or a satisfactory bowel movement ends the uncomfortable abdominal fullness is known as pleasure. A reward system deep in the thalamus is a powerful memory reinforcer which gives enough pleasure to the child so that he pursues those activities again and again to relive that pleasurable feeling.

Joy is a step or so above this and is related to the exciting awareness a person has when he alters his level of activity. The child and his environment work out a balance in an effort to reproduce this joy.

Areas associated with pleasure or reward have been mapped out in the median forebrain bundle (MFB, a collection of nerve cells and fibers in the hypothalamus which receives and sends stimuli from all parts of the brain and the spinal cord) and other discrete areas of the limbic system. The neurotransmitter is predominantly norepinephrine; this is one reason that amphetamines, coffee, alcohol, and other stimulants may make you feel good. This must also be the area that behavior-modification therapists are trying to light up properly; the child does or says something socially acceptable, he is rewarded by loving parents, and his pleasure center makes him "feel good." This is the object of parenting: Reward the children for positive social acts, and the resourceful child sees the world as a challenge. He should grow up to become a responsible social human being. But a number of forces can sabotage this master plan. Since childhood memories, reinforced by pleasure or pain, remain through life locked into the cortical and subcortical and limbic memory system, it is reasonably easy to understand that adult psychopathology can have its origins in traumatic events. (I read of a woman who thought of death whenever she had an orgasm. This unpleasant feeling was finally resolved when she was able to remember falling on and killing her pet canary while masturbating in childhood.)

Too often, unfortunately, some other area of the brain seems to be dominant. When God or evolution added our neocortex, He left those remnants of that archaic system still operative in our midbrain. The old brain, with its built-in responses for aggression, sex, pleasure, and unpleasure, was not eliminated in the developmental processes because of the proximal positioning of the centers for breathing, heartbeat, temperature control, and hunger. (We also need to be aggressive and sexual every once in a while, but in a more socially acceptable way than the impulsive animal.) Experiments with animals indicate we have —in the amazing limbic system between the new brain on top and the spinal cord below—a vast storehouse of built-in, ready-to-go potentials for emotional response. The amygdala, deep in the temporal lobe but still a part of the limbic system, must be the devil in all of us. Stimulation in this area almost always makes experimental animals mean, aggressive, sullen, vicious. The mad dog with rabies has the virus localized in this area.

It was hoped that the cortex, with its innate ability to allow humane responses to give an individual pleasure, would be strong enough to control the animal brain (the emotional or limbic system). Some criminals, however, have temporal-lobe epilepsy. Some irritable focus (due perhaps to a scar from an injury to the temporal-lobe cortex) near the amygdala must stimulate it at odd times to account for their sudden fits of rage. Psychosurgery has brought some relief to these individuals, who are a menace to themselves and society.

I wonder, though, how the neurosurgeons got these hostile people to sign the consent for surgery. ("Hi there; we're going to cut a little piece out of your brain. You won't miss it. Doesn't hurt a bit. Just sign here.") They may not be having any "fun" being aggressive; it just seems that nothing else is working to counteract the amygdala's evil influence. It should be more appropriately used in times of personal attack. I remember reading of a man who was always late for work. He was a good worker, but his tardiness was so flagrant the boss felt he had to intercede: "I like your work, Charlie, but I'll have to insist you get here on time. Can't you get up earlier?" "I get up in plenty of time, but some jerk always passes me on the freeway." "Passes you on the freeway?" "Yeah. I don't like that, so I take out after him, force him over, pull him out of his car and beat him up. They don't do it again."

Charlie felt these people were making him look foolish. They didn't make obscene gestures or shoot at him; they just passed him. They stimulated his amygdala, which must have been supersensitive. The police became involved and the court recommended treatment or jail. An odd electroencephalogram was found. Medicine was not helpful, so a neurosurgeon reamed out the focus in his temporal lobe. He is now getting to work on time. He's not a perfectly acceptable human being, but society can tolerate him now. And vice versa.

Despite some of these therapeutic triumphs, we can't cut up the brains of all evil, sad, or nervous people. And it often wouldn't work, because the site of the problem is not always strictly physical. When the brain makes a value judgment, pain or pleasure is still the determining factor.

Our culture still puts a premium on suffering, but research indicates that pain and stress will frustrate normal cognitive and personality development. If the child perceives the world as overwhelming or a threat, his development will be compromised.

Now we're getting close to the heart of the problem. The cerebral cortex's ability to make a valid decision compatible with the human response breaks down if the cortex receives too many stimuli or if the stimuli are too intense or painful.

A doctor was chastised by the head nurse because of something he said to one of the student nurses. To be fair, the doctor had been forced by his wife to play bridge, which he hates, the night before. He lost and suffered his wife's verbal abuse of his inadequacies all the way home. He developed a headache; he slept poorly. The next morning he cut himself shaving, spotted his last clean shirt with blood. He pulled a dirty one from the laundry hamper while his toast was burning, arrived late to the hospital, found no parking place, and had to walk six blocks through the rain, only to find the surgical patient was not prepped and had to be rescheduled. It was at this time the student nurse asked him, "Doctor, I have twenty rectal thermometers here; what should I do with them?" The doctor's response should not have been laid on her tender, youthful ears.

One can always find stress in the human; just getting up in the morning and going to the toilet can be a hassle to some people. But we all have our breaking point. With some it comes sooner; others thrive on it. A psychiatrist said there are three general types of people—glass dolls that shatter, plastic ones that dent, and tempered steel ones that "boing" and rise to the challenge. What accounts for the difference?

The human personality is too complex to allow a simplistic approach, but a few genetic, environmental, nutritional, and toxic influences are known to reduce an individual's ability to handle stress—in such forms as noise, lack of sleep, starvation, lead poisoning, physical illness, allergy, anemia, parasitic infestation, deafness, blindness, dyslexia, lack of love, gas, trauma, fear, rape, battering, disappointment, non-recognition, and a few thousand other obvious and/or subtle forces. The limbic system interposed between the spinal cord and the cortex acts as the repository of emotional response, but has the additional function of acting as a filtering device to modulate the incoming stimuli that come from all the sense organs. It, plus the reticular activating system (RAS), helps determine the intensity of the stimuli arriving at the sensory cortex. They have a unifying or integrating function and allow for a coordination of input and outflow. Fibers run to the cortex, and cortical fibers return impulses to the limbic system and RAS in an example of the feedback mechanism. In general, this action has an inhibitory effect and tends to screen out extraneous stimuli; otherwise we would have to notice every heartbeat and gas pain and dog barking and leaf falling.

Most of these fibers release norepinephrine (basically a stimulant related to adrenaline) at the synaptic (junction with another nerve fiber) end of the axon. This appears to be the reason why stimulants have an inhibitory effect on this system and is supposed to be the reason that dextroamphetamine (Dexedrine®) and methylphenidate (Ritalin®) have a calming effect on most hyperactive children. Stimulants adumbrate the incoming stimuli so that the cortex can attend to one sensory input at a time.

We all have our limbic thresholds above which we notice anxiety. I remember a recent reception my wife and I attended. Forty people must have been milling in the living room, dining room, and kitchen, smoking, drinking, and talking. Rock music was playing. It was hard to discern conversation from background noise. I grew uncomfortable but not frightened. I experimented by saying, "My grandmother just died," and noted that people smiled and nodded affably. I lasted about twenty minutes, excused myself, and sat in the car awaiting my wife. Her limbic system is better; she took another thirty minutes of it.

A poorly operating limbic system is not only a feeble filtering system but may let sudden and bizarre feelings and emotions surface (inappropriate aggression, stubborn noncompliance, sexual assaults).

A feedback mechanism is also constantly operating between the living organism and its environment. Although the brain seems remotely locked away inside the skull, it is really the body's extension into the environment. Environmental messages impinge upon the brain via receptors in the skin, eyes, ears, muscles, mouth, nose; the brain must readjust to the change by telling the body to withdraw or approach. It is constantly sending messages to the body via nerves and hormones.

If our eyes tell the brain that the horizon is on a tilt, the cortex sends the appropriate nerve impulses to the muscles to shift the body until the perception of the world is again level.

A state of equilibrium must exist between the environment and these various nerve-conduction pathways of the sensory areas of the cortex of the brain. Our perception of the world depends on this base-line input. If the cortex perceives the world unrealistically, it may overreact and upset the physiological balance of the body.

It is obvious we must protect the cortex—it's really our only hope of a comfortable existence. It must be nourished while growing, both prenatally and postbirth, and the child's growing brain has two to three times the energy requirements of the adult's. And it has no storage capacity for energy (glucose) so must be provided with food constantly. It must have a constant supply of nutriments day and night. If the supply of glucose in the bloodstream falls, the cortex simply does not perform and a number of cognitive, memory, and motor skills will suffer.

Just last week, I had to stay at the office doing paperwork until 8 P.M. When I got home my wife said something about my priorities. I began to cry.

Had I been at school, the teacher would have called me neurotic (and sometimes did) and would have recommended psychiatric counseling, a spanking, or more love. I recall a vague sense of standing in the middle of my head and watching my body do this weepy thing. It was as if I didn't care or couldn't do anything about it anyway, or I'll-show-her-she-can't-talk-to-me-that-way. Although I cry at parades and basketball games, I usually do not cry when my wife speaks to me. I can only assume that the stress of her moderate derogation at my tardiness, coupled with a falling blood sugar level, pushed me into a situational depression. You will be happy to learn that I recovered after a bowl of lentil soup.

If the conductivity of the nerve cells in the sensory areas of the brain are altered, a false message or dysperception occurs. Things or people may appear larger or smaller or unfamiliar enough to be menacing. The panic that may overtake an LSD user on a bad trip is the result of a chemical dysperception. ("That telephone pole is coming right at me!") But the point is, simple glucose starvation will produce the same effect.

I know a touchy, sensitive, and frequently suspicious girl in her twenties who had a restless, difficult, almost friendless life. She is bright and is trying to get an education, but problems seem to surface and interfere.

Jane, as I'll call her, knows the value of eating properly, but her mind gets to racing along and she becomes forgetful. She eats eggs, toast, and fruit for breakfast and vows that this day will be different. It's usually different; what she wants is *better*.

For some reason known only to her, Jane frequently ignores lunch, and by 3 P.M. the world appears to tilt. I assume her blood sugar dips to a level low enough that her visual cortex fails to perceive reality effectively. It is frightening, as she feels she may slide off. This triggers the feeling that someone is doing something evil to her.

It is conceivable that when the cortex slips, the animal, emotional, limbic brain might take over and the input from the environment might elicit only mean, impulsive, aggressive responses (the hibernating bear syndrome). Thus the anxiety that follows such unfamiliar impressions often lead to withdrawal or approach, hyper- or hypoactivity, depression or somatic symptoms. In Jane's case, she becomes paranoid. She calls out to some campus idlers standing on the downhill side of her visual field, "Hey, you guys, move over there," pointing to the uphill side. They go along with the joke and move. But she doesn't laugh or smile (flattened affect). Jane is deadly serious. They assume she is crazy, and try to humor her. Despite this weight shift, her horizon is still at a slant.

Then some feeble ray of sanity pops through to some other, maybe noninvolved part of her brain: "You forgot to eat lunch." Jane gets a chunk of cheese. In a half-hour the world settles back to its original position and she relaxes. "Sorry, guys; you can go back. It's O.K. now."

But they have already assumed that she is odd, so they treat her oddly, and she suspects everyone knows she is different. She is effectively trapped into her oddness.

She has been incarcerated in the past and placed on tranquilizers which took the anxiety out of her misperceptions, but she felt dull and stoned, so quit them after a few weeks.

A psychiatrist is trying to help her, but she becomes paranoid about his interpretation of her sickness. I have no doubt that early (before age thirteen years) intervention with diet, vitamins, and psychotherapy would have precluded what now seems to be an irreversible syndrome.

Of course the cortex may also be unable to handle what appears to be a normal load because it is in beta waves; because its cells are rendered nonoperative or malfunctioning because of amino acid, mineral, or enzyme defects; or due to a drug, infection, anoxic, or traumatic insult. If so, sensitive people become fixed into deviant behavior by a biochemical idiosyncrasy. Perception is altered and the brain makes the body act in such a way that the environment (people) perceives a strangeness. The world is uncomfortable with people who get the wrong message from the environment or interpret what they "perceive" as a threat. Because there is no way to talk them out of it, we label them as lunatics and lock them up. We are more comfortable if they are not part of our environment. Then their caretakers treat them commensurate with the label which serves to fix the behavior. All because the cortex-environment-feedback loop, once established, is difficult to interrupt.

Therefore, parents need to know if the environment they are providing is too much or too little for their particular child. Some effort must be initiated early to help any infant or child who demonstrates any evidence of an overreaction to stress. Fortunately, we now have some ways to determine whether children feel they are being hassled by their environment. But any name we give them soon becomes a label which is pejorative and destructive. "Sensitive" suggests the artist and might be resented by an active athlete. "Notices things" fits many of them; but some sensitive people purposely turn off their environment (autism). "Freak," "Goosy," "Weirdo," "Oddball" all may fit, but tend to put these people at the lower end of the pecking order. "Excitement-oriented" is good but doesn't tell the whole story. "Hyperactive" has been overused and does not fit some hyperactive hypoactives; girl hyperactives are usually greater talkers than movers.

"Approachers" and "withdrawers" might be the best terms, as they suggest the neuro-chemo behavior going on in the brain. Approaching and withdrawing are two extremes of human behavior. Most of us fall somewhere in the middle; we respond to our environment by approaching some things and withdrawing from others. But isolation, limitation of action, and narrowness of interest to the point of monomania would describe the real withdrawer:

"My boy is a lazy dawdler. I drag him out of bed, give him plenty of time to get dressed, but after ten minutes he's only got one sock on and he is fooling with his toys. I get mad and he cries, then he can't eat. My husband swats him one, then the coffee spills or the toast burns, and I cry. He loves school (where things are quiet and orderly) when he gets there, so why isn't he motivated to get a move on?"

"She clings to me like a ball and chain. She acts like a scared rabbit. People think someone has been beating her or that she is just spoiled. She needs constant reassurance that she will not be left, that we will have supper as usual, that the bath water is not too hot, and that I'm not going to die. She cries for an hour after I leave her at the nursery school. The teacher says she is imma- ture, as she just stands there with her thumb in her mouth, watching the others have fun. I love her and compliment her and try to get her to play alone or with others but she just puts her head between her knees like. a turtle in its shell. Is she crazy?"

The withdrawn, unhappy, sullen, won't-do-anything, has-no- friends, and avoids-eye-contact child perceives the world as a threat. He retreats from the environment as if paralyzed. Don't get mad at his noncompliance; assume he is being bombarded with too many incoming stimuli and/or has low blood sugar and/or has some abnormal brain waves.

Withdrawers would more likely become librarians, neuro- surgeons, CPA's, chess players, and research statisticians. The autistic child must represent the ultimate stage of sensory over- load.

An autistic child seems to be run entirely by internal stimuli, as shown by his paucity of affective facial expression. He has found his environment unbearably overwhelming. The child cannot stand even eye contact; so he makes his own stimuli to crowd out what he perceives as a frightening world. He repeats stereo- typed, rhythmical motions or sounds in an effort to fill his cortex with comfortable brain waves, as the painful-to-him stimuli from his scary environment are too much for him to handle. Even "normal" withdrawers exhibit some of this same behavior.

"Well, now she's found her bottom. It was bad enough that she pulled her earlobe, sucked her thumb, and picked her nose. Maybe she finally took our advice but could only think of this as a substitute. She rocks back and forth on the pillow, mattress, or anything handy, then gets a dreamy look and relaxes and sometimes sleeps."

Pure approachers are unable to disregard stimuli. The hyperactive child handles the stimuli by overreacting in a physical way to whatever reaches their eyes, ears, or skin. Like the knee-jerk reflex, their response is automatic. See a rock, throw it; hear the phone ring, answer it. The candy at eye level at the checkout counter is irresistible; take it.

"I remember when I first realized he was going to be difficult. He was only four and a half months old. You would expect a baby that age to remain pretty much where he's put, like a turtle on its back. So when I came in his room after his nap and found the crib empty, I assumed he had been kidnapped. As I turned I caught a glimpse of something moving on top of the chest of drawers. There he was! He had pulled himself up the crib slats, jiggled the crib over to the nearest eye-catching thing—the chest—and slithered up on top. He was busy trying to swallow the baby lotion and eat the diapers; I grabbed him before he fell to the floor. Needless to say, he seemed delighted by my attention. Now he sleeps on a mattress on the floor of an empty room."

Does he notice things the others don't? Is he forced by some exquisitely acute perception to do things that other infants can ignore?

"He doesn't know when to quit. We were walking beside a picket fence, and he touched everyone of the slats. When we got to the end he ran back and touched one he thought he had missed. He repeats some nonsense syllable over and over again. We ignore it, hoping it will stop, but he goes on for hours! He will only eat certain foods for weeks, then have nothing to do with them for months. He is stubborn and inflexible."

"I can't take him to the store, he gets so excited. He has to touch everything he sees or he screams so loudly I worry that the manager will throw us out. I can't leave him in the car or he screams and passers-by think I have abandoned him. I try to ignore the noise like the behavior-modification experts say, but people look at me as if to say, 'What a bad mother; she has no control over that spoiled brat. No wonder we have so much crime nowadays.' "

The aggressive child also senses a threat, but fights back. A cold hand touches warm skin, he jumps and screams: "He has been jumping about for an hour since his bath saying his dink hurts. I don't see anything. Is it the new soap? It's a new bubble-bath type. Did he suck in his stomach and some soapy water ran up inside?"

The more stimuli crowding in from the environment, the more active the behavior. Noisy classrooms, circuses, and supermarkets become cruel punishments to these people.

"The worst day he had was when the phone and doorbell rang at the same time. He stood tense, feet apart, teeth clenched, like a quarterback waiting for the ball to be snapped. That lasted about five seconds. Then he fell in a heap on the floor, a quivering mass of gelatin."

Among humans, approachers would more likely become actors, legislators, hosts of talk shows, truck drivers, and doers and organizers. Both modalities of response, however, are the result of overwhelming incoming stimuli. There are corollaries in the animal world: The poodle must bark at every leaf that falls and urinate on every tree he sees, in contrast to the St. Bernard who might ignore his environment unless he needs food or sex.

If a set of stimuli causes anxiety, then an overload must have occurred and some remedy must be attempted. Constant panic will prevent normal psychic growth.

If nothing is done to get the pressure off them, they will learn that the world is a threat and will withdraw or fight. These responses cause the environment to treat them as social misfits, so they become locked into this behavioral fix.

If a doctor has developed an empathy with the mother, if he has a little time and hasn't any big hang-ups himself, he might dig about and discover the stress that is behind the symptoms.

In an effort to isolate the various factors that seem to be responsible for odd, unacceptable, or otherwise unexplained behavior, I compiled the questionnaires that run throughout this book. (Really I did it because it was fun.)

The following rather common behavior categories might help the reader find himself and/or members of his family. The general idea is that the more observations circled in the right-hand column, the more likely is the child (or adult) to have the problems this book is all about.

The following group of observations (numbers 1 to 20) are at the heart of the problem. These are the key signs that give away the diagnosis, so there must be a high score here. Score double for the italicized clues. Remember the global evaluation: unable to disregard unimportant stimuli, approach rather than withdraw, and never satisfied.

		0	1	2
1	*Hyperactive*, easily stimulated in crowds or with stress	No	Occasionally	Yes
2	Motor-driven, constantly moving, walked by ten months	No	Occasionally	Yes
3	Responds to stimuli in a physical way; touches everything	No	Occasionally	Yes
4	Fidgeting, wiggling, foot-tapping	No	Occasionally	Yes
5	Climbs, daredevil, accident-prone	No	Occasionally	Yes
6	*Attention span*	OK		Short
7	Exuberant, impatient, cannot wait turn	No	Some	Overly
8	Demands met	Later	Soon	Immediately
9	Can only attend to one command at a time	No	Occasionally	Yes
10	No self-control, waits until last minute to urinate	No	Occasionally	Yes
11	*Ticklish*, overreacts to pain, touch, heat, cold	No	Occasionally	Yes
12	Laughs and cries easily	No	Occasionally	Yes
13	Talks, interrupts, class clown	No	Occasionally	Yes
14	Cheerful pest	No	Occasionally	Yes

		0	1	2
15	Distractible, unfinished work, jumps from one thing to another	No	Occasionally	Yes
16	Unaware of time of day or household rhythm	No	Occasionally	Yes
17	Throws, breaks things, toys taken apart or destroyed	No	Occasionally	Yes
18	Bites or picks nails, twists hair, bangs head	No	Occasionally	Yes
19	Tics, twitches, bed-rocking, sucks thumb or pacifier	No	Occasionally	Much
20	Chews on clothes, blankets, buttons, and furniture	No	Occasionally	Much

Can we recognize them at birth or perinatally and take remedial action? Do infants *have* to learn to "sweat" it out? Definitely not. Many irritable, overresponding approachers (or miserable, depressed, scared withdrawers) can be made more comfortable early in life. And as we'll see in later chapters there are solutions available short of neurosurgery, tranquilizers, and shock treatment.

3 · Intrauterine Insults: The Self-Perpetuating Vicious Circle

We were taught in medical school that difficult children were the result of noxious influences in the womb, at birth, or shortly thereafter. Although it was rare to find any anatomical defect in these children's brains, a history of some deviation from normal was usually present. The list included uterine immaturity, bleeding in the first few months of pregnancy, drug ingestion, alcohol or drug abuse, lack of protein in the mother's diet, anemia, toxemia, and severe infection or high fever.

If the baby suffered from birth trauma or lack of oxygen or was born prematurely, his chances of having minimal cerebral dysfunction were almost assured. If he survived all these hazards, he might still be struck down with asthma, pneumonia, meningitis, or dehydration, all of which could affect his nervous system and make him sensitive, hyperactive, suspicious, immature, fearful—or just odd. Difficulty with differential calculus in college could be traced to something in his past. What child has *not* hit his head at least once on the coffee table?

However, a significant percentage of our youth perpetuate a self- and society- destroying injury. It is a complicated interplay of the forces of love, hate, depression, nutrition, hope, chemistry, and pejorative labeling. The condition is centered about the young adolescent female who finds her life meaningless, boring, painful, and depressing for a variety of reasons.

Notice these elements in the story of Clovis, a black prostitute, who came to me a couple of years ago to see if I had anything to offer her. "Mother had three girls and two boys. Chicago was home (the city where the big rats eat up the little ones). Somewhere in the hard years my Dad left mother alone to care for

22

five kids. My mother knew nothing but cooking red beans and rice and doing everyday things in the home."

Her mother may have wanted her when she arrived, but soon found the stress of survival when the father disappeared was too much to allow real family fun and mutual acceptance. The young child must frequently hear, "If I didn't have all these children to feed" or "What do you want now? You're always after something."

"Mother loved us in her way. We got food to eat, clothing to wear, a nice house to live in; but still, something important just wasn't there. Crying a great deal, that was me. In size I was small, so went from doctor to doctor; always the same. 'There is nothing wrong with your size; your size is right for your age, etc.' My oldest sister was more mother to me than Mother."

She is lonely, feels unloved and depressed. Strange eating patterns and ingestion of junk foods exaggerate her weak, tired, depressed feelings. Such a girl may even be involved in incest with a stepfather or with casual male friends of her mother. She suspects she is a thing and not a person. Her self-respect drops along with her schoolwork.

"After a while, I felt as though school had nothing for me."

She finds, however, that she can attract a certain kind of love by becoming sexually active.

"Then just before my fourteenth birthday an old man at the picture show gave me forty dollars to feel and do other things to me. So that was the first money that a man gave to me for a date."

It's not perfect, but at least someone is paying attention to her as a person, she thinks.

Such a girl doesn't *have* to be hyperactive, although restless, sensitive people are more likely to split when they feel any pressure. If she is at all restless and feels the world closing in, she will run away. Runaway girls outnumber boys about two to one.

"At thirteen my mind was made up to leave home and Chicago far behind. But go where? Who knows? I was in the street out in the big cold world at fourteen and stopped school in the ninth grade. Now tell me where was I, knowing nothing? I got too smart for myself and left Chicago, left home.

"After four days on the bus getting to L.A., I felt dead tired, with seventy-five dollars and all the clothing I had on my back, not knowing which way to go. In a few days I was together and had the feel of the town and knew what street to work and the times. Money was good but policemen bad, so after a year I went to Fresno, a small town, but not too small."

It may be one boy, then any boy, then many boys. If syphilis or gonorrhea doesn't get her, pregnancy is almost a sure bet.

"The man I married I knew thirty days; that man is my son's father. I was fifteen years old, him twenty-five. Not bad, I felt at the time.

"Fifteen and what a fool I was. He was in the Army. At that time he made me out a check for $91.30. I was never a wife nor he a husband. By the time we both realized we weren't meant for each other, I also found out that I was going to have the baby we both wanted. So we would try and stay together for our child."

It's almost as if she purposely set out to do the one thing her mother didn't want her to. She may have felt that somehow this baby would enrich her dull, unloved life.

"In my seventh month I was big with child, and my husband was running around with one woman, then another. Before my baby was born we both went different ways. When his son came into this world, he did not even know he was a father. My son is named after his father; his father gave it to him long before he came into the world. As a little boy my son had everything that money could buy. But just a little bit of mother was what he wanted and needed."

The under-eighteen-year-old pregnant single girl has a high risk of delivering a premature baby or one with an anomaly. Pregnancy complications such as toxemia are more common. The baby's brain is more likely to be protein-starved because of the mother's diet as well as some poorly understood immaturity of the uterus. The father of the child, when confronted with the news of his potency, may feel the world is closing in on *him* and become disinterested or absent.

Some recent evidence suggests that deficient protein intake *in utero* precludes adequate production of the normal number of brain cells. Later deprivation after nine to ten months of life may alter brain-cell *growth* but might not affect *number*, so is remedial.

But a chronic inadequate diet—especially the protein portion—may affect the individual cells' ability to produce the proper amount or distinctive structure of not just enzymes but RNA and even chromosomes. This is pretty basic to life and who we are; our personalities are tied up in these chromosomes and the genes they carry for our characteristics, not only how we look but how we act. This might be the reason why it is difficult, and frequently impossible, to treat "character disorders"—antisocial, drug addicted, psychopathic, alcoholic, schizophrenic, hypochondriacal, some depressives and other variant or deviant lifestyles.

A baby with an irreversible brain defect reared in a home without love will usually grow up to be an inadequate adult who hates his mother, his school, and his society. He feels gypped, and he was. His poor self-image and inability to cope with the demands of the world alienate him further. Drugs, psychosis, depression, suicide, and crime are unacceptable but understandable solutions.

Growing into a responsible social adult is difficult enough in a family where a child is wanted, loved, and planned for. But to be unwanted, unloved, unaccepted, *plus* being brain damaged from the mother's drug ingestion and poor nutrition is an intolerable burden for a child. Clovis did not mention how her son did in school, if he is working or how he gets along with his peers, but I'm sure it has not been easy for him, even though his mother obviously extended as much love as she could muster. Usually these people are so strange or hostile that finding a mate is difficult, but enough of them do, and enough of them have children that an extra burden is placed upon society to nurture these social misfits and alienated misanthropes.

"Today is ugly and dark with as many fears to go with it. No looking back on my life. How can one person feel as much as to realize right from wrong, and then think and do everything wrong?

"Today, nineteen years ago today, my son was born in Fresno, California. At the time it was just him and me. I had nothing to give him then—after nineteen years only worse. Still have nothing to give my son.

"My age is thirty-four and what a fight! I've been off dope for fourteen months now. March 1973, I got married. That helped me and my husband. We need each other and so much help.

"All our days are a fight. Every day we both go to the Owl Drugstore to get our dose of methadone, the only dope that we both take now, although this is no good for us. To stay on too long kills you. But how many got the strength to get up and not go back to the hard dope?

"Yes, I am so afraid. God, please help me, for I can't help myself. I reach out to help of any kind.

"Now I ask you, What's to become of me? Who can I turn to?"

The theme of Clovis's story seems to be that her son was the best therapy she has had in the past twenty years. All the social agencies in the world will not get her off the street, and one dope will only replace another, but without her son to live for she would have left us a long time ago.

Society should be able to provide a few more options than she is aware of. The real message in her story is that some intervention should have been undertaken with Clovis's mother (or even grandmother). She did contact a few doctors about Clovis's size, but got the old routine. I have the feeling that her mother was reaching out for help for herself and didn't know how to say the words, so she used Clovis's height as a door opener.

School problems, growth problems, nutrition problems (only beans and rice) should have signalled someone that this was a crisis family and one or all of its members were about to slip away.

You may look on this as a plea for the Planned Parenthood groups about the country. So be it, if you like their philosophy. I think they are a beautiful group that's trying to give people options. I would also like to make normal people and loving parents aware of the importance of the intrauterine nutrition and environment.

Statistics show that a woman pregnant under age seventeen or over thirty-five has a much greater chance of having a "problem child" than those women who conceive in their twenties. And children who are more aware of their environment and react more violently to it have a high incidence of similarities in their case histories.

During the pregnancy, the baby is maybe very active—even to the extreme of "pushing" the mother out of bed. This report would be difficult to assess with only one pregnancy, because the phenomenon would have to be a comparative observation. Women report different symptoms with each different pregnancy: *First child*: "I was depressed the whole time, even though we had planned for this one." *Second child*: "I was in pain the whole time; I hated every minute." *Then*: "I never felt better. I was calm, there was no monthly distress; I'd like to be pregnant all the time." "This baby was so quiet compared to the last one. I thought something was wrong." "It was great; my neurodermatitis was gone for nine months."

The unborn baby may already be hyperactive, but his wild gyrations may not bother the mother because she is not hyperactive or sensitive herself and therefore doesn't notice such things. If she feels her pregnancy is a desirable and wonderful thing, then the punching she is getting is only a happy reminder of her beautiful condition. She won't look on the intruder as a threat. But if her husband is a difficult person who is not terribly fond of the responsibilities that go with nesting, and the baby seems to be as restless as the old man, the woman might just feel she is surrounded with oddballs, inside and out. Only a woman with a high tolerance to frustration would remain calm through nine months of that sort of stress.

We doctors have assumed that only the mother could influence the baby because of her large size compared to the fetus. But the baby's chemicals are also transmitted to the mother, and obviously his position and activity level must create some discomfort. The mother's ability to handle the stress of a baby, whether she wants it or not; her relationship to the father; her concept of herself as a woman and a future mother; her needs and a few other emotion-charged factors all must play a role.

Her relationship to her obstetrician is terribly important and sometimes frustrating when he is a rigid, unsympathetic technician; he may have strict guidelines—about weight gain ("no more than twenty pounds") and diet ("drink a quart of milk a day")—rules the woman may not be able to follow. She may become guilty or angry, which is a further stress. I am surprised that more women don't have vomiting, hypertension, headaches, backaches, lethargy during their pregnancies; apparently Mother Nature knows that problems are exaggerated during this time and provides extra hormones to hold the ladies together.

Infectious, nutritional, or anoxic insults to the mother during the pregnancy, at the time of delivery, or to the young infant are known to hurt the baby's nervous system at a critical time: hypertension, threatened miscarriage or bleeding, drug ingestion, inadequate protein intake, high fever, premature delivery of a small baby, small baby born after a full-term pregnancy, much anesthesia, Caesarean section (the operation may not be traumatic, but the reason for this type of delivery may be the trauma), cord about the neck, knot in the cord, breech delivery, transverse arrest, abruptio placenta (placenta separates before the baby is delivered, thus depriving him of oxygen), collapsed lung, respiratory distress syndrome, erythroblastosis (Rh blood type incompatibility causing anemia and bile staining in the brain), anomalies of the heart, lungs, intestines, or kidneys requiring early surgery.

Infections in the first year or two can affect the developing nervous system, especially dehydration, pneumonia, asthmatic bronchitis, meningitis, and fever with convulsions. Head injuries leading to coma or requiring neurosurgery may have an adverse effect. Pyloric stenosis (swollen, hypertrophic muscles at outlet of stomach causing obstruction) causes weight loss and carbohydrate and protein deprivation in the critical first month; surgery superimposed is one more insult to the body. A cow's milk allergy can lead to vomiting, diarrhea, and dehydration. Intestinal flu can flush out many of the enzyme-containing cells of the intestines; food is not digested nor absorbed and brain cells may be starved of important amino acids. Dehydration requiring intravenous feedings in the hospital can be a serious deprivation; too much or too little water and/or sodium may hurt the brain cells. Each injury to the body from gestation on just takes its toll; some are afflicted more than others.

In the old days, many of these babies did not survive; if they did, we had no way to follow their intellectual or social progress. But today these problems are recognized and treated early and vigorously, and only temporary setbacks are noted. If a sixteen-year-old does poorly in languages, it may be some consolation to blame a high fever and convulsion from roseola at age one year. Still, the baby can suffer any of these problems and still come through with no apparent effect.

The sensitive, touchy baby who is destined to have difficulty with his environment can sometimes be recognized early by any or all of the following problems:

Social overresponse: uncuddleable, frightened or stimulated by lights and noise, cannot relax and sleep, very ticklish, didn't sleep through the night by two to three months, upset in crowds, separation cry by six months, prolonged and early temper tantrums.

Motor dysfunction: held up head early or late; sat early or late; did not crawl but pulled self to standing position at six to seven months and walked; walked after eighteen months; approached, touched, and bit everything in sight; accident prone; "no" had no meaning.

A high score in the next grouping (numbers 21 to 44) might lead one to think about getting an EEG, as these insults may produce a touchiness that may have to be medicated.

History of the pregnancy involving the patient

		0	1	2
21	Mother's age	18-32	16-18 32-36	Under 16 Over 36
22	Anemia, high blood pressure, toxemia, convulsions	None	Some	Severe
23	Many medications, alcohol, narcotics, hormones, bleeding, threatened miscarriage	None	Some	Much
24	High fever, rubella, infections, herpes, pneumonia	None	Mild	Severe
25	Smoked more than one pack a day; ate little protein, much junk	No	Some	True
26	Weight gain (pounds)	20-25	18-20 25-30	Less than 18 More than 30

		0	1	2
27	Length (weeks)	38-42	36-38 42-44	Less than 36 More than 44
28	Accident or injury	None	?	Almost lost him
29	Baby very active in the uterus	No	?	Kicked me out of bed

Maybe we should have a law that states that any girl who misses one period has to be brought to a federally funded nutrition center where she would be fed and cared for like a queen bee. The possible baby in her uterus is a human being and has some sort of rights. He should spend nine months in a well-nourished womb and be wanted when he arrives. (I'm so discouraged about our government's priorities that I believe if something like this were ever set up, the agency in charge would only be allowed to feed the girls surplus sugar, white flour, and powdered milk.)

Birth History		0	1	2
30	Weight (pounds)	6-8	4½-6 8-10	Less than 4½ More than 10
31	Length of labor (hours)	6-12	10-20	Less than 1 More than 20
32	Anesthesia	None or local	twilight	Deep, out whole time
33	Caesarean section; placenta praevia; abruption; compli- cations; breech, face, or transverse presentation	No	Some	One or two
34	Color and cry	OK	Slow	Blue, needed oxygen, feeble cry
35	Head molding, forceps marks, bumps on head, jaundice, needed oxygen, incubator, poor sucking	None	Slight	Severe, or two of these

		0	**1**	**2**
36	Exchange transfusion	No	Once	Twice
37	Activity level after a few hours	OK		Limp or twitchy, convulsion

When a parent (usually the mother) tells us that she had a comfortable pregnancy and an uncomplicated delivery with little anesthesia; when her baby cried lustily, was active and kicking immediately, we would assume that there were few or no insults to his nervous system. We ask about severe infections, head injuries, respiratory infections requiring oxygen, high fevers, and convulsions, all of which could disturb his perceptual or motor functions.

Postnatal Medical History		**0**	**2**
38	Hospitalized, operation	No	Yes
39	Head injury, concussion	No	Yes
40	Dehydration, pneumonia, high fever, inhaled object, meningitis, encephalitis	No	Yes
41	Convulsions, twitches, loss of consciousness	No	Yes
42	Fainting spells, dizziness	No	Many
43	Blank or staring spells	No	Yes
44	Weakness, numbness, tingling	No	Yes

As the practice of obstetrics improved the intrauterine existence and arrival circumstances of our infants, we assumed that the number of these children with nervous system hurts would decrease. But as there seems to be no decrease in the percentage rate of hyperactive or deviant children, it suggests that hereditary factors are playing a significant role.

4 · When Heredity Meets Environment: The Genetic Connection

Hurts to the nervous system due to pregnancy events and difficult births (especially anoxia) have usually been blamed for distractibility and impulsiveness, but now it seems that other factors, frequently genetically imposed and hence chemical and enzymatic, can prevent the nervous system from responding appropriately to its environment (internal and external).

A mother once asked me, "How is he able to imitate his father so perfectly—mean, defiant, spiteful—when he has never seen him? His father split about two minutes after he got me pregnant."

My wife uses a great quote that seems to explain to her and to many of her friends a wide variety of childhood traits: "The rotten behavior of the children is due to the inheritance of bad genes from the father's side of the family."

This is not without some scientific basis. Genetic differences can help to explain unusual responses to family or school stresses. Fifty percent of truants go into crime. Dr. Lee Robins, author of *Deviant Children Grow Up*, found that if a boy was a truant and a thief and his father—not his mother, who is usually assumed to be the major influence on the offspring's personality—was a criminal and/or alcoholic, he had an eighty percent chance of being a criminal. This is pretty heavy news in a day when it is axiomatic that poor parenting and bad environmental influence are the major causes of crime. Poverty, race, and intelligence seemed to have no special influence.

Statistics indicate that diabetes, alcoholism, manic-depressive psychosis, schizophrenia, obesity, and other chronic afflictions are genetically related, and frequently cluster in the families of these delinquent children.

If a boy is born to alcoholic parents, he has a fifty percent chance of developing the same problem. A girl has only a ten percent chance. The Chinese claim they have virtually no hyperactive children, and there is little alcoholism among Chinese adults.

We doctors were told that the usual rheumatic fever patient is fair, freckled, and red-haired. The disease is supposed to occur in northern climes (England, Germany, Scandinavia, United States). Is it the cold crowded conditions, or is it related to milk drinking? Some doctors feel that strep infections are more likely seen in milk drinkers and, of course, strep is more likely to lead to rheumatic fever. Allergic people have many allergic relatives. Migraine is often family related. Height, weight, flat feet, age of menarche, and color of eyes are largely genetically determined.

As I toted up the genetic factors to find some common symptom or sign that might diagnose the condition more accurately, I discovered that these hyperactive children are more likely to be male (four to one) and blue-, green-, or hazel-eyed as opposed to brown-eyed (three to one). Such a child is usually thin, is ticklish, loves sugar, and is either a deep sleeper and wets the bed or has trouble falling asleep and is a restless sleeper, often arising early.

But if blue-eyed blondes are more likely to be hyperactive, how come we haven't noticed this before? Did the princess who could feel the pea through twenty mattresses have blue eyes? Perhaps when the world was larger, there was more room for such high-spirited types.

It is the year A.D. 1000. You are an eighteen-year-old blue-eyed blond living in a small village on a fjord on the coast of Norway. You are faced with a long, boring, cold winter with nothing to do but cut firewood for your mother, who cannot understand why you don't settle down and carry off Inge, the girl next door. You gather a few of your like-minded friends, and in a fit of derring-do, you all pile into a longboat with a few provisions and sail West. You hit Scotland, wipe out a few of the surprised menfolk, rape a few girls, and come home again with some oatmeal, scones, and some wild story about getting lost looking for firewood.

Your motivating philosophy seems to be, "Don't just stand there; do something."

It is the year 1850. You are twenty years old, and your father is a shoemaker in Dresden. You and your four brothers will inherit the business, and you are supposed to marry Hilda, the girl down the street. You have heard of the opportunities in America and decide to risk it. Your father is upset that you seem so flighty, but he acts as if he is jealous of you and, with a little encouragement, he might go along. You end up in St. Louis with a great number of fellow Germans. It is almost like home. You smoke, drink coffee, and drink fermented apple cider to help you relax.

It is 1970. You are thirteen years old. School is boring, stupid, musty. But the geographic option of moving west is no longer available. Because people under stress can no longer move, they are forced to sit, "get a hold of yourself," "calm down" when they feel the panic of the world closing in; they want to scream and run.

The teacher says you have so much potential, if you would just sit down and apply yourself. But it is more fun to make jokes or faces and get the class to laugh. An hour's worth of homework takes you four hours, and then the teacher complains about mistakes. Your parents are drinking more vodka before and after dinner than ever before. You feel their marriage is a sham and that they are staying together because a divorce might "upset the children." You love them but don't like what they do. You move from depression to guilt to anger to "who cares?" You don't particularly like yourself. You rarely hear an encouraging word. You occasionally wet the bed, which can only mean you are a worthless baby. You like sports, but someone is always a little better than you are.

Hyperactivity, alcoholism, drug abuse, crime, obesity, and schizophrenia are the "new frontiers."

You gang up with some other losers and smoke cigarettes and pot. You know it is bad for you, but it helps you relax. The vice-principal catches you and says, "You're a bad one. We've been watching you. Shape up or you'll end up a delinquent."

You counter with, "Up yours!" You are expelled. It all seems to fit. You've been told you were a bad boy all your life. Now you might as well act that way. Your parents scream. You are taken to counselors; they all want you back in school and working up to your potential. "You can do it if you try." You have. Forget it. No way. Your parents' drunken arguments seem to be somehow your fault. "Why was I born?"

Studs Terkel, in his book *Working*, has pointed out how few people really like what they are doing. Somehow the world has gotten the idea that restless, moving people are bad or unstable and should be punished for not having a mortgage on their home, or charge and saving accounts. You run away. You shoplift. The police catch you. There is no Scotland or America for you. You're stuck. They treat you as if you're bad. You become bad. Wine and bourbon become your friends because alcohol relaxes you and helps you sleep.

Premedical and medical school education tends to eliminate the hyperactive, although bright, student because of the long, boring lectures we had to sit through. So the students that remain to become doctors are more likely to be calm, good in a crisis, able to stand pressure, and, of course, have trouble understanding the hyperactivity they would see in their offices; they would assume it was due to poor parenting and lack of self-control.

If a genetically hyperactive doctor happened to slip through medical school, he would less likely go into psychiatry, neurosurgery, or internal medicine, which require a longer attention span. I have often thought of what I would do if I were being wheeled in for brain-tumor or blood-clot surgery, and my neurosurgeon came over to reassure me that everything is going to be OK. He's scrubbing up for the surgery and he has a mask on. I look up into his blue eyes and wonder if he will get bored with my brain and quit. (Maybe I'll call his wife the night before and insist she feed him a good breakfast.)

I have found this rule helpful, but there are inconsistencies and contradictions. For instance, many American Indians seem to be more likely to overreact to sugar ingestion but, of course, they usually have brown eyes. One full-blooded Cherokee woman told me, however, that she and her eleven sisters had blue eyes and blonde hair at birth, but they were all black-eyed and black-haired by the age of one year. Brown eyes are dominant over blue eyes, so it is important to know eye coloring of parents and grandparents. I examined a very hyperactive, brown-eyed boy whose mother is a calm, black-eyed, black-haired Spanish woman; but the father is an excitable, long, thin, blue-eyed, blond, evangelistical minister. I am assuming the father's blue eyes and touchy nervous system are inside the boy, behind the brown eyes he inherited from his mother. Spanish people tell me that there is much blue-blonde in their background because they are descendants of the Visigoths. The children most severely afflicted are those whose fathers are alcoholic Indians and their mothers obese Swedes.

Skeptics ask me to explain hyperactive Blacks. I understand that only ten percent of American Negroes are full-blooded Blacks; the remainder are mixed with the genes of Anglo-Saxon plantation owners. Was hyperactive Thomas Jefferson trying to perform a eugenics experiment? I suppose *my* problem is that I've got an idea about genetic influences on human behavior and I'll go to ridiculous lengths to make each individual situation fit into the mold.

Still, when I discovered that Orientals are infrequently saddled with these difficult children and have little problem with alcoholism, I began to ask parents if there was alcoholism in the family background. I was dismayed but excited by the high incidence of this affliction in the families of children who had no nervous-system hurts.

Perhaps it would be better to just take them as they come in the door; to inquire only about diabetes, obesity, and alcoholism in the family and let it go at that. However, the summation of all genetic influences and individual eye-and-hair color does seem to help me predict which child will respond to which modality of treatment. Hyperactivity, allergy, and reaction to sugar are not all-or-none phenomena, but surface on a sliding scale or continuum from minimal involvement that requires maximum school and home stress to produce symptoms all the way to the wild, active child who leaps through life in the calmest home.

In our search to identify the children who will have the greatest risks of physical and mental disability, we must include the following.

Genetic traits: strong family history of obesity, diabetes, hypoglycemia, alcoholism, allergies, migraine, insomnia, schizophrenia, and manic-depressive psychosis. (American Indians have a higher incidence of the above familiar problems.) Blue or green eyes in the child, usually a boy. The higher the score, i.e., the greater number of 'yes' responses to the right column observations, the more likely is the child to be genetically hyperactive.

Nationality or Ethnic Background (If adopted, skip to number 70)

45	Oriental	Black	Indian (skip to number 70)
46	Jewish	Spanish-American	Irish
47	Medit.	French	Nordic

Grandparents (and their siblings if strongly afflicted)

48	Eyes (majority)	Brown	Hazel	Blue, green
49	Hair (majority)	Black	Brown	Blond, red
50	Diabetes	None	1 or 2	3 or 4 had it
51	Alcoholism	None	1 or 2	3 or 4
52	Obesity	None	1 or 2	3 or 4
53	Migraine, allergies	None	1 or 2	3 or 4
54	Temper or crime	None	1	2 or 3

Parents

55	Father's eyes	Brown	Hazel	Blue or green
56	Father's hair	Black	Brown	Blond or red
57	Mother's eyes	Brown	Hazel	Blue or green
58	Mother's hair	Black	Brown	Blond or red
59	Parents' siblings' eyes	Brown	Hazel	Blue or green
60	Parents' siblings' hair	Black	Brown	Blond or red
61	Diabetes	None	One	Both
62	Alcoholism	Neither	One	Both
63	Obesity	Neither	One	Both
64	Coffee, cola	Upsets	Occasional	Both love them
65	Bad temper, crime	Neither	Once	Both in trouble
66	School failure, dyslexia	Neither	Rept. grade	Both did poorly
67	Bed-wetter	Neither	One, a little	Both, or one till age twelve

68	Allergies	Occasional, sneeze	Hay fever	Eczema, asthma needs shots
69	Insomnia	No problem	Occasionally	Up late, takes pills
The Patient				
70	Eyes	Brown	Hazel	Blue, green
71	Hair	Black	Brown	Blond, red
72	Activity	Normal	Busy	Constant
73	Ticklish	Slightly	Some	Very, painful
74	Nibbles	Never	Some	Always
75	Craves sugar	Never	If offered	Steals it
76	Sleep resistance	Never	Occasional	Up late always
77	Deep sleep and bed wetting	Never	Twice	Constant

If all the four grandparents of your child have diabetes, alcoholism, obesity, migraine, allergies, and/or violent tempers, and are fair with blue or green eyes, you already know that he has a higher chance to develop the problems I have outlined. It would be prudent to breast-feed him, to avoid pets and early feeding of solids, to have no sugar or white flour in the house, to stimulate without exciting, and to add vitamins C and B to his diet. If symptoms develop, increased surveillance should lead to the cause and its removal.

Genetic weakness or constitutional inadequacy is a weak explanation in the light of present-day knowledge of cellular biology. It also discourages the hope of improvement.

But how about a genetic weakness that allows enzyme systems to malfunction, permitting environmental forces to gain entrance to the body? Viruses and bacteria invade because these enzymes did not manufacture enough immunoglobulins and/or white blood cells with defense properties sufficient to protect the host. Upsetting stimuli can gain entrance if there is a genetic weakness of the limbic system. Just one more environmental pressure that makes the world too close for comfort.

5 · The Blood-Sugar Cycle

Why does a conscientious boy have stomachaches Monday through Friday in the fourth grade, yet is free of them in the fifth grade? Why don't all the children develop stomachaches in this teacher's class? Why are these nervous, ticklish people more likely to be sensitive to their environment?

As we've seen, the above pediatric problems are the end result of some environmental stress: pollens, bacteria, viruses, teething, weather changes, school—or the thought of it, need to succeed, parental pressure to conform, exertion beyond the body's capacity, maturity, unfamiliar hormones, anemia, to list but a few. But what is the final common pathway? Why do some bodies respond in different ways, and others, given the same stress, not respond at all? What are the body cells doing or not doing to allow these frustrating problems to surface?

A thousand times a day some germ, pollen, pollutant, or trauma acts upon the body; usually the body reacts imperceptibly and wins the battle. But occasionally some environmental threat gets a foothold at a time when the defenses were busy elsewhere:

"He went swimming in a cold mountain stream, and three days later he had polio."

"Every time my ex-husband has the children for his weekend, they come home overexcited and complaining of stomachaches. The next day they have bad colds and miss school for three days."

Dr. Peterson, in his *The Patient and the Weather* noted an increase in the hospital admission rate of patients with heart failure, pneumonia, and appendicitis at the time of "polar wave fronts." We all expect a flood of colds and flu right after Hal-

39

loween (cold, rain, up late, excitement, and candy). When a hundred people are exposed to tuberculosis and only twenty become infected, why didn't the other eighty get it? Were they exhaling at the time? Did they have a better night's sleep the night before? Did they eat a better breakfast, or were they excited about some new challenge in their life?

Acupuncturists know that skin stimulation in key spots can change the brain waves. The cerebral cortex can affect the thalamus and hypothalamus and hence the pituitary, which might increase or decrease in function, thus affecting all the glands in the body. These glands secrete hormones which by a biochemical feedback will signal the pituitary to selectively decrease the original stimulating hormone.

These genetically determined enzyme systems allow for an equanimity or smoothness in body growth, digestion, sleep rhythms, responses to allergy and infection, energy maintenance, and sexual and aggressive drives.

Research has indicated that every communication system of the body has a feedback control which limits its action. ACTH (adrenocorticotrophic hormone) from the pituitary gland stimulates the adrenal cortex to produce its hormones; these have an inhibitory effect upon the production of ACTH. There are nerve circuits that control the action of the nerves on the muscles; receptors in the muscles send messages to the cortex of the brain to modify the impulses being sent to the muscles. When the level of glucose rises in the blood, the beta cells of the pancreas are activated to release insulin, which, of course, serves to lower the blood glucose level by promoting transport into muscles and fat tissues. Nerve cells themselves secrete chemicals (norepinephrine, serotonin); these chemicals have a rate-limiting effect on their own precursors.

Once the cerebral cortex is activated, an impulse is sent to the hypothalamus at the base of the brain which stimulates the pituitary to secrete hormones to call the adrenal glands into action: the final common pathway of stress. If the adrenal glands cannot respond adequately due to exhaustion, the host becomes ill. The particular type of "psychosomatic disease" would in part be determined by other familial-genetic weaknesses and by the nature of the initiating environmental force.

Most medical observers now believe that a variety of inadequate enzyme systems allow some people to succumb to environmental forces. Genes are responsible for enzymes, and enzymes make the chemicals or hormones that carry out the work of the body and maintain it in a state of homeostasis.

Environmental imbalances produce an overload, causing an enzyme exhaustion and consequent inadequate chemical production—the body becomes sick. A vicious cycle is produced: The protective hormones of the body try to combat the malady. If adequate, the body recovers. Frequently, however, the body is so busy with one stress (fever, fear, anxiety, anemia, insomnia) that a few other enzyme systems become exhausted and the whole system falls apart—a breakdown. (It is interesting to note that serotonin and norepinephrine, both normal brain chemicals, are only a methyl [CH_3] group or two away from LSD and mescaline.) Maybe mother was right: "Wear your galoshes, dear, or you'll get a cold, then pneumonia, and you'll die."

Thinking perhaps that sugar metabolism might be the cause or at least an aggravating factor, I obtained the five-hour glucose-tolerance test on some of the children and, not surprisingly, found abnormal curves. The blood-sugar curves resemble the response seen in patients who have reactive hypoglycemia.

The human brain has a high metabolic rate which must be satisfied with a continuous supply of glucose—not an amount that varies from 150 milligram percent down to 60 milligram percent in the space of an hour or two. (It is estimated that the glucose requirement of an infant or child's brain is about double that of the adult.) The suddenness of this drop is a threat to the body, and stimulates the adrenal glands to secrete adrenaline and other hormones that release glucose from glycogen stores within the body, chiefly the liver.

This may be the explanation for the apparent increase in incidence of hyperactivity. It is no secret that we are eating more sugar than we did just a few years ago. (Indeed, the sale of sugary breakfast foods has increased seventeen percent in the last year.) It may be that children with sensitive nervous systems cannot handle sudden rises in quick sugar. Their bodies overreact to the sudden increase by excreting extra insulin. The resulting sudden drop in the sugar level in the bloodstream may be the stress that triggers frantic, purposeless muscular activity. Suspecting that hyperactivity can be related to a defective sugar metabolism, I asked about obesity, alcoholism, and diabetes. Not surprisingly, I learned of the high incidence of these three problems in these families. Is it possible that hyperactive approachers grow up to become obese, alcoholic, or diabetic?

A doctor recently recommended that booties may be a colic preventer. We all thought it was silly, but he says it works. Maybe a baby gets a cramp from eating green beans. He cries because it hurts. His crying is a further stress, which uses up some of his blood sugar. This drop in blood sugar is a threat to the smooth, even functioning of the body. The adrenal glands are triggered by the fall of the fuel supply, glucose, and pour out adrenaline, one function of which is to release sugar from the liver.

This readjustment to normal may be all he needs, and he will sleep it off. But if he had too many beans or if he is genetically unable to compensate because of an inadequate enzyme system, he may become prey to some other problem sneaking in the back way—fever, diarrhea, convulsion. If the extra adrenaline constricts his skin capillaries and his feet become painfully cold, he may continue to cry. If his usually responsive parents think he is spoiled, or if they themselves are sensitive or under stress because the neighbors are pounding on the wall (because all this is inevitably happening in the middle of the night), the parents may respond with anger and/or abuse—a further stress. Therefore, wearing booties may prevent a child from being battered.

If our hypothesis is correct, these children have two basic but interrelating problems: One is a sensitive nervous system that is unable to filter out the environment. This increased sensory input suggests to the cerebral cortex that the environment is a threat. It reacts by sending hormonal or neuronal messages to the adrenal and thyroid glands, to the intestines and muscles to do something. The activities deplete the sugar stores in the blood and liver. This secondary problem of falling sugar reserves is related to the rapid utilization of energy due to stress. It is aggravated by the inability of the endocrine glands (especially the adrenals) to readjust the blood glucose to an appropriate level. Many children and adults can cope with all these internal adjustments, but if we add one more insult—sugar ingestion—the whole system bottoms out.

Hyperactive approachers and these sensitive people in general are usually very thin. It is axiomatic: If a child is fat, he is probably not hyperactive. He may even be hypoactive; his low blood sugar may be because he stores it as soon as he ingests it—it doesn't have a chance to give him any energy before his body turns it into fat. They may still become obese *after* adolescence, which suggests some other mechanism of glucose metabolism has taken over. Some people can be tense, sensitive, ticklish, thin nibblers as youngsters, but their adult hormones change their metabolism so that they deposit the sugars and carbohydrates they eat as fat or glycogen. They remain obese, and constantly hungry.

Headaches are a frequent family trait, especially migraine, a hereditary vascular headache which seems related to stress. Many parents report increased excitement, activity, appetite, and/or insomnia in the hours before an attack. Children (usually boys) have a related condition called periodic or acetonuric vomiting. It is assumed that the victim cannot get sugar fast enough from the liver for energy needs, so the body burns fat, which causes acidosis. The acidosis triggers vomiting. Antiemetic suppositories and intravenous glucose may be necessary to terminate an attack.

As these children mature, the vomiting becomes less of a problem, but the "sick headache that pounds" becomes worse. It is a logical assumption that the cerebral blood vessels are enlarged to increase the available blood sugar to the starved brain, which has the highest priority of all the organs in the body. The caffeine in coffee and headache remedies may constrict the cerebral vessels and slow down the pounding, as well as releasing some sugar from the liver.

Why do more boys than girls develop cyclic vomiting? And if it is related to migraine, why do more women than men have migraine? As we've seen, hyperactivity is more common in boys, thus probably boys would respond with the more physical reaction of vomiting, while a girl more likely would respond with the more passive method of dealing with stress by psychosomatic means. Dr. Walter C. Alvarez, a longtime student of human behavior, said that he could diagnose migraine sufferers because they usually beat him to the office door when the interview was over. I have been able to diagnose hyperactive adults by observing that they are the first ones to rise at the end of a meal. They volunteer to clear the table, offer to get the coffee, and suggest we all move into the living room. Maybe migraine sufferers are really hyperactive people who burn up sugar faster than the liver can release it. Maybe hyperactive adults cannot stand the closeness of the crowded dinner table. Do people need wine at the table so they can tolerate eating together?

Although traditionally considered to be the result of stress, the migraine headache is really due to the swollen blood vessels, resulting from a chemical or neural influence on the vessel wall muscles. Some chemical receptor in the brain or adrenal glands receives the message that the blood-sugar level is falling. Another chemical or nerve impulse dilates the blood vessels in an effort to restore an optimum flow of glucose to the brain.

If a fall in the blood sugar is the trigger mechanism for the miserable headache, it makes sense to provide the body with a constant supply of sugar. Does the falling glucose level cause the victim to feel tense and become irritable, thus making the environment appear hostile? Or does some slight stress or excitement use up enough sugar to make the blood sugar drop, thus initiating the inevitable? Remember, these people notice their environment more than others. Little things get right through to where they live.

Bed-wetting or enuresis is found frequently in these children. Parents may call it laziness, or excuse it on the grounds that this active child sleeps too soundly to notice the message from his distended bladder. His deep sleep is attributed to the high activity level during the day; by nightfall he is so exhausted that he sleeps as if dead, sometimes remaining in one position all night. One explanation may be that his blood-sugar level falls so low after sugar ingestion in the evening. Thus his nervous system does not have enough energy to transmit the message of the full bladder up to the area of social concern in his cerebral cortex.

Some children will not wet if they get a protein snack at bedtime, but will flood the sheets after pie, cake, or ice cream. Allergic bed-wetters may wet after a small dish of sherbet (milk), but not after a generous piece of watermelon. Is it the sugar or the milk? Is the bladder sneezing? But stress is still not ruled out as an inciting factor; a day of excitement or fear or worry may cause the child's blood sugar to fall during sleep just as rapidly or just as low as if he had sugar and his insulin drove it down. All factors may operate to reduce the fuel supply to a level that compromises the smooth operation of the nervous system.

Even though they have a conscience, these overreactive kids lie, cheat, and steal. Charlie is in the supermarket in front of the candy shelf just three to four hours after a breakfast of jam, sugary cereal, and a doughnut. His blood sugar is dropping rapidly; his body screams for some quick sugar. There is not enough energy to keep the circuits in his conscience operative. He steals the candy. He may even deny that he did it; the brain needs energy simply to store memories.

What starts as a chemical, neurological, genetic imbalance becomes a psychiatric problem. Once this "badness" concept becomes established, it is extremely difficult to chisel it out of the brain, where it has become part of the psyche.

Basically, everything we are or do is chemically mediated— and can be chemically medicated.

We are individuals with unique enzyme-biochemical systems and different environments and life experiences from which we have stored memories for emotional responses. The trick is to minimize these adrenaline-producing events and their memories so we may face the challenge of life, look back and say, "Hey, that was fun." If we can accept the concept that we are all chemically different and we all respond differently to stress, then we should be able to accept the premise that we are able to alter our response to stress by fortifying the enzyme systems that are responsive to stress.

We know that enzymes are put together by minute amounts of amino acids, vitamins, and minerals, plus an energy source, usually glucose. As Ray Gilman, pharmacist, points out (in an unpublished manuscript), "If a gross deficiency of these essential chemical ingredients leads to death, and an adequate supply creates health, there is a whole range in between in which an increased deficiency will result in the appearance of an increasing number of symptoms."

We can all accept the fact that our genes are responsible for the enzymes that make the chemicals that operate our bodies. Is it too big a step to say that hyperactivity occurs because the victim does not have enough norepinephrine in his limbic system?

The fun part of all this is that many of our somatic symptoms due to life's problems are remedial. But the remedy is more preventative or prophylactic than therapeutic.

Doctors are trained to treat the end result of enzymatic malfunction. Can't we help patients become less responsive to environmental stress rather than trying to treat them for nauseating, throbbing headache with caffeine and aspirin *after* the symptoms develop? As the ads say, extra ingredients are what count.

In a way it is unfortunate that antibiotics, tranquilizers, cortisone, and antihistaminics all came into widespread use at about the same time in the early 1950s, just as we were beginning to understand what cheap, safe benefits could be derived if the doctor would listen to the patient telling him what the patient's body was telling the patient. The doctor treats the end product of the body's imbalance because he gets quick results. But if he would move up the chemical chain a couple of links, he could be more permanently helpful and produce fewer side effects on the way.

Until now we have all been taught that everything was psychological or environmentally produced or the result of bad parenting. All this created depression and guilt in the victim's caretakers and little improvement in his behavior. We must get the general medical school philosophy to change from "you are weak and sick because your mother fixed you at the anal level," to "people who have allergies, nervous symptoms, insomnia, obesity, alcoholism, migraine, and hyperactivity are suffering from enzyme-chemical dysfunctions and you must add the nutrients to activate the enzymes, or supply the missing chemicals."

If our environment could supply everything we needed, the stresses of gravity, light, sickness, heat, tough teachers, getting up in the morning, and thoughtless peers could be character-building challenges rather than depressing put-downs. We have ways of guessing what to do, and we have sophisticated tests to help pinpoint deficiencies or poisonings that preclude optimal enzymatic functions.

The key role of carbohydrates as a source of deviant behavior has been emphasized all through the book. The increased incidence of hyperactivity and so-called psychological problems can be related with the increased use of sugar and white flour:

"We sleep in on Sunday morning, have pancakes and syrup, go to church, and miss most of the service because we are constantly shushing the children. It's all very embarrassing, and we end up with headaches and are hostile for the rest of the day. The sermon is usually something about being nice to one another."

The delight of this new view of cause-and-effect relationships is that one can find the answer to the irritable household without going through the time and discouragement of the nondiagnosis at the doctor's office. Manipulation of the diet can be begun simultaneously with behavior modification or whatever other environmental changes are necessary to reduce stress and cheer up the body.

Sugar, white flour, and carbohydrates can only be utilized in the body when enzyme systems are adequate. The presence of most of the B vitamins, many minerals, cortisone, and thyroid are minimal requirements of these systems.

In some people, vitamins may not be absorbed adequately or provided in sufficient quantity to be available as enzyme precursors.

If the usual criteria of the approacher can be met and one can be assured that the home has a basic stability about it, and we are in essential agreement that the child's enzyme systems are inefficient, a vitamin injection seems appropriate.

I once believed that if a doctor gave vitamin injections he was a quack or at least bilking the public, because we have all been taught that if one ate the usual nutriments, he would get enough for his needs. I now feel that some people are unable to absorb the amino acids and nutriments because they have an inefficient intestinal tract due to poor absorption of these nutriments which are necessary to make the enzymes that help absorb the nutriments. These enzymes are necessary to do the work of the body. Digestive enzymes by mouth or a vitamin shot or two may get the whole system working again.

Vitamin A is necessary for normal skin and nasal and mouth membrane integrity. Dark adaptation is decreased if A levels are down. Rough, nutmeg-grater texture of the skin of thighs and upper arms may be a sign of inadequate A intake. Zinc is necessary to make vitamin A work. Those white spots in the nails (part of skin), which we used to think were related to the number of girl friends one had, are really due to a zinc deficiency present when that section of the nail was being formed.

Nicotinic acid (niacinamide is chemically related) is vitamin B_3 and has been given credit in the demethylation of cerebral chemicals (adrenochrome) that may be increased in schizophrenia.

B_6 is involved in the metabolism of almost all nutriments. Severe deficiencies may lead to convulsions. (Some babies had convulsions in the 1950s when fed a milk with a deficient amount of B_6.)

If a person appears to be twitchy, jumpy, restless, a worrier, or have insomnia, extra B_6 might relieve these symptoms. Magnesium might be given with it as high doses of B_6 (more than 600 milligrams) might deplete this mineral.

And just as a little aside, hyperactivity is inversely related to serotonin levels in the platelets in the blood; the more hyperactive a child is, the lower his serotonin levels. Vitamin B_6 in large doses will increase the brain serotonin levels. (Maybe hyperactivity is due to a relative insufficiency of norepinephrine in the limbic system plus decreased amounts of serotonin in the other areas of the brain served by that brain chemical.)

All the other B vitamins are essential in the proper use of ingested carbohydrates; some people simply do not ingest enough of these in their diets.

Vitamin D is necessary for the absorption of calcium. Calcium and magnesium seem to be related. Calcium has an effect on cell walls; magnesium is involved with a number of carbohydrate metabolic processes. If the calcium level is low, norepinephrine may not be released from the nerve cells; calcium and dolomite have a calming effect on hyperactive children. Some patients are relaxed and sleep well on dolomite; others find that calcium alone is best for them. Calcium is involved in the release of insulin from the beta cells of the pancreas. When insulin levels rise in the blood, the magnesium levels are lowered.

Vitamin E has been found effective in protecting cells from toxic environmental influences. It has an effect on many enzyme systems; it aids the liver enzyme systems involved with the metabolism of drugs and poisons. The Russians have found that exercise reduces the body stores of vitamin E. This must explain why it has proved effective in reducing muscle cramps (calcium, vitamin D, and aspirin also work). E is an antioxidant and free radical "scavenger;" its recent reputation as a panacea for heart attacks, strokes, and tiredness is largely unjustified. But the increased air, water, and food pollution must be doing something to our bodies. Vitamin E, from 100 to 400 units daily, seems like a good idea for anyone who is breathing, drinking, or eating.

In summary, biochemical events profoundly alter the ability of the cortex to perceive the "truth" of its environment. Inadequate enzyme functioning is due to faulty genetic inheritance made manifest by environmental influences (diet, poisons, psychic stress). If the proper chemicals are not produced, the cortex does not receive the environment's input correctly.

To think and feel properly and comfortably, these neurons must be nourished adequately and completely with amino acids, energy, oxygen, and minerals. Malfunction of neuron firing will lead to a dysperception; the cortex reacts inappropriately. The body gets sick as a consequence.

Humans trying to cope need all the help they can get. Assuming we have made an effort to eliminate the stress, the psychiatrist should nourish his patients right along with psychotherapy and tranquilizers. The allergist should refuse to treat patients if they eat sugar and white flour; he should insist his patients get vitamin C and pantothenic acid right along with the desensitizing shots. The pediatrician should insist that all his patients nibble on protein; sugar should not be in any home. He might even experiment with a little thyroid on his hyperactive patients. He should walk into schools and ax down the candy machines and get protein snacks in all the classrooms. Criminals and alcoholics should all have five-hour glucose-tolerance tests.

And pregnant women should be encouraged (forced?) to nibble on protein and be given extra vitamins and glutamic acid from the moment of conception if not for years before. And if her child is moody, depressed, or violent, is upset by crowds and cries more than he laughs, an analysis of his body, his diet, and his environment is in order.

PART TWO

SOLVING THE "BODY" PROBLEMS

6 · What You *Don't* Have to Worry About

Our daughter knows how to use the pot, but she is lazy or doesn't notice, and she has damp panties all the time. I ask her in a nice way why she doesn't use the toilet. She says she forgot or looks at me in a surprised way, saying, 'I spilled my milk.' The doctor checked the urine, and there's no infection. He says I should reward her for progressively longer periods of dryness. I can't go around lock step with her holding my hand on her bottom. There must be a better way."

"We finally made it through the 'terrible twos' and find ourselves in the 'troublesome threes.' I have taken a crummy job as a secretary hoping that if I am away from him I won't scream at him so much. The baby sitter doesn't care if he sucks his thumb, pulls his hair, and clutches his bottom or has temper fits. She figures it is not *her* problem, so pays little attention; therefore he behaves better for her sometimes. When he acts up on my arrival after work, I can pass it off as 'he's hungry and tired.' I feed him, bathe him, try to read a story to him, and 'interact' in a positive way, partly because I feel guilty that I have been avoiding him all day. He jumps down, runs about the room, interrupts what I was hoping would be a fun time. He finally falls asleep at 10 P.M., then has a BM at 10:30 and we go through the whole night ritual again. He acts hurt because I don't appreciate that nocturnal gift. Can I give him an enema at 7 P.M. to clean him out before bedtime?"

"We cannot toilet train her. I sing and act happy when I use the toilet to suggest it is a fun thing to do ('Mommy's going grunt-grunt-grunt, etcetera'). She's supposed to want to imitate me. She stares at me as if I've flipped. I put her in old training pants so the teacher would think that she has control. She has no problem at school because she can hold everything until she gets home. When she sees my concerned face, she dumps it. I'm the laughingstock of the neighborhood."

"Our three-year-old boy refuses to use the toilet. We put him in training pants and sent him to nursery school as you suggested. He got the message from his peer group that it is unacceptable to poop in your pants at school, so somehow he saves it until nap or bedtime when he relaxes and lets it go in bed. I have shown him what fun it is to use the toilet in the bathroom; I'm singing and laughing in there. But he just stares at me. I feel like an idiot."

Parents who cannot abide thumb-sucking, bed-wetting, nervousness, sleep resistance, or general irritability indicate to that child by word, or deed, or facial expression that that child is unacceptable:

"I suspect he could try a little harder. It's difficult for me to be sympathetic when he could straighten out the whole mess by a little effort. The house is beginning to take on a disagreeable odor. Would it be bad to have him sleep sitting on the toilet? He's less likely to wet during school vacation. Is school too tough? He isn't wildly enthusiastic about school, and, as the teacher says, he could do better if he would try. Laziness, I guess. Much looking around, much talking, much unfinished work; he'll probably grow up to be a bum. How do we motivate him to shape up and show some real old American responsibility?"

Fifteen percent of males wet the bed after age five years, but only eight percent of girls. This two-to-one ratio suggests genetic factors, although for years it was assumed to be a form of aggression, called urethral aggression. The child felt put down, was unable or unwilling to use physical or vocal aggression, so the only way left for him was to empty his bladder in the bed. The soft, warm bed was equated with the soft, warm mother. When examined psychologically, these children usually had evidence of guilt and remorse over the problem, showed a poor self-image, and in general were loners or misfits in school. It was easy to see the natural progression to crime or depression or alcoholism in later life.

But ask any parent of an enuretic child and the fact of deep sleep is usually elicited. The child's brain simply does not know what the bladder is doing. The full bladder sends messages to the spinal cord, which is supposed to transmit them to the cortex, the awareness part of the brain, for the final disposition of the problem.

"Ring. Hello, brain, this is the spinal cord," comes the message, "Bladder says you better move legs to the toilet, or Mother will be mad. It doesn't bother *me*, but I thought you ought to know." But brain doesn't respond because of dream commitments or closed circuits because of low sugar levels in crucial areas. The persistent stimuli to the spinal cord finally elicit a reflex message back to the bladder, "OK, OK, let it go."

The next morning mother complains, "Not again!" But she is talking to the conscious or cortical area of the child's brain, which didn't know anything about it. If you are on the first floor shouting at the janitor on the third floor about a leak in the basement, don't be mad that he doesn't respond. Maybe the wild party on the second floor prevented him from hearing you.

Obviously, soiling oneself is appropriate for the infant, but is a sign of trouble in the four-year-old or over.

The bed-wetter and the child with encopresis may not be displaying nonverbal urethral and anal aggression. He truly may not be able to respond to the messages from his body to his brain. No milk, no sugar, no white food ingestion, plus adding roughage and bulk laxative, may allow the child to notice his rectum and respond in a socially acceptable way.

Every child needs some rules or guidelines; if they don't get them, they will act up until some restrictions are placed upon them. They feel safer if someone cares. Discipline should be invoked initially for safety (avoid fires, knives, stairs, street, etc.). But any child may be unacceptable in a home with high standards of performance. A rigid home is a stress:

"He's eight months old now and has been sitting well for two months. Now he wants to walk; he's already up and moving about the furniture, holding on. Didn't I read somewhere if a baby doesn't crawl, he will have trouble with reading in the first grade? I crawl to show him what to do, but he just looks at me as if I'm stupid."

"I love to keep house, or I did until my daughter began to help. I want her to enjoy housework and the fun of cooking, but everything she does in the kitchen is a smarmy mess. I go over things with her sixteen times, but she always manages to break, spill, burn, or ruin something. Pouring out a bowl of dry cereal is too complicated for her. Am I expecting too much from an almost six-year-old? She seems stuck at the two-year-old level."

Learning waits on maturation; when the nervous system can tell the muscles what to do, then the muscles will respond to the brain's messages. But the brain has to *want* to tell the muscles, so motivation is the triggering factor. This is all predicated on the supposition that the brain is nourished properly.

"She still picks her nose and sucks her thumb. How do we get her to stop that?"

Do parents scream at them and pound on these children because they don't fit into the idealized conception of the obedient child, or are they noncompliant because they have learned that this is a sure way to get attention?

Years of parental dissatisfaction must tip the scales in favor of a bad self-concept. No wonder the old adages become truisms: "Children who suck their thumbs (wet the bed, bite their nails, clutch their bottoms, etc.) will grow up to become criminals (alcoholics, crazy, etc.)." Advertisers and propagandists know the technique; repeat something long and loudly enough, and someone will believe it.

In varying degrees we are all programmed to the old wives' tale that thumb-sucking is a sign of nervousness or insecurity. Ask any three-month-old baby who has his thumb in his mouth all the time he is not feeding. It must provide some freedom from anxiety; witness the kicking and screaming that follows the forcible removal of his thumb from his mouth. He is an expert in this activity and may have been doing it even before birth.

The amount of parental concern invested in this normal, healthy (at least to the infant) activity *has* to mean that someone has made these people believe it is a sign of poor parenting and/or a harbinger of crime or neurosis. Of course, if parents believe such foolishness and respond negatively by voice, expression, or gesture to thumb-sucking, the infant gets the message that he himself is a bad person. He cannot divorce the feelings he is receiving about his sucking from the feelings he has about himself as a person.

We now know that thumb-sucking, bed-rocking, hair-pulling, bottom-clutching, and other rhythmical activities that children do are a form of acupuncture or acupressure, or acukinesthesia.'

It has been known for some time that traditional acupuncture alters the brain waves in animal and human subjects. Veterinarians tell us that touchy animals will submit to painful procedures with equanimity if under the influence of acupuncture. Simultaneous needle placement and EEG's clearly show this change. This could explain why people receiving acupuncture treatment are able to reduce their tranquilizer intake.

The whole business of life is to get what one wants without suffering uncomfortable anxiety. The cortex is the first reception area for incoming stimuli; if it senses an overload, it will push the panic button and initiate fight or avoidance responses.

But the sensory input from the lips, mouth, and muscles can have a calming effect on the cerebral cortex and effectively block out noxious or uncomfortable incoming stimuli. The gate theory may be appropriately applied here: One set of incoming stimuli may occupy the nervous system to such a degree that painful messages may lose some of their emotional impact. (If I can get a five-year-old to blow up a balloon or pinch the skin of his neck, he doesn't overreact to the DPT booster I have to give for school entrance.)

If you are a small baby and discover that thumb-sucking takes the edge off a bad gas pain, you will tend to continue the rewarding activity. If your parents pull your thumb out of your mouth and frown at you, your cortex will signal "tilt," and pain and anxiety will cause crying, insomnia, uncuddleability, and other clues to grandmother, who summarizes, "He seems so nervous and unhappy; what are you doing wrong, dear?" I assume people smoke because they feel thumb-sucking is no longer an appropriate form of tension reduction. Are smokers asking for extra niacinamide (equals nicotinic acid)? It is possible that thumb-suckers have a higher risk of developing alcoholism because oral pleasures are high on their list of fun things; it also may be true that thumb-suckers are sensitive to incoming stimuli and need both these age-appropriate methods of tension reduction to control anxiety.

An infant or child who sucks his thumb or does some rhythmical self-stimulation is telling us that he is trying to keep the world from overwhelming him. If he is cheerful and seems content, nothing need be done. If he is wakeful, touchy, and backs off from his environment, *then* our vitamin, protein, and no-milk program might help.

But if your child sucks his thumb, then he *has* to suck his thumb. Pretend it is his own self-administered acupressure, if that label allows you to accept this behavior.

Maybe only actors and actresses should have children. They could be provided with a script, "Hey, I see you sucking your thumb. I bet that's fun. You're a nice baby. I love you." If they are convincing enough, they might pull it off, even though deep in their heart of hearts they hate thumb-sucking because they were told it was evil and dirty.

But remember, if you want to remove one habit, you must be prepared to accept a substitute. Children who are forced to give up thumb-sucking may become bottom clutchers (button chewers, hair pullers, ear-lobe pullers). There is nothing more embarrassing and difficult to ignore in our culture than the child who is forever grabbing his/her genitalia.

Crime and sociopathy are more related to school failure, truancy, and lack of peer acceptance (externalizing symptoms or acting out behavior).

Parents, on the other hand, are more likely to call the doctor's attention to signs of immaturity which they assume are due to insecurity or represent a neurosis and, hence, a parenting failure. Hair twisting, stuttering, tics, thumb-sucking, nail-biting, encopresis, enuresis, stomachaches, headaches, fear of the dark, night terrors, frantic attachment to toys, and poor socialization are but a few of the many traits that we parents think will give friends and relatives the clue that we are not rearing our children properly. It's all very embarrassing, so parents turn to their friendly pediatrician for help.

Because the doctor has no clear idea of the etiology of these behavior patterns, and because he *has* seen most of them disappear in other children, he will try to be as sanguine as possible with, "It's a phase; he'll outgrow it." Every once in a while this works. If the parents truly have faith in their doctor, they will be reassured by his unconcern. They will stop paying attention to the behavior and it often does go away. Even if it doesn't, no consistent predictive significance has been found in children who suck their thumbs, rock the bed, clutch their bottoms, or have headaches and stomachaches (so-called internalizing symptoms). We may be worrying about the wrong things.

Acceptance of the child as he comes in the door is the key to satisfactory child-rearing. A child who discovers he is not up to the standards of the particular household in which he finds himself has great difficulty in developing a good self-image. In our efforts to feed, clothe, love, protect from danger, and educate these children, they just seem to get in the way. We find when we analyze our responses to them, we are constantly correcting, disciplining, complaining, and sighing. They seldom hear a compliment; they feel gypped.

Just a few years ago school failure, reading difficulties, and poor coordination were felt to be due to a right-left dominance confusion. The idea was something like this: The child was genetically destined to be left-handed, and the naive parents had forced right-handedness on him. This somehow allowed him to reverse letters, words, and, in general, do everything backwards, as if he viewed the world through a mirror.

We have all heard stories of tough parents or teachers attempting to change a leftie to the more "natural" right-dominant function; the usual result of such pressure is anxiety, stomachaches, hives, tears, or at least some kind of psychosomatic distress.

Research has indicated that this is true for only a small number of children afflicted with learning difficulties. Today parents allow their infants to develop hand dominance without pressure or interference; about a third are left-handed and suffer only slightly in a right-handed world (gear shift, scissors, machine handles, some musical instruments, etc.)

All normal infants demonstrate bilaterality in the first few months of life. Arms and legs move symmetrically, with little or no preference of one side over the other. Bottle grabbing and toy scooping is usually done with both hands operating simultaneously. After eight to ten months, right- or left-hand movement preference can be observed. A right-handed child will grab a bit of food or a toy and, guided with his right eye, will stick it in his mouth. He is reinforced by his own reward, and right-eye, right-hand coordination is established, usually firmly by the age of one year or so.

Unpredictable variants have been recorded. Just last week a

mother told me her left-handed three-year-old switched to
right-handedness overnight without antecedent clue or trauma
to explain it.

A sign suggesting the genetic influence of handedness is the
difference in the breadth of the thumbnails (also seen in the
big-toe nails). A right-handed person usually has a right thumbnail that is broader than the left thumbnail. It is not from use or
being sucked upon; the difference is present at birth.

A right-handed child will hold his left hand still and scrub with
the nail brush in his right hand. With the brush in left hand, he
moves the nails of the right hand back and forth against the
stationary brush.

Right cerebral dominance, which should be correlated with
left-handedness and a broader left thumbnail, is more likely
associated with activities and interests in form, design, perspec-
tive, architecture, and decorating. My wife feels her perfect taste
is due to being Swedish; I believe it is somehow related to her
left-handedness. She cannot sing a note; something had to give.
Is her soul also in her right cerebral hemisphere?

If a right-handed person has a broader left thumbnail, it suggests that he is genetically *supposed* to be left-handed but was
pushed into right-handedness, or something happened to his
right cerebral cortex which prevented him from becoming a
proficient left-handed performer.

This distorted dominance may be associated with maladroitness, hyperactivity, mirror motion (when one hand is alternately
turned palm up and palm down rapidly by the child, the other
hand imitating the action), and some other "soft" neurological
signs. This phenomenon of handedness correlation with
thumbnail breadth is interesting, but has no significance unless
associated with sensitivity, school failure, and trouble concentrating. I have found an increase in EEG (brain wave) abnormalities
in children who aren't functioning socially or academically, and
who display this left-handed-broad-right-nail (or right-handed-
broad-left-nail). Maladroitness seems to increase when other
signs of mixed dominance are present e.g., right-eyed, left-
handed, right-footed, cannot hop on left foot, plus broad right
thumbnail.

It must be remembered, however, that all the above may have

absolutely no significance for the individual case sitting in the doctor's office with a problem; it is a *trend* that someday may turn into a helpful diagnostic clue.

Mixed cerebral dominance is just one more clue to indicate that the child has the potential of an exaggerated response to stress. He may not, however. He should be guided, not pushed, into some hobby or sport where he has a reasonable chance of success, but at the first (or maybe the second) manifestation of anxiety, he should be allowed to retreat gracefully, without embarrassment or loss of prestige. I am left-eyed, right-handed, and have a broad right thumbnail. I had much difficulty trying to play ball with my peer group. Stamp collecting and swimming were OK, but what if my father had been a pushy jock and insisted that I practice "to make it perfect?" He would have become angry and discouraged, and I would have become depressed and probably developed some convenient escape symptoms.

We must be willing to accept differences in our children and reward these differences as expressions of uniqueness and individuality. Don't force a way of life on a child that the nervous system is going to reject. The elbow bends only one way.

7 · Normal Neurological Development

In our country especially, because of the tremendous difference in biochemistries and life styles, any attempt to set rigid standards of behavior, growth, and development of motor skills will only be confusing to some, inappropriate for most, and the cause of grief and guilt to a few. The doctor tries to be reassuring—or wishy-washy—as he does not want to lay heavy news on parents who are already unsure of themselves in their role.

Still, the doctor is getting better at assaying the integrity of the nervous system, so he can help dispel fears or suggest further consultation if a metabolic, genetic, endocrine, or growth defect is suspected. The doctor should be supportive, interested, and sympathetic. He shouldn't make you feel guilty. If you feel let down after a visit, you may have gone to the wrong doctor (or he shouldn't have gone into medicine, or you gave him the wrong clues).

What follows—a few of the really basic neural-muscular and social acts a growing child should be able to perform—is only a rough guide to the parents of any child.

One month—Lying prone, the baby should be able to lift his head high enough so that his chin clears the bed. Can focus on a person's face if they are about a yard away; will follow a moving object a few degrees.

Trouble: Vomits more than an ounce at each feeding; stools too hard or too loose and frequent; cries after feedings; upset with cuddling; phlegm; wheeze; eczema; persistent diaper rash.

Two months—Baby has good head control; can raise head to full vertical position when prone; can follow moving object one hundred eighty degrees; will stop movements and listen when hears voices; social smile present.

Trouble: No smile; does not focus on sights or respond to sounds; pushes away from cuddling; arms and legs do not move equally bilaterally.

Three months—Baby lifts head and chest on outstretched arms when prone; swings at toys; sustained social contact; listens to voices and music; babbles—"ba-ba," "ngah;" smiling and laughing.

Trouble: Not happy and laughing with social contacts; frightened at sudden noises and movements; no body, eye, or hand response to objects clearly in view.

Six months—Rolls over, almost sits with rounded back leaning forward on hands; grabs large objects; responds to emotional tone; talking begins—repetition of self-produced sounds; head turns to sounds.

Trouble: Ear infections already; constant mouth or noisy breathing; sneezes more than six times a day; chronic cough; all solids cause gas; changed formula at least twice already; constipation alternates with diarrhea; tenseness and touchiness alternate with lethargy and withdrawnness; cannot relax and sleep when obviously tired; crawls all over bed; cries out or wakeful at night; still hungry at 2 A.M.; stops babbling; does not repeat sounds (own or others); no interest in toys.

Nine months—Sits alone well with back straight; pulls to standing; crawls; pinches with thumb and forefinger; pokes with forefinger, persistence of interest in one toy or object; understands that something out of sight may still exist; cries on separation; vocalizes demands; "mama," "dada;" responds to name; loves peek-a-boo; waves bye-bye; laughs a lot; pleasure at familiar voices or faces.

Trouble: Falls over if left sitting unsupported (motor retardation) or approacher (got up by nine months to walk with little or no crawling); touches, destroys, or eats everything in sight; over-reacts to tickling, noises, or separation—cries until exhausted; little or no response to voices.

One year—Walks holding on to hand; has anticipatory gestures: holds up arms to be picked up; releases object on request; can retrieve hidden objects; imitates words and inflections of sound;

understands "no-no;" has vocabulary of three or four words; rolls ball back; holds still for dressing, hand-to-mouth feeding. *Trouble:* Too distractible to eat with family; definite food likes and dislikes; cries in crowd; clings in panic to mother in strange situations or may leap in to any situation despite obvious danger; red perianal rash with many foods; chronic runny nose not related to teething; fever with each tooth; many ear infections or attacks of wheezing bronchitis; sick on holidays when routine changes occur; no facial expression of emotion; appears depressed; dark circles under eyes.

Eighteen months—Runs; seats self in small chair; into drawers; piles three cubes; scribbles; imitates vertical strokes with crayon; four to fifteen words; names objects; echoes words; jargon: imitates speed and inflection; uses m, n, p, b, and d; uses spoon crudely; may indicate soiled diaper.

Trouble: Constantly moving; accident prone; ingests poisons; "no" has no meaning; climbs and falls; daredevil; picky eater; prefers many small feedings; loves starches and sweets; hates to chew meat; thin or fat; easily frustrated; never satisfied; approaches and destroys; breaks toys; repeats one word for hours; cries out or still wakeful at night; eczema gone but now has asthma.

Two years—Runs well; climbs stairs; opens doors; piles six cubes into tower; imitates circular scribbling and horizontal strokes; helps to undress; turns pages of books singly; listens to stories with pictures; puts three words together ("I go bye-bye"); nouns are half the vocabulary, understands twenty to one hundred words; points to own body parts.

Much emphasis has been put on the acquisition of linguistic skills because facility with language is a reflection of the integrity of various areas of the cortex and is little-influenced or only temporarily warped by environmental factors. Speech development of normal-hearing children of deaf parents is virtually unaffected by the minimal language stimulation in their homes. Institutionalized children may show some delays, but with adequate stimulation they catch up rapidly.

The importance of early detection of hearing loss seems justified as communication is based on adequate auditory input. Early proper training can prevent language retardation. Children with hearing loss and language delay are frequently considered stupid, and suffer all the stresses that their peer group and school can heap on them.

Trouble: May have been quiet and compliant—now runs, hits, and whines; bent on destruction; mean; cuddling impossible; squirmy; won't sit and listen to story; tears book apart; "I hit you;" parents find they say "no" to everything he does; worse in crowd or supermarket; refuses nap; up late or on different timetable; speech is a word salad; frequent earaches, snoring, wheezing, or intestinal upsets.

Three years—Alternates feet going up the stairs; can ride tricycle; can stand momentarily on one foot; makes tower of nine cubes; copies a circle; knows age and sex; counts three objects; makes simple declarative sentences; pronounces all vowels; five-hundred-plus words in vocabulary; responds to simple commands; understands opposites (come/go, push/pull, etc.); unbuttons clothes; puts on shoes; washes hands; plays games in parallel with other children.

Trouble: Appears frightened in new situations—sits quietly wide-eyed, sucking thumb, twisting hair, withdrawn; refuses to join in on nursery school activities; holds back; screams if forced into new activity, or may dash headlong into everything; accidents; showoff; communicates by hitting, biting, scratching; runs over pets with tricycle; aggressive; fights when put to bed; ticklish—laughs till cries or vomits; noticeably upset (withdrawn or hyperactive) when parents argue; scribbles violently, holding crayon in fist; tears clothes off, ignoring buttons; washes whole bathroom but stays dirty; hard to understand; very frightened of doctor; trouble imitating words, designs, movements; does not understand games, but able to take machines apart; lights fires; still picky about food; fat or thin; craves sugar; may love beer, wine, or cola beverages.

Four years—Hops on one foot; throws overhand; uses scissors; climbs well; copies cross and square; draws a man with two parts besides head; counts four objects; tells a story; can transform declarative sentences by using adjectives, contractions, negatives, conjunctions; knows what objects are used for; vocabulary about one thousand words; can execute two-part commands; should articulate correctly *m*, *b*, *d*, *n*, *p*, *f*, *h*, *w* most of the time; social interaction with other children; toilet alone.

Trouble: Either clumsy or very adroit; speech too fast or too slow;

unsure of eye and hand preference; still needs to suck thumb, rock bed, or do some rhythmical activity; stereotyped behavior; avoids eye contact; cannot be talked out of fears; too shy or too forward in social contacts; temper outbursts, isolates self; soils self; Jekyll and Hyde personality.

Five years—Skips; copies triangles; knows four colors; counts to ten accurately; dresses and undresses; can repeat a ten to twelve syllable sentence; vocabulary of two thousand words; can articulate k, t, g, ng most of time.

Trouble: Can skip on one foot but not the other; marked difference in rapid-movement skills of hands; clothes on backwards; selfish; sullen; makes odd noises; no friends; fiddles with objects or buttons; no self-control; confused when given too many directions; needs to win; everything must go his way; teases others, but cannot take criticism; selfish; never does fair share of chores; night terrors or deep sleep and bed-wetting; stuttering, stammering.

Six to seven years—Use of future tense; understands left and right; qualitative (little and big, fast and slow); articulates wh, j, f, l, r, sh, ch, s, th, v; knows phone number; can repeat five numbers in sequence; good auditory perception (can distinguish *cat* from *cap*, and *pat* from *pet*).

For auditory stimuli to be meaningful, there must be an intact auditory perceptual system which transmits, processes, stores, and retrieves information provided by the peripheral hearing mechanism. It allows focusing on words while blocking out irrelevant stimuli. It enables identification of a single voice. It allows recognition of *hat* as one of the *-at* words that rhymes with *cat*.

About one third of deaf people have a hereditary factor that predisposes them; others have been hurt because of congenital rubella or other diseases, prematurity, or newborn jaundice. Repeated ear infections and allergies cause much hearing loss, but this type of loss usually occurs after infancy and is less likely to be permanent.

Trouble: Other children pick on him; he responds with tears or fighting; chip on shoulder; never satisfied; plays with children younger than he; bossy; with authority he is stubborn, defiant, impudent, or shy, fearful, or submissive; fidgets constantly when concentrating; inconsistent—seems to understand letters, words, and numbers one day, then it is all lost the very next day, as if a trap door in his brain opened and all the carefully stacked information fell out; circles under eyes; pale despite a normal hemoglobin level in blood (not anemic); tired; cannot keep up, discouraged; headaches and stomachaches; muscle aches; shin splints; prefers things or spirited animals (dogs and horses) to people.

Finger agnosia—the inability to lift fingers or identify fingers or note difference between them—is abnormal by age six years. Over the age of six there should be no confusion between left and right. Involuntary motions of the left hand that mirror the activity of the right hand may be normal in a seven-year-old but not in a nine-year-old. A nine-year-old should be able to separate eye motion and head motion.

A few *yeses* in the right-hand column in the following grouping (numbers 78 to 101) are compatible with normality, but are more likely associated with developmental lags. Primary retardation has to be thought of if the child is slow in *all* areas: motor, speech, cognitive, and social. It can be a result of perception difficultie∷ (vision and hearing inadequacies, or a problem with the cortex getting the message accurately). "Yes" responses in the following group of observations are usually the result of "yes" difficulties in group 21 to 44. Anemia, sickness, low thyroid, PKU, autism, and a general lack of environmental stimulation must be considered. Extra diagnostic help for children involved with these problems may be sought from the testing psychologist, the perception-motor testing specialist, and sometimes from the EEG.

General motor, cognitive, speech and social development

		0	1
78	Smiled socially	by 6 weeks	after 6 weeks
79	Turned over	by 6 months	after 6 months
80	Sat well	by 8 months	after 8 months
81	Crawled	by 9 months	after 9 months
82	Stood with support	by 1 year	after 1 year
83	Walked alone	by 15 months	after 15 months
84	Fed self with fingers	by 1 year	after 1 year
85	Fed self with spoon	by 18 months	after 18 months

		0	1
86	Understood "no-no"	by 1 year	after 1 year
87	Played pat-a-cake	by 1 year	after 1 year
88	Two- or three-word sentences	by 2 years	after 2 years
89	Toilet trained (girl)	by 2 years	after 2 years
	(boy)	by 3 years	after 3 years
90	Dressed self without help	by 5 years	after 5 years
91	Threw, caught ball; rode tricycle	by 5 years	after 6 years

After 6 years of age:

		0	1
92	Accident prone, clumsy	no	yes
93	Prefers younger playmates	no	yes
94	Refuses to try new things	no	yes
95	Odd gait; walks on toes	no	yes
96	Stutter, stammer, baby talk, fumbles for right words	no	yes
97	Reading problem, glasses, lazy eye	no	yes
98	Handwriting	legible	awful
99	Arithmetic	understands	trouble
100	Right-left confusion	none	yes
101	Laces and zippers always open	no	yes

The doctor's examination—Most parents who bring their children into the pediatrician regularly are already aware of the need for and are practicing love and meaningful stimulation for their children. They usually know more about the child's strengths and weaknesses than the doctor could possibly find out with all his tests. Still, if the doctor has known the child all his life, he usually has some suspicion about his patient's competence long before he gets to school. Each doctor has his own method of examining a child for clues that tell him there is a problem.

Palpating the abdomen is very upsetting to these sensitive people. I have acoustical tile on my office ceiling and if he is old enough to count, I have him—while supine—count the number of holes in one row of one square while I poke about in the liver and spleen areas. If he is truly hyperactive, he is really ticklish and cannot count beyond five holes without breaking up and almost rolling on the floor. The finger-in-the-groin check for hernia is virtually impossible with his back against the wall, me on the floor, and our heads banging together.

How much of a threat does his environment seem to him? Does he panic at the thought of a shot? Some subtle things like unwillingness to undress, how well he leaps up on the table, how he winces when an instrument touches him, are all being graded in the doctor's mind on a scale of zero to two that indicates the child's ability to handle stress, and of course suggests his chances of success in school.

I have used a few tests of fine and gross motor skills to give me clues as to the child's neurological integrity; the following observations are general signs of the genetic, hyperactive, sensitive child:

		0	1	2
102	Complains of temperature of room, stethoscope	no	some	a lot
103	Climbs or jumps onto table	can't or won't	needs help	easily
104	Restless, moving, swings legs	none	some	constant
105	Pulse rate	90-120	60-90	less than 60

(One would think that these active people would have a rapid pulse, but it is slow. I assume that because they are always running, their hearts are at maximum efficiency, i.e., slow.)

106	Ticklish. (Can't count more than five holes on the ceiling when abdomen is palpated)	23	5-20	less than 5

		0	1	2
107	Hernia check	OK	backs up	impossible
108	Mirror motion, arms at sides (when one arm is turned back and forth, the other arm imitates that motion)	1+	2-3+	4+
109	Mirror motion, seated, hands on thighs. (Rapidly turn palms up then palms down, slapping the thighs each time; repeat with one hand in air. If the raised hand imitates the turning on the thigh hand, that's mirror motion.)	1+	2-3+	4+

The following group, if scored high, would reflect more neurological trouble and perception-motor difficulties and reading problems. If associated with a high score in group 21 to 44, a neurological workup and/or an EEG might be worthwhile.

		0	1	2
110	Gross motor (walks backwards on heels, hops on one foot)	OK	difficult	clumsy
111	Fine motor (rapid fingers-thumb)	OK	hard	impossible
112	Eye tracking (follows examiner's finger without moving head)	OK		moves head
113	Establish handedness (check breadth of thumb nails)	same		broad right nail, left-handed
114	Establish eye preference	same		different
115	Establish foot preference	same		different
116	Touch left hand to right ear, etc.	OK		confused

	0	**1**	**2**
117 Writing. Dictate: "The boy had a dog."		OK for age	impossible reckless speed
118 Reversals ("was" for "saw")		none	many
119 Clumsy, crude, slow, disjointed		no	really awful
Copy:		OK for age	can't do it
○		3	3
+		4	4
□		5	5
△		6	6
◇— (diamond with line)		9-10	9-10

We also watch for failure to touch fingers rapidly and in sequence with thumb of same hand; difficulty in walking along a narrow line; accentuated extension of arms when walking on tip-toe. How long can the child sit still with the hands relaxed hanging between knees? Dextroamphetamine responders twitched a finger in less than thirty seconds.

I use the *Cognitive Skills Assessment Battery* (Boehm and Slater, published by Teachers College Press) and find it useful in evaluating kindergarten and first-grade readiness.

The Denver Development Test is valuable to assess a child's neuromuscular, social, language, and cognitive skills; and all doctors, counselors, and teachers (and probably parents) should be familiar with it. Most of us have the child draw a man. It's a rough little IQ test as well as a fair perception-motor abilities test, and has some predictive ability for academic performance.

The child has to be comfortably seated with a pencil and an 8½-by-11-inch piece of paper. Beginning at a basal level of three years, the maturational level is determined by adding one-quarter year for each point as determined by the number of parts drawn. Hence, if a four-year-old child can draw a head (one point), legs (one point), arms (one point), eyes (one point), and mouth (one point), his level is four and one-quarter years. This would indicate that his perception of the world and his ability to reproduce his perception are on a par with his age. Dr. Louise Bates Ames told me that having the child *complete* a man may even be a better way to test the perception-motor integrity.

It is difficult to tell sometimes if the problem lies in the reception of the incoming stimuli or if the brain is having trouble telling the muscles exactly what it wants them to do. But one thing *is* clear: It is no surprise to note a difference in the drawings from the same child depending on his recent diet.

8 · Allergies and Adrenaline

Allergic symptoms include—but are not limited to—colic, many necessary changes of milk, gas, eczema, asthma, chronic nasal discharge, repeated rashes, constipation, and diarrhea.

Parents report: "He had a stuffy nose from birth. Snort, gasp, gag, zonk, sneeze, sniff, and cough were constant indoors and out, night and day. Antihistamines helped temporarily. Aspirin stimulated him. Actifed® quieted him, as did your gin-lemon juice-honey remedy for croup. Every cold led to an ear infection or bronchitis or asthma, requiring antibiotics. He always ran a fever with tooth eruptions. He had a convulsion when he had baby measles (roseola). Every time I introduced some new food, he would have terrible gas and sloppy stools for three days. Our daughter had several bladder or kidney infections, but the X-ray investigation showed no structural anomalies. He had pimples and boils on his buttocks after Easter and Halloween. Soap dried out his skin; the supposedly relaxing bath ended with a night of restlessness and scratching. Instead of dandruff he had crusty eyelids and thick scabby sores. He got huge reactions to flea and mosquito bites; he would dig the tops off and then get impetigo, requiring some antibiotic treatment. Cracks in the skin just behind his ears had to be treated with cortisone ointment or they got infected. He had severe eczema for his whole first year; we must have spent thirty dollars a month on medicines, soaps, and lubricants for his dry, itchy skin. He's got this red patch on his cheek that won't go away. Some days it is very red and he digs at it. Last summer it turned into a white, scaly area surrounded by

71

his tanned skin. Some cortisone ointment I had lying around
helped for a while, but it soon came back. Orange juice makes it
worse."

Parents report that allergy-prone children also have much gas,
vomiting, diarrhea, wheeze, croup, phlegm, noisy breathing, ear
infections, deafness from fluid accumulation behind the eardrums necessitating allergy testing and desensitizing shots, ton-
sillectomy and adenoidectomy, tubes placed in the eardrums to
aerate the middle ear, many antibiotics and hospitalizations for
asthma, bronchitis, fevers, and dehydration.

It is quite obvious to anyone who is a parent of more than one
child that there are individual differences in activity level and in
susceptibility to infections. Evidence is accumulating to indicate
that behavior problems, allergies, and infections are more likely
to occur in the same children. The concept of psychosomatic
illness is based on this relationship. Nervous people have a high
rate of asthma, hypertension, ulcers, irritable bowels, migraine,
weak feelings, tiredness, and anxiety attacks.

Doctors are reasonably skilled in the detection and the treatment of disease, but unsure of the reason for the persistence of
symptoms or the frequency of the recurrence of some diseases.
Perhaps if we could find a common factor, we could eliminate
the susceptibility to the diseases (somatic end result) as well as
the triggering factor in the psyche.

The asthma or hay fever sufferer gets antihistamines, cortisone, and desensitizing shots, but we should explore the reason
why he developed the allergy in the first place.

Allergy is a complicated phenomenon, but its secrets are being
exposed by research. Allergy is a familial trait; afflicted children
come from families that seem to have more than their share of
victims of hay fever, asthma, hives, gas from foods, bouts of
diarrhea, pimples on their buttocks from chocolate, and a collection of symptoms called tension-fatigue syndrome. We can understand the genetic passage of these undesirable traits, but not
how this information is passed from the DNA to the RNA to the
cytoplasmic chemicals that must cause the intestinal muscle to
contract or the nasal mucous cells to pour out secretions.

Abnormalities of a blood protein, globulin E, is found in
atopic people. (Atopy is the familial condition which creates a

susceptibility to eczema, asthma, hay fever, and hives.) Environmental stress, pollutants, dust, and some foods make these people worse, another example of the environment acting upon a weak enzyme which is due to a defective gene. Treatment with antihistamines, cortisone, and desensitization has been largely to control the flare-ups, but little has been done until recently to change the E globulin or to support the faltering enzymes:

"Our neighbors reported us to the local county social agency because she looked so malnourished: pale and potbellied. We finally found a doctor who discovered a wheat intolerance. She's perfect now on protein, fruit, and rice."

Is it enough to find out that grandmother has asthma and father has hay fever? "Aha! That's it! He's allergic." But *why* is allergy?

Immune mechanisms, chemical mediators such as histamine and some globulins are involved. Emotion and excitement are known to trigger attacks, and hypnosis can stop attacks. It is not too far-fetched to relate some of the susceptibility to exhausted adrenal glands.

Hyperactivity is basically a sensory overload due to improper filtering or a malfunctioning cortex or both. Hay fever is the result of an environmental pollen overload that impinges on the nasal mucosa, which is inadequately protected by cortisone from the adrenal glands. The frequent association of hyperactivity and allergy is related to the reciprocal exhaustion produced in the brain and the adrenal glands.

We know that cortisone is manufactured in the adrenal cortex, its excretion stimulated and controlled by the secretion of ACTH from the pituitary gland, which is connected to and interacts with the brain by chemicals and nerves. The adrenal cortex also provides hormones for carbohydrate metabolism, salt maintenance, and male and female sexual characteristics. We use synthetic cortisone for short-term allergy control.

We know if a sufferer produces enough of his own cortisone, he would not have any allergy symptoms. But the adrenal glands have been exhausted for any of several reasons: 1) Because they have not been adequately supplied with enzyme precursors (vitamin C and pantothenic acid). It is interesting to note that most babies do not become allergic to cow's milk until about three to four weeks after birth. Why did he wait so long? Why not with the first ounce? What is wrong with the lining cells, that they don't make the proper enzymes to split the protein or the lactose into small, innocuous, useful nutrients? This is about the time it takes for the enzyme systems to run out after the termination of support from his parasitic uterine involvement with his mother. 2) Because these glands have been overstimulated by some psychic stress due to an overload of the cortical-pituitary-adrenal hookup:

"I thought after our divorce my five-year-old son would settle down, but he seems tense and twitchy. He has developed a wheeze which is worse after a visit with his father. When he gets home he seems pale, has a stomachache, can't eat, and tosses in his sleep. I try to let him know we both love him even though apart and his daddy is a nice man (ugh). Are the visits making him sick? Should I get the attorney to stop visitation rights? He's also developed an itchy rash in the last month."

Hence, allergy could be produced by psychological, and not just pollen, overload. If the adrenals are responding to stress, maybe they are unable to manufacture enough cortisone to interrupt the allergic response.

3) Low blood sugar has forced these glands to devote their secretion to the maintenance of an adequate blood-sugar level:

"We can always tell it's time to get up because my husband and the children start to strangle, choke, snort, gasp, cough, wheeze, and zonk at about six every morning. Don't tell me it's an allergy. We got rid of the animals, feather pillows, wool blankets, covered the mattresses, and have a precipitator attached to the furnace to clean the air. They are better about noontime, even with the furnace on. Should I awaken them at 4 A.M. to give everyone a decongestant?"

4) Or all of these. But once the allergic reaction begins, it sets up its own vicious cycle of stress which further exhausts enzymes, amino acids, glucose, and hormones, thus allowing the cramps, skin rashes, snorts, drips, and wheezes to upset the baby (and the household) further. "Approacher" babies notice their bodies more than others. This excess input of stimuli signals the brain that some attack is in progress.

The signal from the cortex of the brain to the pituitary is the chief method the body uses to stabilize the imbalance. The pituitary sends hormones to the thyroid and adrenal glands to do what they can. These glands can do just so much; if depleted of enzymes and hormone precursors they will be unable to relieve the target cells of the skin, respiratory tract, and the intestines from the allergenic poison. Itch, cough, sneeze, and cramp will tell the brain that the last bit of help was insufficient. Further attempts at internal stabilization fall on unresponsive glands.

The above intertwining chemical phenomena are mentioned not to confuse the reader, but only to indicate how complicated are the biochemical and neurological feedback mechanisms and how difficult it would be for a doctor to prescribe for a patient with an allergy, a neurosis, a pain, a depression, or a psychosis without upsetting some other enzyme-chemical system.

"We paid a lot of money to send our three-year-old to a nursery school so he could learn how to get along with others, but he has been home more than there. He always has junk in his nose and they don't want him; they say he is sick. We can't teach him to blow his nose so he at least looks better, nor can we get our money back."

"Our baby is twelve months old and gets an ear infection every month. We are going broke buying antibiotics. In between he has green stuff crusted about his nostrils. My mother-in-law looks at me as if I'm doing something wrong. If it's due to milk, which I have limited, why isn't the stuff white or clear like an allergy?"

It has been known for a long time that allergic people are susceptible to infections. The phlegm in the nasal and bronchial passages from milk, dust, mold, or other inhalants is a good medium for bacterial growth. Sinusitis sufferers usually end up in the allergists' offices. Allergic children are more prone to ear, respiratory, intestinal, urinary, and skin infections. They have more than their share of virus infections and high fevers.

The rather obvious association of the touchy, hyperactive blue-eyed approacher with allergies and infections suggest a common fault, some breakdown in the neurochemical-humoral defense system that gets overloaded with stress: namely, milk,

food additives, and colorings; dust; germs; low sugar; low cortisone; excess light; sound; etc.

A premature or traumatic birth represents such stress overload. The exhaustion of the body's chemical and enzyme system
because the cortex-pituitary-adrenal mechanism was overstimulated from that stress must be the reason why those babies are so
frequently saddled with allergies and infections. An uncomfortable baby is so busy with internal problems he cannot possibly
find much joy in his environment.

Stress means different things to different people. It is obvious
that some people can handle stress and others cannot.

It is difficult to determine whether the stress of living causes
this genetic predisposition to allergy to surface, or whether the
allergy merely adds one more stress to an overtaxed metabolism.
But it seems that these children's bodies are so busy with one
problem that something else gets hold of them.

If the adrenal glands are busy trying to control a familial
allergic tendency to milk, for instance, a bacterial invasion might
not be combatted before a full-blown ear infection has been
established with all the recognized findings: fever, screaming,
bulging eardrum, etc.:

"We all got the flu shots last fall because we were sick constantly last winter. We all had fever and were sicker than if we
had had the flu itself. My husband never gets sick, but the rest of
us cough, snort, wheeze, and feel dull and achy for weeks.
What's the matter with us?"

Someone did a longitudinal study on the frequency of
children's respiratory infections, and came up with the observation that the average one- to four-year-old has six to eight respiratory infections a year; that's one every one and one-half to
two months. Some had none; some had twelve a year, or a constant drip. If allergies are controlled, would the child become
less sick?

"He gets a cold about every two months. We have to give him
an antibiotic because he always gets a greenish nasal discharge
and an ear infection. He is deaf and nasal-sounding for a month.
For about two days he seems normal, then the whole cycle begins

again. Does he need his tonsils and adenoids removed or do we
sweat it out?"

What are too many colds? Draw the line at one every three
months. Obviously allergies must be considered when the frequency gets above the average. If tonsils and adenoids are enlarged enough to need removal, it suggests a milk allergy.

Someone with this amount of sickness can't help but feel irritable, lose his appetite, and have disturbed sleep.

The doctor is trained to treat the disease at the end of a complicated string of chemical defects. The doctor does what he can
to control the allergy and treat the infections and usually adds,
"Avoid stress." Penicillin helps the body kill the bacteria and
recovery follows, but the victim might still remain on the edge of
tenuous control.

We should be better able to relate to our environment; we
need to develop our body sense. The doctor must learn (or teach
the parents) to recognize the *first* slip in the body's interaction
with the environment—internal or external. If we don't think
straight, something has happened to our brains. Even a cerebral
allergy has been postulated as the cause of certain psychic and
behavioral phenomena. (Most frequently implicated foods: milk,
meat and wheat.) When we have an allergy, we must first understand that something has reduced the effectiveness of our adrenal glands.

If the adrenal glands are the key organs in the constant daily
battles with stress, then we should be able to discover which
people will be at greater risk for stress in childhood and adulthood by the frequency and severity of allergic and infectious
problems in the first few years.

Allergy symptoms	0	1	2
120 Eczema, hay fever, hives, asthma in relatives	no	some	much
121 Many formula changes, used soy or goat's milk	no	once	yes

		0	1	2
122	Watery nasal discharge; rubs nose; sneezes, snorts, zonks; more than eight colds a year	no	some	yes
123	Many ear infections; purulent nasal discharge; constant cough, wheeze, bronchitis; pneumonia; needed antibiotics	no	occasionally	yes
124	Vomiting, diarrhea, gas, constipation	no	occasionally	frequent
125	Tension-fatigue: zonks, circles under eyes, pale, tired, aches	no	occasionally	yes

It seems logical to attempt to reduce the inciting stress that exhausts the adrenal glands and the body's immunity systems. Eliminating the ingested, inhaled, or contacted offenders may be enough. Something has to be done about the inhalants around the house—dust, cats, dogs, birds, wool blankets and rugs, feather pillows, cottonseed in the mattress, mold in the wall, and the uncovered-dirt basement. These irritants would more likely be the offenders if the child is a great sneezer or nose manipulator.

"Every time he goes to grandmother's he gets asthma, but we have the pets at *our house.* Is it her face powder?" Allergists can do skin tests and discover the offenders more accurately, with the exception of the foods (i.e., milk).

Milk is the usual villain if the child snorts or zonks, and if his frequent colds lead to ear infections, asthmatic bronchitis or croup attacks. Eliminating milk and dairy products is a valuable rule that all pediatricians use if a patient seems sick too much.

If the doctor recognizes eczema, antihistamines, soothing baths, and oil plus cortisone ointment provide relief and may break the cycle while the initiating allergen (milk) is eliminated. Soybean milk is the usual substitute, but if the worn-out enzymes are not restored, the baby soon falls apart with similar symptoms. Goat's milk, amino acid milk, and meat milk might all have to be tried.

The chronic wheeze and snort might respond to the same formula manipulations plus some decongestant-antihistamine preparation (Actifed®, Triaminic®, Novahistine®, etc.) but a new threat can be anticipated: ear infections. Small tubes that serve to equalize the air pressure between the pharynx and the inner ears frequently become occluded by swelling of the lining cells and accumulated mucus. This now unaerated, undrained dead space promotes bacteria growth and subsequent otitis media (middle ear infection) requiring antibiotic treatment and possible surgical drainage.

The tired child with headaches, stomachaches, and circles under the eyes gives away the diagnosis when he starts to zonk. Milk or wheat or eggs are surely the culprits, but sugar and white flour can do the same damage.

You must remember the debilitating effect the ingestion of sugar has on the bodily defenses. Some parents have noted the absence of the common cold and many allergies by merely eliminating desserts and sugar from their meals. But this is not a sugar allergy. In some people a fluctuating blood-sugar response is stressful enough to overstimulate the pituitary-adrenal axis.

If all of the above allergens have been eliminated as much as possible (short of moving), and each cold ends up as a bacterial infection (green or yellow mucus) requiring antibiotics, the doctor might try injections of a vaccine of dead bacteria usually found in the average nose and throat. Some doctors believe that an allergy to one's own bacteria is a real possibility. Injections of a vaccine made from the bacteria from the patient's nose (autogenous vaccine) might help develop an improved immunity.

Cortisone for asthma (or arthritis) can lead to a psychosis or stomach ulcers. If we could find natural biodegradable ways to make the body function for us, we might end up with a better body, inside of which we could live quite comfortably. So supporting the internal control mechanisms may be just as important.

Since the adrenal glands secrete hormones that help the body control the allergic reaction to foreign irritants, it follows that the adrenal glands should be protected — no sugar is primary.

Now that we know what exhausted his adrenal glands or what nutriments he needs to help him make cortisone more easily, we are in a position to help in a more effective, natural, physiological, long-lasting way. Then an effort to recharge the adrenal glands so they may produce the appropriate amounts of cortisone would be in order.

Supplying the adrenals with protein and enzyme and hormone precursors boosts the glands' ability to make their protective chemicals. Vitamin C, pantothenic acid, and a good amount of most of the B-complex vitamins are helpful.

Linus Pauling insisted that vitamin C helps fight infection. Everyone laughed. But it was proved valid in some double-blind studies (subjects and investigators did not know who had the C or the placebo). It helped twenty percent or so. The use of vitamin C in doses of 250 milligrams and upwards daily was effective in some people in warding off colds, virus infections, and secondary bacterial infections. Some need more and others less. If a patient has too many respiratory infections, we know that his immunity systems are overtaxed and unable to function. Question for Linus: Did you find out if those benefitted were fair and/or eating sugar and/or had allergies? The adrenal glands are full of vitamin C; does the C go to these glands to help them pump out the allergy- and infection-controlling chemicals?

The trick seems to lie in the ability to predict the onset of an infection and loading the system with three to five times the maintenance dose. If 250 milligrams of vitamin C seems to be doing something, such as no colds for three months, then at the first sign of a disease process, (sneeze, scratchy throat, slight fever, three coughs, etc.) the dose should immediately be quadrupled to at least 500 milligrams, two or three times a day. Aspirin, antihistamines, and a decongestant may all be given in the usual doctor-recommended doses.

Extra vitamin C and B complex are especially helpful in those fair, light-eyed children with multiple allergies. A vitamin C and B injection at the time of the initial examination is a good therapeutic test; if sneezing, wheezing, diarrhea, skin rash, etc., are improved in two days, it indicates that this patient would profit from diet and oral vitamin therapy. The above vitamins are enzyme precursors, so they must be begun right after birth if you are going to preclude the development of the allergy.

This is not to suggest that the allergist is obsolete—far from it. Allergic people need all the help they can get, but the above do-it-yourself remedies may make the allergist's job easier, or his allergy shots may produce improvement a little faster than usual. This makes the allergist feel that he is helpful; people in the helping professions need to feel worthwhile, or they get grumpy. But if a child demonstrates the sickness and behavior clues outlined above, a concerted effort must be made to correct his biochemical and nutritional defect and help him—with medicine, if need be—achieve a little control over the short circuits in his nervous system. Again, early remedial action is mandatory before secondary psychological damage becomes permanent, before sickness and/or delinquency become a way of life for these people.

9 · Early Food Problems: Colic, Diarrhea, and Obesity

We could never fill him up with enough milk so he would last more than two or three hours. He had to have small frequent feedings; he was a nibbler. I often thought while I was sitting there in the middle of the night how great it would be if we had a tube running down to his stomach! We could regulate the milk so he could get about an ounce every hour or so, and we would all get some sleep. We did try to flood him with a lot of milk at one time using a nipple with a huge hole, but he would either scream with colic or threw up the whole mess and we would start all over again. He always seemed so bloated, like a spider: scrawny arms and a gross abdomen.

"Instead of improving after three to five weeks, he got worse. When he wasn't crying he was vomiting, straining, or grunting. After what seemed like an hour of monumental pushing, he would deliver about a tablespoon of green slime. We changed to soybean milk and he was OK for about three weeks. Then we went through it all again; in those first few months we must have changed his formula six times. The milk had to be at body temperature or he wouldn't drink it. He refused solids until he was eight months old. He seemed to choke easily; we never gave him junior foods [strained baby foods with lumps] because he had such a gag reflex. He had definite likes and dislikes. He needed to suck on his thumb or a pacifier when he wasn't eating. We usually had to pull his hand out of his mouth to get the food in.

"He cried every time he passed gas or urinated; he would look at me as if I had poked him. We had to change him every time he had a small bit of urine or stool; he seemed to notice even a wrinkle in the diaper. He cried during the changes as if the urine evaporating from his skin was too chilling. He always seemed to have a rash somewhere, and frequently had an ammonia sore on the end of his penis."

Such a child seems active, sensitive to stimuli, and colicky.

Eating and food-related problems

		0	1	2
126	Weight gain as infant pounds/month for first 3 months	1 to 3	?	Less than 1
127	Colic, many formula changes	no	some	constant
128	Gas, cramps, sloppy stools	no	occasionally	constant
129	Vomits if excited or over-fed	no	occasionally	frequent
130	Wants small amounts	no	occasionally	frequently
131	Sedatives, aspirin, vitamins, excited	no	?	always
Older Child:				
132	Prefers candy and cookies	no	occasionally	steals
133	Eats a lot, stays thin	no	?	yes
134	Picky and finicky	no	occasionally	always
135	Loves chocolate, cola and/or coffee	no	occasionally	addict
136	Wild for two hours after sweets	no	?	yes
137	Headaches, stomachaches, periodic attacks of vomiting	no	occasionally	yes
138	Jekyll-Hyde behavior, good and bad days, temper outbursts	no	occasionally	life style
139	Hypoactive, withdrawn, daydreams, far away	no	occasionally	frequent

These symptoms suggests two things: The infant is allergy prone and he is a sensitive person, susceptible to stress. Therefore, nothing is gained by waiting for rashes, colds, diarrhea,

and irritability to occur. The diet change is fundamental to comfort and minimizes stress for everyone, but we know allergic
babies continue on for a lifetime of colds, sinus trouble, gas,
rashes, and misery. Prevention is the key.

The following would be a tentative plan to decrease a child's
susceptibility to uncomfortable symptoms and recurrent ill-
nesses, which could result in an improper response to the environment, which might lead to psychological problems, which
could result in more sickness, which might weaken ego strength,
which etc., etc.

Avoid stress: "He was uncuddleable. He had to be removed to the
neighbors when I did the vacuuming. A door slamming set him
off and he kept crying because he was crying."

A violinist father I know could not play above middle C until
his baby was over four months of age. Calm, quiet surroundings,
and a minimum of light and noise is mandatory. An even air
temperature of sixty-five to seventy degrees is better than a fluctuating sixty to eighty. The air should have some moisture in it;
if the air is dry, hanging wet sheets and towels about may be
sufficient. There should be no animal products in the room
(feather pillows or wool blankets). Electric floor heat, which
kicks up less dust, is better than circulating warm air from a
furnace. A minimum of handling may be better, but since touching, holding, rocking, and fondling are important in the development of the child's self-concept, an effort should be made
to see what the baby's stress tolerance is. If he cries or vomits
when handled, he may feel you are crowding him and/or his
territory. Handle him enough less often to avoid those symptoms.

Consider milk allergy: The La Leche advocates have been screaming at pediatricians to insist that new mothers breast-feed their
babies this natural way and leave cow's milk to the calves. Our
problem is that if we insist that a mother nurse her baby, and her
milk supply is inadequate for some reason, she feels guilty. This
discouragement usually cuts the supply further. Instead of fill-
ing the breasts with milk, the baby's insistent hunger cry may
produce enough stress in her to further decrease the supply. To
provide proper protein nutrition we switch the baby to cow's
milk, but these are the very babies that so often become allergic
to cow's milk.

The pediatrician is caught between the guilty mother and the allergic baby, so for us to avoid our own uncomfortable stress headaches, we become wishy-washy. "Try to nurse," we say, "but if it's a big drag, use the bottle." (A mother breast-feeding her infant sometimes finds the baby is happier if *she* does not ingest dairy products.)

If the baby is breast-fed and gaining well (at least four ounces a week or one pound a month as a minimun), but is screaming inconsolably, the mother must assume she is eating something that is offending her baby's intestines. Anything *might* be responsible, but onions, garlic, and beans are the worst. Whatever is irritating in green vegetables, tuna fish, pork, nuts, eggs, and milk can get into the breast milk and create gas and cramps. But nursing should not be discontinued; these babies usually do worse on cow's milk.

Remember, this problem tends to run in families. If the mother is fair, or has many of the genetic factors previously alluded to, and has had a debilitating pregnancy and delivery, her bodily coping systems may be depleted. No amount of will power can make her pituitary, adrenal, thyroid, and breast glands function if her enzymes aren't supplied with the proper or sufficient nutrients. The mothers of these babies need psychological as well as protein, vitamin, and chemical support. The babies doing poorly at the breast are the very ones we should *not* allow to switch to the bottle. They have already demonstrated their susceptibility to the problems this book is all about.

The mother should have been involved with the La Leche League and the Association for Childbirth Education long before the delivery. These and others are psychologically supportive and great stress relievers, especially after a frustrating visit to some obstetricians' offices. The nutritional drain and the physical exhaustion of pregnancy and childbirth can be partially ameliorated by the following schedule during pregnancy and breast-feeding:

No sugar or foods containing sugar, food additives, or colorings should be eaten. She should nibble on protein and add extra vitamins and minerals to her diet. She should gain eighteen to twenty-four pounds during the nine months; pregnancy is no time to go on a starvation diet. If she is enormously obese, however, she might be able to gain less than the above figure if she is good about nibbling on protein. Take Vitamin C, 500 milligrams (at least), and big doses of all the B complex vitamins, but especially niacinamide (300 to 500 milligrams), B6 up to 300 milligrams a day, pantothenic acid (at least 100 milligrams a day), B12, folic acid, and lecithin. If milk is eliminated because it is an allergen, she should take two grams of calcium a day, or calcium lactate or dolomite to supply that amount, and extra fluids to a total of two quarts a day. Coffee, tea, chocolate, and cola beverages should be limited.

The breast-fed baby should be given extra vitamin C—at least 50 milligrams; some doctors recommend 100 milligrams. Cecon® is a fairly palatable way to do this. B6 (50 milligrams) and calcium (one gram of Neocalglucon® calcium-lactate solution) should produce calmness without dopiness.

If he is bottle-fed, a change to soybean milk may be a godsend. Several kinds may have to be tried before the most suitable one is found. It takes about two to four days to clear out the intestinal tract of the cow's milk protein and calm it and everyone down.

Many parents report that everything went well for a week or so, then all the symptoms recurred. The assumption is that the baby has become allergic to soy protein.

I once was faced with a baby who had cramps and diarrhea from cow's milk, eczema from soybean milk, and a wheeze from lamb meat milk. The mother alternated the milks so that the baby had a few of all the symptoms but not enough to upset him to the point of crying. Time and maturity finally controlled the problems. He is a fine young man today but is restless, ticklish, and has hay fever when he mows the lawn.

A disaccharide (double sugar such as lactose) intolerance is not uncommon, so a milk without carbohydrates may solve both the cramps and sloppy stool problems.

All these stresses use up energy, depress the blood sugar, and exhaust enzymes. It makes sense to provide low allergenic protein and extra vitamin C and the B-complex vitamins. Calcium can ameliorate cramps, irritability, and insomnia, so an extra gram a day (in addition to what is in the milk) is worthwhile. Bone meal is one way.

If the baby must drink cow's milk, Enfamil, Similac, SMA, etc.

are probably better because the processing has decreased the allergenic properties inherent in raw cow's milk. If he has the familial tendencies listed earlier, extra vitamins should be added to bring his total daily intake up to 100 milligrams of vitamin C, all the vitamin B complex up to about three times the recommended daily requirements, B_6 up to 100 milligrams, B_{12} to 25 micrograms, calcium to more than one gram a day. Pantothenic acid is supposed to be beneficial if allergies are suspected; 50 milligrams a day or more should help.

Feed frequently and moderately: A heavy meal and a full stomach encourage regurgitation and/or a cramp. Because of his inability to disregard things, this baby notices a full stomach more readily than others. He begins to fuss after three ounces because he is acutely aware of the stretched stomach walls. A full comfortable feeling to the average baby is perceived as an appendicitis attack; he thinks he is going to die and acts accordingly.

Moreover, these people are calmer if they nibble; otherwise the level of blood sugar fluctuates too much—another stress. Some babies are so touchy that they cannot be held when fed, and the bottle has to be propped. If the baby is sensitive and being breast-fed, it is difficult to prop the mother, so it may be necessary for her to leave the baby supine and slide into position over him, like an airplane landing. Burping is usually not necessary for the breast-fed baby, but swallowed air—which these babies notice—can be tested for by thumping lightly on his abdomen in the upper left quadrant. A tightness detected here like a ripe melon suggests trapped air. Roll him on his right side for a few seconds. This shifts the air to the top of the milk. Then when you sit him up and tilt him gently back and forth—don't pound on his back—he may reward you with a dry burp.

Most gas is from swallowed air, so the above maneuver is important. The big problem is the gas that moves into the intestinal tract, which joins the bubbles from fermentation of the foods (especially sugars) due to bacterial action. There is about twenty feet of intestine from the stomach to the rectum, all lined with nerve cells sensitive to stretching of the muscular walls. One dollop of gas takes about twenty-four hours to pass from top to bottom; an aware baby might scream the whole time. The baby who is not so aware might be full of the same amount of gas but only giggle when he passes his wind. Gas pains in the bowel suggests to the baby that he might have a load in his rectum, so he grunts and strains. His bearing-down noises then suggest to the parents to check the diapers; they find nothing or a scant teaspoon of green slime after what seems like a monumental effort. Glycerin suppositories may help evacuate the last six inches of the lower bowel, but the unreachable nineteen and one-half feet above are still cramping.

Massage and warm soothing applications to the abdomen are only temporary distractions. Medicines are important for comfort, as crying and wakefulness are stress factors for the baby as well as the parents. Atropine (as in Donnatal®) or antihistamines (Benadryl® is standard) or sedative-antihistamines (Phenergan®) are useful here while waiting for the "immature" nervous system to develop to the point that it does not respond to a stomach cramp as if it were a knifing. Barbiturates (Nembutal®) have been a standard treatment, but most parents—and now many doctors—have discovered that this class of sedatives usually makes these touchy people worse. Apparently they suppress the activity of the cortical nerves in the surface of the brain, but not the frequency and intensity of the incoming stimuli; these babies act like drunks who have hurt themselves—thrashing, wildly screaming, and flopping their heads about.

"The doctor gave him some colic medicine with phenobarbital in it. After one dose he was wild and excited for twenty-four hours. He does a lot better if he gets Phenergan® or Benadryl® antihistamine-tranquilizer-type medicines."

Although the doctor is necessary to help with appropriate medicine, the very fact of the appearance of these symptoms has to mean the neurochemical control is depleted. His reassurance and treatment are necessary, but wise parents should add the following supportive ingredients to help hold their child together; vitamin C, 100 to 200 milligrams; B complex (brewers' yeast protein powder in two or three bottles a day); extra calcium (one to two grams), and pantothenic acid (100 milligrams). These things are slow to effect the necessary control, so the doctor's prescription may be necessary for weeks or months before any benefit is seen. Each flare-up (triggered by a cold, attack of the flu, upset in the household, allergy to a wool blanket, introduction of a new food; or falling out of bed) would set the whole timetable back. Sometimes a stress can be anticipated (holidays; visitors; a trip; divorce; older sibling brings a cold home; weather change like sudden dry, cold, clear winter nights) and the vitamin intake, especially C, can be tripled to prepare for the onslaught.

The crampy, colicky, grunting baby with loose, green, frequent stools may respond to the same formula change plus medicines to decrease the awareness he has to his distress (Donnatal®, Phenergan®, Benadryl®). Does camomile tea work because it turns on his limbic system? Does a little bit of alcohol work because it sedates his cortex and makes him less responsive?

True diarrhea usually means an attack of intestinal flu, a virus disease characterized by a day of vomiting and fever, then seven days of diarrhea. If it lasts longer, it suggests a bacterial superinfection, or more commonly, that the lining cells of the intestinal tract have sloughed off or are nonfunctioning because the virus has temporarily disabled them. Complete rest may revive them, but the infection may leave the patient open to an enzyme deficiency (he cannot split carbohydrate or sugar molecules, which remain undigested and act as a purge) or a milk allergy (the milk protein has become a foreign irritant, so the cells secrete fluid to wash it away). In either case the patient continues with gas, bloat, and diarrhea until the carbohydrate is removed from the diet (CHO-free milk) or he is placed on a milk to which he is not sensitive or given an antibiotic if he has a bacterial infection or a vitamin C and B complex injection to revitalize the enzymes in these lining cells.

Recognizing that he has a stress condition and that he might not be able to handle the added burdens to his system, it would be prudent to withhold complex carbohydrates and milk to avoid taxing the decreased capacities of the enzymes. Extra vitamins B and C should be added in small frequent amounts to supply these cells with their nutrients. Some water to prevent dehydration and glucose (the simplest of sugar; some parents find honey or fructose is safe if not overdone) should only be allowed for the first day; anything else adds fuel to the intestinal fire. If urine is excreted at least twice a day and the diarrhea is subsiding, very weak milk (one part milk to four parts water) might be tried after the initial twenty-four hours of rest. This is gradually strengthened depending on the message from the rectum. If stools increase in volume, moisture, and frequency, cut back to sugar water. If seven days elapse and normal stools are not forthcoming, assume the problem is sugar or milk protein and switch to CHO-free milk. Stools should appear reasonably normal in forty-eight hours; if that change is not satisfactory, try soy, goat, or meat milk.

Never use boiled milk without diluting it well above the original water concentration; it has too much sodium and babies get a devastating type of high-sodium dehydration.

Diarrhea alternating with constipation should alert the parent to an allergy or an enzyme problem. It may mean that the milk forms a thick heavy curd which becomes dehydrated as it progresses through the intestinal tract. When it arrives at the rectal outlet, it is a hard golf ball that defies expulsion. If some solids are given, like barley, pears, or carrots, they would hold moisture so when they arrived at the nether end, some sloppiness could be expected.

If, however, the *milk* overtaxed the intestinal enzymes, *it* would cause the loose, bubbly bowel movements. If the child is eating constipating solids such as rice, applesauce, or bananas, then his BM's may alternate between loose and hard, but for different reasons.

An attempt to achieve reasonably "decent" stools would involve (1) feeding only milk (breast, modified cow's, or soy) in the first four to six months, (2) beginning safe solids (least allergenic: rice, barley, yellow vegetables, pears, bananas, applesauce) only after the first three to five months of life, and (3) introducing but one solid food a month. This is all very boring, but if this routine is not followed, there is risk of developing an allergy which may never be outgrown, and some evidence indicates that babies given solids early are more likely to be obese adults.

The pediatrician has recently been blamed for a variety of

adult ills including neuroses, psychoses, and alcoholism. Now the latest load dumped on him is adult obesity. Maybe frustrated internists or psychiatrists thought up this idea because their treatment failure rates are so high. They would get a bad self-image if they couldn't pass this blame on to the child watchers. The large number of lay organizations (Weight Watchers, TOPS, Medical Diet Service, etc.) is patent testimony to the medical failure in treating this lifelong debility.

Fat children equal fat adults Sociohistorical studies suggest that in the old days, a corpulent body was like driving a Cadillac—equated to financial or political success. There was a need to show the town that one had made it; one was successful enough to afford rich food. But more recently success, power, drive, and ambition are associated with thinness. Most models are almost scrawny.

If a man is moving up the socioeconomic ladder, he will likely chose a thin woman whom he finds more energetic and driving than a cute, chubby, cuddly, but somewhat lethargic girl he dated but discarded as she seemed to be more interested in nesting and cooking than did her thin counterpart. Therefore, the theory goes, a natural selection process goes on that tends to put thin people at the top of the business struggle and leave the heavies more or less satisfied with middle management, sales, blue-collar work, and the less demanding nine-to-five jobs that suit their energy level. I would have no doubt that these thin families in top management come from the ranks of the hyperactive approachers and would have more than the average share of migraine, ulcers, hypertension, and alcoholism scattered amongst their ranks. Stress diseases, but they couldn't help but get to what they think is the top, because they need to win.

Genetic knowledge indicates that obesity runs (rolls?) in families; if both parents are fat, half the offspring will have to contend with ease of weight gain all their lives. The endomorph with thick lips, short tapering fingers, and forty feet of intestines doesn't want or need to win as much because he knows he is not as agile, and frequently needs to snooze after lunch anyway. He assumed his destiny was fat, and he might as well accept and enjoy it. But now comes overwhelming evidence indicating a high relationship of obesity and diabetes and cardiovascular disease. The push is to leanness.

More recent studies show that fat cells, once filled in infancy, are more easily filled up again in adulthood, like a balloon— much easier to blow up the second time. This is where the pediatrician is supposed to intervene. If we can keep the mother from rewarding the child with food every time he cries or is frustrated, we are told, the child may be able to keep his fat cells flat all his life.

We have made some headway in spreading the word to avoid solid foods until four to six months of age and stay away from saturated fats and sugar. The baby-food manufacturers have been cooperative by removing salt and sugar from most of their products.

It is difficult, however, for a parent who is orally oriented to let a hungry baby go hungry. Behavior modification experts feel that a child learns to eat not for physical hunger but because an emotional need is rewarded by this oral gratification. We must teach parents to reward their children with love and cuddling when frustrated. But most parents have seen the improved behavior after food ingestion, and hence *they* are rewarded when they see laughter replace tears within minutes after a snack.

Two or three chemical factors must be recognized if we are to avoid avoirdupois. In the genetically programmed obese, the enzyme that helps store sugar as fat is much more efficient than the enzyme that mobilizes fat into burnable energy. Some people—again genetically determined—overreact with an insulin abundance when quick sugar (usually refined sugar or sucrose) is consumed. The blood sugar rises rapidly, more insulin than is really necessary comes pouring out of the pancreas, and the blood sugar drops to such low levels that the victim is overpowered with hunger; he seeks the quickest form of energy available—sweets. It is now known that obese people have higher amounts of insulin in their bloodstreams. It's as if elevated blood sugar represented some sort of threat. As soon as their insulin finds sugar, it stuffs it rapidly into storage. This sets up the craving for the quick relief of that "all gone" feeling.

In the obese, low blood sugar has a tendency to cause drowsiness and tiredness. The very people who should exercise to burn up the storage depots are the ones who are too tired to even get motivated, much less actually move about. Thin, restless people get headaches or migraine when they eat sugar; the obese get tired and fatter.

Psychotherapy is about as useful here as in chronic alcoholism. The patient accepts *intellectually* what he has to do, but when his blood sugar falls, his cortex, which has the memory for this intellectual resolve, is asleep or nonfunctioning because there is no energy source in that area.

Animal and human experiments have indicated that when constant protein nibbling is the life style, weight remains at a normal, stable level. But if the food—even a well-balanced diet—is consumed only once or twice a day, it is more likely to be stored as fat. Then during the twenty or so hours of fasting, the energy requirements of the body may require the use of muscle tissue, because it is harder to get energy from fat stores than glycogen or muscle protein. The net result may be a fat person with thin, weak muscles.

The only fat animals on the earth are humans and their pets. It seems obvious that we have been programmed by grandmother, who served three meals a day because it was a drag to heat up the stove all the time. We should have been listening to Mother Nature, who apparently wants us to nibble. But we must nibble on grass, leaves, berries, nuts, other animals, roots, bark, or whatever else we can grab. If God made it, it's probably OK (He does test us with potato stems, rhubarb leaves, and toadstools); if man made it, it's probably not worth eating or will make you fat, or cause constipation, anemia, or cancer.

A protein diet nibbled on six to eight times a day will maintain the blood sugar at levels that will not trigger the craving. The blood insulin levels will fall to normal levels, and after three weeks the patient can maintain a neat balance between food intake and energy consumption. Another bonus: people who eat six to eight times a day and avoid sugar and white flour tend to have lower cholesterol levels.

Now we know that vitamins are enzyme precursors, and enzymes allow the body to function better. Our enzymes are determined by our genetic background. If there is obesity in your family tree, it seems prudent to try extra C and B-complex vitamins (or a couple of vitamin C and B injections) along with the protein nibbling and sugar and white flour avoidance. Something must be done to stop the bad self-image, ("I'm no good because I have no will power") and blood-sugar vicious cycle. Psychological support will enhance the motivation of these rotund people, but the sugar craving has to be minimized by protein nibbling.

Hilda Bruck says, "Inside every fat person there is a thin person anxious to get out." Many thin people get fat because of some stress that initiated the first drop in blood sugar; sugar ingestion calmed the fluttery feeling, but stimulated the insulin production at the same time. These people store calories too easily and develop obesity, tiredness, and this craving all at the same time. Motivation and self-control are almost impossible when one feels rotten.

10 · Appetite Loss and Cyclic Vomiting

He's so picky with his food. I've understood that if parents eat everything, their children will also. Well, not in our house. He refuses to try anything new. If we force it down, he just brings it back up. If he has to chew something more than twice, he refuses to eat it. Milk, juice, and pudding are his favorites. He cannot sit at the table more than three and a half minutes at a time."

A frustrating loss of appetite makes the whole day a real wall-climber.

Once a child is walking, talking, and feeding himself, we want to assume he is grown up and can be relied upon to act maturely.

He is supposed to eat his supper. We say, "Eat your supper." He may or he may not. If he is about to eat his supper and we tell him to, it might look as if we got him to do it.

You know perfectly well if he would eat he would feel better, but if he snacks, he will lose what little appetite he has and Daddy will scream at him for not eating his supper. Headache number 4,261.

This is also the same child who is up at dawn wondering where his breakfast is. "He's up at 5 A.M. fixing breakfast: a jar of jam in a bowl of Frosted Flakes. I can't get him to eat anything else. I thought the appetite was supposed to pick up after age two. I fix eggs, bacon, cereal, juice, and fruit for him and the dog gets it. He dumped one supper of mashed potatoes and gravy on his head. He's mean, defiant, pouty, grouchy, bitter, angry, and breaks his toys if they don't do his bidding. I know he'd feel

95

better if he'd eat something. He eats candy and junk foods for
grandmother, but I know that is wrong. When I'm exasperated
with him I might slap his behind and say 'No!' Then he gets a
look in his eyes that says, 'I'm going to kill you.' I'm worried."

Your mother says, "Good. Serves you right. That's just what
you did to me at that age."

Your spouse says, "You don't discipline him properly."

Your mother-in-law says, "Maybe it's the way you prepare the
food, dear."

Your psychiatrist says, "You didn't develop your position as
the authority figure in the first few weeks of his life."

Your pediatrician says, "Most two- to three-year-old children
are like that. He'll outgrow it." You harbor the secret thought
that he may not live long enough to outgrow it.

The whiny child may discover another attention-getting act:
namely, ingesting various household poisons and medicines left
unguarded about the house. It is a pediatric maxim that accidents and poisonings (plus fevers and earaches) occur most frequently between 3 P.M. and supper. This "children's hour" must
in part be induced by a falling blood-sugar level that makes some
children (and adults) evil. Some will cry, appear depressed, or
become hyperactive; others will have headaches or stomachaches. Maybe some feel hungry and will eat anything in the
absence of food.

Some biochemical mechanism unlocks his tenuous impulse
control and he becomes an approacher—unable to disregard the
attractive nuisances in his environment. Maybe he's searching
for food; it seems logical to assume that his lunch calories are
pretty well stored or burned up by 3 or 4 P.M. He'll put anything
in his mouth in a desperate effort to satisfy his "all-gone" feeling.

"Twenty minutes after dinner he claims he's hungry. I ask him
why he didn't eat more at supper. He says he wasn't hungry
then."

If he was hungry for supper about an hour *before* it was offered, his blood sugar might have dropped to a point that would
give him symptoms—headache, nausea, vomiting, irritability,
depression—that would prevent him from eating, the very activity he needs to correct the cause of his problems. He would be

labeled neurotic, rotten, and stubborn, or get spanked or sent to bed for disobedience:

"Dinner is a disaster. Everyone is shoving, poking, spilling, or crying. Someone will tickle Charlie and he gets to giggling and cannot stop until he vomits. We try to get each to tell the most fun thing they did that day. When it's Charlie's turn, if he is still with us, he starts to stammer. Frustrated and angry, he rushes from the table. We know if he would eat, he would feel better and be able to handle the excitement. Maybe each should eat separately in different rooms. How do we get family life to be fun?"

Let's start the day again. Maybe if we get a better run at it, you might end up laughing, not crying.

Throw out all sugar. It is an artificial food that should never have been manufactured. Do not use food or drink that contains artificial sweeteners, colorings, or additives. Many people are allergic to these chemicals and become irritable or sick when they eat them. Read all labels before buying food; purchase nothing that has sugar, dextrose, or sweeteners included in the first five items on the label. Have no jam, jellies, canned fruit with syrup, pie, cake, cookies (or anything baked with sugar), ice cream, pop, syrup, molasses, or brown sugar in the house. Foods made for diabetics may be permissible. Honey alone or in recipes may be acceptable, but it still promotes the idea that good things have to taste sweet. Some people are affected by honey almost as much as sucrose. A TV ad implies that sugar made from sugar cane is better because it came from a natural source. It all ends up as sucrose, the villain.

Sometimes simply removing sugar, white flour, milk, food additives, and food colorings is sufficient to produce such a change that nothing else needs to be done. Improvement is usually noted in one day, but you may have to allow a couple of weeks.

"I like what you say, but I can't get him to eat anything now. Before, at least he would eat a doughnut for breakfast." Most people, once trapped into sugar ingestion, find it extremely difficult to stop it cold turkey. They feel tense, have headaches and, of course, a strong craving for sugar. They may be suffering from hypoglycemia because the extra insulin still circulating in the bloodstream is continuing to depress the blood-sugar level.

Sometimes one must start the evening before. If even a quarter of a hamburger patty, or a gob of peanut butter or a handful of almonds could be poked down the child's throat just at bedtime, he might be well enough in the morning to eat another small bit of protein to get his morning going. The grouchiness and anorexia in the morning are due to low blood sugar and depressed cortisone levels and acidosis from the carbohydrate he got after supper and fat metabolism. At least, don't allow the usual ice cream or cookies at bedtime. If food refusal carries on more than two days, the vitamin B and C injection usually allows normal hunger sensations to take over by activating the enzymes that signal the brain to respond to the kitchen smells.

Much of what has to be done for these children (and adults) is a compromise between the practical and the ideal. The memory of tasty, sugary foods is so strong in these people that it usually takes at least three weeks of this protein nibbling to make them feel good enough and strong enough to ignore the sugar cravings. It also takes about this long for the elevated insulin levels to return to normal.

Artificial sweeteners, saccharin, etc., may be substituted with the understanding that it is cheating and will be used as a temporary crutch. Honey, which is largely fructose, can be used as a sweetener in gradually reduced amounts. It must be remembered that it is a carbohydrate and its use is to be discouraged; it still promotes the idea that things have to taste sweet. (Fructose, a ketone, is the fruit sugar, and is metabolized in a different way than dextrose. The liver has to convert it to dextrose, so it does not excite the pancreas as acutely as dextrose or sucrose.) Mothers tell me that if a child eats some cake with white sugar she has to scrape him off the ceiling, but the same recipe, substituting honey, has no great effect on the activity level. Even Mother Nature's own banana can be a poison to some. A mother told me that if she lets her child eat a banana without some balancing protein, her child will roll on the floor and scream for four hours.

We try to force people to have no sugar (white, brown, molasses, corn syrup, candy, or foods with sugar—canned fruits, jams, jellies, pop, and soft drinks) in the house. If they are there, someone is going to eat them. White flour is the other strong taboo, so families who love to bake must use stone-ground, or whole-kernel wheat or bran flour and honey for the recipes. Most dry cereals are empty of anything worthwhile, although in fairness, the breakfast-food manufacturers are making at attempt to provide some natural grains. However, much granola is loaded with molasses. Cereals, even hot oatmeal, Cream of Wheat®, Shredded Wheat, and Grape Nuts® are not high enough in protein to be sustaining for most people for more than two to three hours. If I eat hot cereal with milk, no sugar, two pieces of whole-wheat toast, and some fruit for breakfast, I slip away at about 10:30 A.M. Adding one egg to this will keep me until 11:30. No cereal, but consuming two eggs, toast, and fruit, I will have enough energy to think and write until 1 P.M. lunch. My Sunday school headaches must have been the syrup on the pancakes we had as a variation of the hot oatmeal and egg Mother fixed during the week. (God was punishing me for eating artificial food.)

People who want to change their diets, but find they are locked into the quick carbohydrate breakfast, or Tang (worthless) and coffee with sugar, may find a glass of fresh-squeezed or frozen (read the label) orange juice or unsweetened apple juice laced with a tablespoon of brewers' yeast protein powder is about as quick and tasty and will hold them most of the morning. Sometimes a gob of old-fashioned (no sweeteners) peanut butter on a half piece of whole-wheat toast is quick and nourishing. A cold piece of last night's meat or a cold hard-boiled egg or dish of cottage cheese or yogurt (no additives) will do. I carry nuts—almonds, filberts, walnuts, peanuts—in my pocket and eat two to six every twenty minutes. Chewing these with some of the awful-tasting protein tablets helps gustatory acceptance of the latter.

One mother I know has found her son will eat breakfast if he can have strawberry or raspberry jam on everything. He gets hives from the fruit and headaches from the sugar. He is willing to tolerate the somewhat painful vitamin B and C injection every week or two so he can eat what he loves (or is addicted to). The shot helps his adrenal glands make enough cortisone to suppress the hives, but the headaches may go on until this mother uses up her homemade preserves and tries a different method—i.e., no sugar for home canning, but maybe honey or sorbitol. Compromise, compromise.

The whole family has to change its ways. It is not fair to these sensitive, sugar-loving children to have sugar in the house and expect them to leave it alone. As the condition is frequently hereditary, one does not have to look far to find another family member who is wedded to sugar—usually it's the father. If he is not eating desserts and having three teaspoons of sugar in his coffee, he is into the wine and the bourbon. One woman told me that her husband occasionally just pours the coffee into the sugar bowl and drinks it from that vessel; it saves time.

Shoppers must read every label. If sugar, sweeteners, corn syrup, molasses, or dextrose are listed in the first five items, they should be left on the shelves; the store manager is supposed to get the message and not reorder these dangerous foods.

Ms. Jean Farmer of Bloomington, Indiana, spent her own money and two years getting the school board to ban sugar, candy, and snacks from all the schools in their system. Dallas, Texas, followed in 1975. Boise, Idaho, tried, but it was a big hassle, especially when the teachers refused to give up their cokes and sugar in their coffee. A dangerous situation developed in the street between the local junior high school and the candy store across the street; the students' craving for sweets allowed them to dash willy-nilly out into the traffic. Mrs. Holdman, in Portland, is doing a monumental task of educating parents and school administrators to the evils of sugar ingestion.

The problem is motivation. If we all had headaches or fell on the floor or threw up two minutes after sugar and white flour ingestion, we would have all quit long ago. But the effects are often subtle and become so lost in a myriad of other stress-producing traumata in our environment that we are unable to see the connection. Vague correlations like cancer of the bowel, heart attacks, and hemorrhoids which come thirty years later are too unrelated to become credible to a population that wants a good cause-and-effect connection.

And besides, sugar tastes so good.

Cyclic Vomiting: When a child vomits once or twice, we call it the stomach flu or gastroenteritis, which is always "going around."

This disease is so common we expect it once or twice a year per person as a part of growing up. One day of vomiting and seven days of diarrhea is the usual course, and not much is done except holding the head of the victim over the toilet bowl. But if no diarrhea follows the twenty-four hours of heaving, one should suspect a metabolic dysfunction.

I recall writing a paper during my training days on periodic vomiting in children. Only now do I connect that pediatric problem with the children discussed in this book. I must get a call once a month about this distressing, recurring frustration.

Twenty years ago all that was known was that it is usually seen in boys. Their mothers or maternal aunts frequently have migraine attacks or at least vascular, one-sided, recurrent headaches; it seemed to be associated with some difficulty in releasing stored glycogen (which turns into sugar) from the liver.

If little glucose is available for the body's energy needs, fat may be utilized. The end products of this energy source are acetone and ketone, which are acidic chemicals. The resulting acidosis triggers vomiting; perhaps some occult body wisdom figures that emptying the stomach of its acid may balance the equation. Vomiting, however, leads to dehydration, and a severe case may have to have intravenous water, salt, and glucose to restore the body to normality.

Some astute clinician discovered that ketones show up in the urine as early as twenty-four hours before the vomiting begins. So the trick was to test the urine when the child seemed restless, depressed, or out of sorts. If the urine was positive for acetone, some remedial extra fluid and carbohydrate could be given orally to abort the attack. Now the mechanism seems more logical to me, and I hope to the reader.

These boys seem to share a genetic fault, the overt manifestations of which come to the parents' attention when stress is applied—physical exhaustion from exercise, mental exhaustion from academic overload, domestic pressures, enzymatic depletion from a high carbohydrate diet, or a combination of all. It might appear to be a psychological phenomenon: "He is vomiting because he hates school (or mother, or sister, or teacher, etc.). He throws up as a symbol of his rejection."

But try this on for size: he had pancakes and syrup Sunday morning, a sugary treat at the circus in the afternoon, then he tore around when he got home and went to bed after a dish of ice cream because no one fixed supper and he was fading fast.

His parents are awakened at 2 A.M. by the unmistakable sound of retching coming from his room. But they don't exactly rush in to take care of him, since they both have headaches and nausea, also. (Remember, they all shared the same diet and share similar genes.)

He is sunken-eyed, weak, and feels as if someone kicked him in the stomach. They call the doctor, who diagnoses the flu ("It's going around") and suggests an antivomiting suppository, but, of course, the drug store is closed. So they take turns changing the wet washcloth on his forehead, wondering if it isn't appendicitis.

Since he is still vomiting, they drag him to the doctor. He is mildly dehydrated, has a peculiar fruity odor to his breath, but his blood count is normal and his abdomen is soft and flat, which tends to rule out a surgical problem. Cautious fluid by mouth plus the rectal suppositories get him out of the crisis in a day or so. No diarrhea follows, so it's called one-day flu.

In a month or so the process repeats itself, but now the suppository (Phenergan®, Tigan®, Thorazine®) and some relief is obtained in a few hours. The events preceding the attack may be stressful, so it is called a nervous stomach. A more structured, even uneventful life is recommended and his parents settle for frequent pallor, tiredness, and stomachaches.

If one could just remember to think of this problem, much of the mess could be avoided. Obviously a family history of diabetes, alcoholism, migraine, allergies, and—less likely here—obesity, would help to suggest some disorder of carbohydrate metabolism. A diet calender would be helpful; parents should write down what he ate in the twenty-four hours preceding the onset of vomiting (sugar, milk, chocolate, etc.). Ketostix® can be used to test the urine as soon as his behavior becomes sullen, erratic, or hyperactive. If the ketones are present, oral fluids, fruit juice, and/or honey might turn things around more quickly. Oral tranquilizers may stop the vomiting, but if it has already begun, the rectal route is the next alternative.

The protein-nibbling diet is the answer, especially on exciting or stressful days. Somehow parents must keep him away from the junk and sugary foods at school, grandma's, the circus, and the movies. When he is away from the kitchen a handful of peanuts every twenty to thirty minutes might keep him calm and cheerful through the day.

These children outgrow this usually in adolescence. Hormones must play a role here, as it is less common in adults. Women usually don't have the adult analogue of cyclic vomiting, and migraine, until adulthood. They are usually thin, quick, social, and talkative. They get involved in some exciting, absorbing project and forget to eat or eat handy, sugary foods. When they succumb to an attack, family and friends say, "She exhausts herself; no wonder she gets sick."

11 · Sleep Resistance and Night Wakefulness

If these difficulties are not enough, he still has one more device to unsettle his home—sleep resistance. Most children are reluctant to go to bed at night, but our hero makes the "children need twelve hours of sleep" rule a farce.

"Since eight months of age he has had a terrible separation cry, but I *have* to get out every once in a while. When he sees the sitter come and I pick up my purse, he screams and pounds his head on the floor. I turn and resolutely march out the door. The sitter reports that he goes on like this for thirty to forty-five minutes and ends up asleep or holds his breath, turns blue, and his eyes roll up in the sockets. I thought they were supposed to quit that tantrum thing if no one was watching or responded to it.

"We can never put him to bed without a kicking, screaming scene. We give him a bottle (which he throws back at us), a pacifier, a toy, a song—nothing settles him. A spanking makes him worse. A sedative kept him up singing and jabbering until 3 A.M. Gin and honey quieted him, but I don't want to get that started; there's already too much drinking in my husband's family. I thought that sleep resistance didn't happen until age two years. Is this going to get worse?"

It has long been assumed that the child who is unwilling to go to bed and sleep on command at a reasonable hour is playing a game with his parents. This is so typical of the one-and-a-half- to two-and-a-half-year-old that it is listed as a normal developmental phase.

Usually children give up this phenomenon out of boredom or because they. find some other equally rewarding activity to irritate their parents. Frequently some verbal taunt like "I hate you" or "Drop dead" is substituted for the climbing out of the bed and

104

coming into the living room and interrupting the parents' staring-into-space time.

Angry shouts ("Go to bed or I'll kill you!") and loss of control (spankings) are still forms of attention and serve to reinforce noncompliance. Anger, guilt, remorse, depression, and feelings of inadequacy all descend on the parents, who then argue between themselves about what is right. They consult their friendly pediatrician, who says, "It's a phase. Lock him in his room." A gentle, firm, and nonsmiling return to bed is the recommended method of teaching this child that the day is over. This lesson may take a year to sink in, but at least you have the satisfaction of knowing that you are dealing with the learning center of the brain.

You may, however, have a child who needs little sleep; if a two-year-old finally settles down to sleep at 10 or 11 P.M. and awakens refreshed at 6 or 7 A.M., you are stuck with one of these hyperactive approachers and you may have to learn to live with that fact.

"He never slept in one position; he moved all over the bed as if looking for something or trying to get away from his stomach cramps or wet diaper. We would often find him jammed up in the corner of the bed or way down under the blanket. He awakened at least once or twice every night until he was three years old. He would sleep if I would stand there with a pacifier in his mouth and a finger in his rectum; this maneuver must allow the wind to move from one end to the other more easily. He often slept with his eyes quarter open—like a watchdog, afraid he might miss something. Occasionally as proud parents we would sneak dinner guests in to his room to 'oooh' over our joy. There he would be, staring at us through the slats. Some nights he didn't sleep at all. He constantly rocked the bed when he was asleep, or because he was asleep, or to allow him to sleep. He would stop for a few seconds if we called his name, but would go right back to it. He jiggled the crib around the room until one night he jammed it against the door. We had to break a window to get in to him for his night feeding; all that exercise made him hungry. He broke down two cribs until we got smart and put the mattress on the floor. He was able to climb out of his crib at four months of age! The best solution was to put him in a furniture-less room with wall-to-wall carpeting and let him figure out when and where and how to sleep."

Sleep peculiarities, strange eating habits and allergies are frequently clustered in the hyperactive approachers, so the following subgroups may be artificially contrived.

Sleep pattern		0	1	2
140	Insomnia after four months	no	some	constant
141	Restless, light sleep, bed torn up	no	some	yes
142	Nightmares, terrors, sleep-walk	no	occasionally	frequent
143	Sleep resistance, no naps	no	occasionally	true
144	Asleep after 10 P.M., first one up	no	occasionally	yes
145	Fear of dark, comes into parents' bed at night	no	occasionally	frequent
146	Deep sleep, hard to rouse	no	occasionally	usually
147	Bed-wetting after age five years	no	occasionally	constant

There is no satisfactory answer. If hostility is creeping into your whole child-rearing scene, something has to be done to make the child more acceptable. No amount of pounding on him will change his body rhythm. Cajoling, bribing, spanking, tying him in bed, locking his door all only serve to stimulate these sensitive children more; sleep is even further delayed.

Children do not reason as adults, but they feel or sense emotional tones as well as or better than we do.

Babies who do not sleep through the night because they overreact to their digestive pains may also notice the irritation of their tired, exasperated parents. If they suspect they are unacceptable or a burden to their caretakers, they feel rejected or no good. The bad self-image becomes implanted in their memory storage bank and befouls their entire adult outlook. Remedial adult programs are costly and tardy. If a child knows he is loved, worthwhile, wanted, and needed, he should have little trouble carving out his role as a functional adult.

Counseling may be necessary along with the following techniques. Sleep is responding to other treatment based upon research into its nature. Since stimulation of the ascending neurons from the reticular activating system causes arousal of the cortex and damage leads to sleep, this RAS area deep in the brain has an inhibitory/excitatory effect on the cortex; it is the arousal center of the brain.

Some cyclical factor must be postulated to explain why this arousal center alternates from daytime alertness to nighttime inhibition.

Some of this diurnal rhythm must be related to the influences of the pituitary hormone, which peaks in the bloodstream at about 6 A.M. If the adrenal glands are functioning properly, cortisol levels in the blood reach their highest concentration at about 8 A.M. Our circadian rhythm must be in part regulated by this hormone.

The hippocampus, in the limbic system, attracts much of the adrenal-cortical hormone that reaches the brain. One of the known functions of this area is related to arousal and attention. It is also known that stimulation of the hippocampus produces an inhibitory effect on ACTH secretion (another feedback-inhibitory control).

Thus inadequate amounts of cortisone, as found in allergy, can result in sleep disturbances. Remember the family in Chapter 8 who awoke zonking at 6 A.M.? Allergic victims who are awakened by a full nose or a tight, wheezy chest might be suffering from an inadequate supply of cortisone in the early morning hours because the adrenal glands have been depleted of this hormone due to falling blood sugar.

A large dose of vitamins (especially vitamin C and pantothenic acid, cortisone precursors) plus a protein snack at bedtime to prevent the nocturnal blood-sugar drop should solve this problem rapidly. (A vitamin injection given to a young man eliminated his half-hour nose-blowing session virtually overnight.)

The colicky baby is also noticing his environment and/or his stomach too acutely. He perceives some threat to his comfort. If he cannot suck his thumb or rock the bed to produce alpha waves in his cortex, he can only cry. The parents perceive a baby in pain. The doctor is summoned; he perceives touchy, sensitive people who may be causing the distress. He prescribes a sedative for the baby and a tranquilizer for the parents.

How about another option? Assume the baby has an allergy to

milk (even if breast-fed; cow's milk protein can be a part of a nursing woman's milk if she is drinking it) as well as an inadequate limbic system filtering mechanism. Change the milk, stop flavored vitamins and all solids, provide vitamin C up to 100 milligrams a day and ground-up vitamin B$_6$ (100 milligrams a day) and pantothenic acid (100 milligrams two or three times a day.) A vitamin C and B-complex injection might speed things up. Giving him the precursors to cortisone might allow peaceful sleep and dissipate the allergy all at once. Stopping milk and sugar may allow comfortable sleep as well as disappearance of nasal phlegm.

Many children and adults are stimulated when they eat sugar of any kind, because the adrenaline is released when the blood sugar falls. Others are more somnolent because the increased amounts of insulin produced following a rich carbohydrate meal tends to lower the amounts of amino acids relative to tryptophan—a precursor of serotonin, a neurochemical, and hence more tryptophan is available to enter the brain and become serotonin. (It is known that cats, at least, deprived of tryptophan, have insomnia.) In some studies, feeding one gram of tryptophan induced sleep more quickly. Corticosteroids induce the breakdown of tryptophan: less corticosteroids, more tryptophan. Corticosteroids are at their lowest level in the evening; maybe more tryptophan is available in the evening to induce sleep.

If stress releases cortisol and tryptophan is metabolized perhaps the decrease in serotonin under stress is related to the decrease in available tryptophan. Depression, some forms of hyperactivity, and some psychotic states are associated with decreased amounts of serotonin in the brain. Therefore stress, with its associated excessive excretion of adrenal-cortical hormone, may prevent the body from providing the brain with enough tryptophan to allow an optimum supply of serotonin; depression and insomnia may follow.

Tryptophan, an amino acid, is found in beef and other protein-rich foods. A steak, potato, and rich dessert meal may cause drowsiness—not from a full stomach, but because of the extra tryptophan. Thus protein nibbling from 3 P.M. until bedtime may allow a child to fall into relaxed sleep. Many people try to restrict eating to three meals a day, which may be satisfactory for some, but our flighty hero should be allowed to nibble. Old-fashioned peanut butter, a piece of cheese—a gob of food every two hours may be what his system is crying for. A wise parent might feed the child half of his supper about one hour before the arrival of the stress-producing spouse. Children in nursery school should be given a protein snack half an hour before the arrival of their ride home. The remainder of supper could be offered an hour later.

The touchy, goosy, afraid-of-everything, cannot-relax-and-sleep child may think the world is too close to him. Organize a structured, scheduled environment with definite activities at definite times. Redecorate his room with soft blues, browns, and greens and as few objects as possible short of being sterile. Allow him to attend to one thing at a time. Let him rock and suck or hold a blanket to his ear for as long as he wants. Let him eat by himself. Restrict the afternoon nap. If he takes a three-hour nap, cut him down to two hours. Sleep may come more easily after supper.

A quiet story, a boring TV show, a hot bath, along with another protein snack with prayers and "What was the most fun thing you did today?" might be all that's necessary to allow for that cozy, loved, snuggly feeling so necessary for sleep.

Calcium has long been known to have a calming, beneficial effect on sleep induction. Because of its known action on cell-wall permeability and enzyme activation, an insufficient amount may prevent the release of neurochemicals so that sleep may not occur at the appropriate time. Two to four dolomite tablets (or two teaspoonfuls of Neocalglucon®) at bedtime is usually enough. Some recommend a glass of milk for the calcium, but allergic people might find that the phlegm it produces counteracts all its relaxing benefits. Cheese might be all right.

Phenothiazines, like Thorazine®, make good sleep inducers: They depress the RAS; on the other hand hyperactive children may be put to sleep with stimulants. (An enzyme lack is assumed to explain this paradox.)

Benadryl®, Phenergan®, Thorazine®, Noctec®, and Atarax® all seem to be safe and satisfactory aids to the acceptance of bedtime. Many feel it is cheating to drug a child, but I feel that screaming at or pounding on a child are more harmful to the psyche.

But once he *does* go to bed, will he stay there?

"My two-year-old has been up at night at least twice a week since birth. Even *before* he was born, he kicked me out of bed occasionally with some sort of internal broad jump. He is completely uncuddleable. He may sleep for an hour or two, wet his bed, get cold, then wander into my bed. I can't sleep with his thrashings, so I get up, change the sheets on his bed, and get in. He finds me in an hour, and I move to the couch. We finish up at 5 A.M. on the living room floor—snarling at each other."

In general there are two types of night-wakefulness problems. Some babies drop off to sleep easily but awaken every two to four hours all night, whereupon they insist on some kind of human contact, comforting, food, or just cry a lot as if having a terrifying dream. Others defy their parents because they fail to drop off to sleep at what seems to be an appropriate time for the age.

If we say an infant should sleep through at one month of age and he doesn't until three months, it does *not* mean that he is damaged or sick or hyperactive. If he awakens during the night in the first few months, hunger seems to be the logical cause. He may be growing too fast and cannot get enough calories down during the waking hours to prevent a hunger pain at 2 A.M. Our touchy protagonist may not be able to fill himself up enough during the day because an overdistended stomach is painful, or an incompetent valve at the top of the stomach may not allow distention without regurgitation.

Rapidly growing babies who cannot get all their calories jammed into their intestines to last for the twelve night hours will awaken regularly until their growth slows. Babies destined to be six feet tall may require night feedings until they are five or six months of age. Parents who are five to five and a half feet tall might have babies who sleep through the night from birth on. Refeeding, changing, and a soothing burp should be enough to allow resleep. The problem may only exist if his parents think he should sleep through by one month of age or are showing anger because of this insomnia. They may take it personally and fight back because they feel so rotten at 2 A.M. But some people love to be busy and enjoy a child who needs extra care.

Nocturnal wakefulness is not a habit; *something* awakens these babies. Many normal adults do the same thing without remembering the act the next day. But no one does anything for us when this happens, so we turn over and return to sleep. If we, however, as these wakeful children's parents, reward them with love and food, they learn they are *supposed* to cry until they are comforted. This application of the learning theory of behavior is appropriate in those children who have a responsive cortical memory and so are able to receive and store this function.

If three months have gone by and everyone is bored, angry, and tired, some effort to change the pattern is worthwhile. Adults frequently find it difficult to turn over and drop off to sleep as easily as children seem to be able to do. This up-for-two-hours-and-sleep-for-one-hour all night does not promote a happy, rested, accepting attitude to face the stressful responsibilities of the next day. One can be sympathetic with women experiencing postpartum depression or with parents who might be angry enough to batter their children. At least some tension at best or seething resentment at worst would be expected. A few headaches would suggest at least a strain on the body's reserves.

If you are tired of waiting for him to outgrow this loathsome trait, the following may be helpful: Stop the milk or change to soy bean milk. It may be a cramp.

Three or four teaspoonfuls of protein (strained beef or lamb) in the last bottle offered at the 9 to 11 P.M. feeding may sustain the blood sugar through most of the night and postpone the hunger sensation.

Offering fewer ounces per bottle or less time at the breast at the 2 A.M. feeding may discourage the "rhythm" of nocturnal feedings.

A time-release capsule of an antihistamine (Contac® or Teldrin®) or a tranquilizer (Thorazine®) may prevent the message of the empty stomach from reaching the brain. The former would be especially helpful if a stuffy nose might be the irritant that helps make him wakeful.

We forced one of ours to sleep through the night by giving him a dose of chloral hydrate (Noctec®) at 2 A.M. when he awakened for a feeding. The sedative confused him so he didn't care that he got only three-fourths of his usual eight-ounce bottle. Each night we gave him the medicine and about an ounce less milk; in a week he was sleeping through. During the day he gradually increased his intake so that his twenty-four-hour intake remained the same, but it was obviously more convenient for all. He was a more acceptable baby.

If these methods are ineffective, the baby must surely be one of these oversensitive types and some other methods must be tried. We now venture into the area of guesswork, but some scientific rationale exists for most of these ideas:

Give calcium at bedtime; it has a calming effect on many people. Too little calcium causes a twitchy irritability, so one or two grams might soothe the baby's nervous system.

The absence of pyridoxine or B_6 has been known to cause convulsions and fretfulness; 100 milligrams of this daily might relax a baby.

Magnesium has been used as a nervous-system sedative and may be found in dolomite along with calcium.

If all else fails, one should consider nocturnal seizures, but a brain-wave test (EEG) may not be confirmatory. Dilantin® or Valium® may be useful, but should be used as the last item on the list.

Do not forget pinworms as one of the most common causes of night wakefulness.

One of the most frightening, heart-pounding events that parents deal with is the child who awakens out of a sound sleep at 2 A.M. with a bloodcurdling scream, and sits bolt upright in bed, eyes wide open and looking terrified.

"We thought we had the bed-rocking problem solved when we put his mattress on the floor. He can't rock the mattress, or at least it's not so noisy, but now he is having terrible nightmares. Some nights he is just panicky and other nights he wanders about the house. Once we found him on the porch. He has had the worm medicine. What causes this?"

"She awakens at about 1 A.M., screams, and acts as if someone is attacking her. Why is she so susceptible?"

"He's four years old now. Last month he heard a fire engine in the neighborhood and he is still having nightmares about it. He wakes up in a sweat and shouts that he is on fire. It takes about an hour to settle him down again. How long will this go on?"

"She is an active eight-year-old. For two years she has been awakening about an hour after she falls asleep with a piercing scream and clutching her shin as if she had been kicked. Is this a shin splint or rheumatic fever?"

No amount of cajoling, shouting, ice water, or shaking can abort one of these attacks. It just finally disappears, and normal sleep resumes. The concerned parents, however, have a little difficulty getting back to sleep.

Thoughts of poisoning, epilepsy, worms, or at least insecurity run through their minds. They try to remember what grandmother said about the bad effects of cherries and milk or ice cream and pickles for supper.

(Recently there has been some interest in exorcism as a treatment, assuming the reaction is the battle of the soul and the devil trying to take possession.)

Our training in medical school allowed us only a few diagnostic options: pinworms (always more troublesome at night), earache, some odd form of epilepsy, and, of course, insecurity or psychic stress. It was always hard for me to understand the latter mechanism. How could psychic phenomena actually produce a bad dream? Where is the terrifying thought stored, and why does it appear in the middle of the night as if the projectionist in the brain pulled the wrong switch?

The insecurity theory has some validity, since these episodes frequently occur the night following a strenuous day—athletics, party plus a movie and junk food, or a tough day at school with a teacher glaring. Occasionally the anticipation of a stressful event will allow this night terror to occupy the dream time. A friend of mine in medical school used to dream of taking the next day's exams. He would sweat through the terrible trauma and awaken thinking, "Well, I'm glad that's over," then realize he had the whole awful squeeze to do again. Indeed, many children suffer from these nocturnal terrors and grow up to be perfectly normal adults. It doesn't seem to bother them or lead to any psychopathology; and they have no memory of these vivid episodes the next day.

Sleep and dream research has indicated that all of us must devote twenty-five to fifty percent of our sleep time to dreaming. If dream deprived, paranoidlike feelings overwhelm our waking state. Stored memories are the dreams' content; the plot is woven with psychological wishes, however distorted or disguised in symbols. Some evil people have sweet dreams; some lovely people have unreportably foul nightmares. Inconsistencies are frequent. Freud thought that the dream is the psyche's way of dealing with unconscious (limbic system?) wishes in a socially acceptable way—symbols in dreams allow the material to get by the dream censor (superego) without anxiety. It is a method of release that allows sleep to continue. (Some bed-wetters dream up a toilet so they can wet without guilt.) We all would appreciate pleasant dreams. But our nocturnal screamers may have an immature nervous system, a low threshold for incoming stimuli (limbic system allows raw stimuli to ascend to the receptive centers), or a falling blood-sugar level which triggers an epilepticlike electrical shock wave or the release of adrenaline.

The sequence might occur something like this: A stressful day depletes sugar stores in the muscles and liver, leaving little reserve for the work of the brain (one quarter of the blood volume of each heartbeat must go to the brain because of its high energy needs and its inability to store sugar for future needs). A carbohydrate or sugary dessert or bedtime snack might precipitate a further reduction in the level of sugar available. The cortex, thus deprived, cannot function properly; the limbic system would fill the void with, and/or send overwhelming images of violence, sex, food, unpleasure, or pain to the area where dream awareness is projected. These animal feelings are just there; there is no surfacing needed to relieve psychic pressure.

A further physiological event might produce just plain panic: When the blood sugar falls, adrenaline comes pouring out of the adrenal glands to help extract sugar from the stored glycogen in the liver. Adrenaline is responsible for the feeling of anxiety, and in some people, impending doom (final exams or root canal work).

Everyone secretes adrenaline in response to fear or anger or tension. In the dream state the fear, anger, or tension may be the *result* of adrenaline secretion. The dream may not be as bad as the feeling accompanying it. This would produce the manifestations of fear that the parents observe: dilated pupils, rapid heart, sweaty palms, and readiness for flight.

The parents have heard that ignoring "bad" behavior will help extinguish it, but they don't realize that they are trying to communicate with the wrong part of the nervous system.

He is unable to learn anything in the middle of the night

because he is operating at a subcortical level, at about the gorilla level.

The cortex is necessary for the storage of memory or learning in general, and if a neurobiochemical defect prevents its operation, the message almost literally goes in one ear and out the other. Nocturnal wanderings, sleep resistance, insomnia, 3 A.M. depression (and associated suicide and homicide) could all be classified as a dysperception. The brain is getting the wrong message from the environment. The latter did not change; the only thing left to blame for these discomfitures is a distorted reception of the incoming stimuli.

It now seems obvious that much can be done to prevent frightening night experiences during the dream state by reorganizing or rerouting the electrochemical pathways. If we could keep the evil, animal, or vicious limbic system emotions from welling up to the cortical areas where the dream is viewed, our patient might sleep peacefully and awaken rested.

The therapy would be the manipulation of the environment, internal and external. Talking out the events of the day (or the next day) in a calm, accepting manner will defuse much stored anxiety. A hot relaxing bath plus a big glass of "calcium" (don't use the standard milk as these people may be allergic to this therapy) and some protein snack is frequently all that is necessary to provide the nutriments that the brain requires for one of its busiest times—one to two grams of some calcium (dolomite, bone meal, or calcium lactate) about an hour before bed, along with some nuts or meat or a hard-boiled egg. Vitamin B_6 (100 to 300 milligrams) at this time may be required. Pantothenic acid as a cortisone precursor might hold the adrenal glands together.

If the night is better, the morning is good. If the morning is good, the day is better. If no response occurs in just a few days, a sleeping EEG might be revealing. We have assumed the pinworms were treated at the first sign of night restlessness weeks before.

Grandmother was right, the pickles are OK (vitamin C) but the ice cream is the villain. But it is necessary to point out that normal people sleep more deeply when they consume sugar at bedtime; the resulting hypoglycemic attack may prevent the brain from working at all, and they would not even notice a bad dream.

PART THREE

YOUR CHILD AND--
OR VERSUS--
SOCIETY

12 · Why Are Children Battered?

An obstetrician told me how he almost ruined the warm doctor-patient rapport he had established with a lovely woman at the end of her first pregnancy. He delivered her of a baby whose eyes were a little widely set, whose ears were a little too low on the head, and whose neck seemed a little short.

He would have told the mother of the unfortunate circumstances, but the anesthetist had put her under for the repair. When he was satisfied that she was safely recovering, he went to the waiting room to tell the father the disturbing news.

His concern was immediately dispelled when he called out for the woman's husband. The new father's wide-set eyes beamed. His low-set ears perked up when the doctor was able to reassure him that he had a lovely baby boy and his wife was doing fine. If this woman loved her husband, she should be able to love this baby, who seemed to be created in his image. This father should have no trouble accepting this boy, as he is programmed to accept this constellation of features as friendly, or at least non-threatening.

Mother Nature must have discovered that if the baby has most of the features of one or the other of the parents, the child would be more fully accepted, loved, and appreciated.

Consequently, he would be more likely to develop a good self-image, grow up to accept his role as an adult in his family or tribe, and pass on this love and acceptance to the next generation. Comfort should be the criterion of a satisfactory human existence, a feeling of pleasure derived from present events or the hope, at least, that the future will be better than the now—a sense of belonging or worthwhileness.

117

Just wanting a child doesn't seem to be quite enough. A child who doesn't fit into the mold of what we expect is going to have a little difficulty feeling accepted. If a two-year-old whines because he is cutting molars and is constipated, we may find it difficult to show love and acceptance—especially if he is reluctant to become toilet-trained until he is three.

But parents who want children, who have planned for them, pour love into them, follow all the guidebooks, and listen to everything their pediatrician suggests are frequently disappointed in the results. The children may seem to defy them, be on a different time schedule, be active in a home that loves tranquility, or be withdrawn in an outgoing family. They just do not seem to fit in. They often seem to intuit—and perform—the very trait the parents find least desirable. If they take pride in neatness, the child is messy. If they are health nuts, the child is sickly. If they are athletic, the child is maladroit and prefers sedentary activities. (Maybe a method should be established to allow parents to swap children when they realize there is some distortion in the parent-child relationship.)

"My John is completely unpredictable. He's a Jekyll and Hyde," says the father. "I feel guilty and embarrassed now, because almost every night my wife told me what a monster he had been all day, and I would tell her, 'He's all boy,' or 'He's testing you; you've got to give him more definite limits. Maybe you're not forceful enough,' or 'He'll outgrow it.' Now she's sick in the hospital and I'm the baby sitter, and I know what she means. Today he seemed calm and responsive to my suggestions, but yesterday and the day before he was all over me, the street, the store—whining, running, falling on the ground, shouting 'I want' or 'No' or 'Gimme.' During visiting hours at the hospital I turned around for a second and he got on the elevator. When I finally caught up to him, he was about to assist in surgery. People give me that look that says, 'You shouldn't have a child if you don't know how to discipline him.'

"My wife is full of love; we wanted him when he arrived. We've disciplined him about danger and tried not to beat him down for every transgression, but I'll have to admit, my wife is right—he is two people: a beautiful, curious, thoughtful angel, and a mean, short-tempered, unfeeling gorilla."

"We got up late this morning; I was tense and had a headache. Everyone got something for breakfast—juice, toast, cereal—not adequate, but something. I didn't want them to be late for work and school. And then this Kevin in the midst of the scramble asks, 'What's for supper?' Couldn't he just keep his mouth shut when he knows I'm under pressure? He seems to know my bad days and zeros in on me.

"Supper was little better; I had some time to balance things up—protein, fruit, vegetables, grain, and some dairy products. I served this with positive thoughts: cheerfulness, optimism, don't put anyone down, ignore bad manners and fighting. And then, as if Kevin knew the one thing that would get me, said, 'What are we doing next Saturday'?

" 'I don't know what we're doing next Saturday!' I burst into tears and rushed out of the room. I quit! I can't go on pouring out love, security, and food without a little bit of positive feed-back. I need to have a little joy, a little fun, too. I can't cuddle him, read to him, or have a little rewarding one-to-one interaction without him appearing bored, disinterested, cheated, or asking, 'What's next?' He is never satisfied. He needs to win at everything. If he doesn't, he is mad, or bitter, or exquisitely depressed, and I can't talk him out of it."

"If she weren't so nervous, her baby wouldn't be so fussy and colicky," is a half-truth. Most women are calm, resourceful, and can usually withstand chronic pain. But when their own flesh and blood keeps screaming, scratching, coughing, wheezing, vomiting, breaking out, and generally being a real twitch, it drives the best of them up the wall. How does it make a parent feel when he has done his best to soothe a baby, to cuddle, hold, and rock, and then be rewarded with a cupful of sour milk all over a clean shirt? This injury becomes insult when the neighbor or mother-in-law can feed the child and put him down with nary a peep. What a blow to the psyche! Remember your mother's threat: "You should have a baby just like you!" You did. How did she know so much about genetics?

So you have accepted this somewhat less-than-perfect baby and resigned yourself to a never-paid-up bill at the drugstore, but at least his intellectual potential seems to be intact. Or is it?

It must be obvious to the reader what I am leading up to:

Genetic factors of hyperactivity certainly are expressing themselves here.

The usual story is of the baby who holds his head up early, peers out at the world when an attempt is made to cuddle him as if to say, "Is this all there is?" These babies relate to their environment in an exaggerated way; all stimuli seem to be a threat (as the germs, viruses, and allergens mentioned earlier) or as unignorable attractions. Most of them are approachers and respond physically by actively regarding whatever comes to sight, hearing, or feeling. (Some, however, appear to overreact by withdrawal as if slow, frightened, or paranoid.) The common denominator of all is that environmental messages are noticed more acutely. It's as if the environment were too close.

He is so goosy that tickling makes him cry, and he thinks diaper, temperature, and food changes are some personal attack. He stands and walks early (often forgetting to crawl) only to get into attractive dangers. Teething suggests to him that someone hit him on the jaw. He thinks the world is conspiring to make him miserable. He is either laughing until he vomits or is crying until he holds his breath and turns blue. He finds it impossible to fit into the family routine, no matter how structured, calm, nontraumatic, and routine his parents have tried to make it.

Most busy, hyperactive approachers are cheerful pests, but many go through life with a chip on their shoulder, feeling gypped—as if the world owes then a living:

"She's furious if she doesn't win at everything. She kicked her bike because she couldn't ride it the first time up. She cried and pouted because she didn't win all the prizes at her own birthday party. She is all take and no give, a complete narcissist. She carries a grudge for weeks." They never quite get the message that we are all in this together and need to help each other out. They don't sense the mutuality of the human social experience. Everything must go their way. Parents may find these children a drag; every family decision must first consider the child's over-responsiveness. They ruin every outing, visit, picnic, or party because of their twitchy, impulsive behavior. And if everyone survives some carefully planned activity, he will come down with a fever, a cold, or hives.

I assume that we all need rules to live by. But what of those who cannot fit into the rules? Are they necessarily bad? I maintain that the baby usually starts the cycle. But any reasonably responsive, caring person will become tense, irritable, and a little resentful when there seems to be no relief in sight. But what's really tragic is the genetic connection discussed earlier. Remember your mother saying to you, "I hope you have a child just as awful as you are; it'll serve you right!" It often happens. Children who are sensitive, touchy, who act out, wake up at night, and are severely disciplined will grow up to have children who do the same thing. Thus the very people who are the *least* equipped neurologically, chemically, and physiologically to have such a difficult child are the very ones who are more likely to have them! Does the parents' subliminal irritation about the time, financial, and emotional drain suggest to the child that he is less than appreciated? Or does he thrive on their negative attention?

We know that battered children number in the thousands. But from the stories parents tell me about the awful behavior of their children, I am surprised that there are so *few* battered children. Most parents do call for help when they realize how close they have come to damaging their child for some persistent mischief. Their tears, shakiness, and anger give away the loss of self-control that precedes either flight or a vicious counterattack:

"If I don't entertain her every minute she goes clunking about the house whining and flicking her hands as if shaking water off. Does she have arthritis? We've dewormed her, checked for teeth (always coming in), made sure she had no ear infection, corrected a mild anemia, and have tried to reward her with a smile and a love pat when she seems cheerful. We try to ignore her bad behavior. We even stopped serving foods with artificial coloring or additives (it helped). We wanted her and always love her but as she is sensitive, I suspect she knows we don't like her behavior. Basically we *don't* like what she does. She will sit sucking her thumb and be calm when she hears her father's deep voice say, 'Be quiet and sit down, please.' Are we expecting too much from this narcissistic age? Why is she such a grouch? So we just wait? Or is she being psychologically damaged now? We have read all the books, consulted two pediatricians, and are

completely baffled. We need to have a little reward for the time
and effort we spend on her. She turns every fun thing into a
shambles. I feel I'm about to lose control and really hurt her."

"Would you give me the number of Parents Anonymous, the
hot line for parents about to batter their children? I can't take it
anymore. He comes in at 4 A.M. and wants to know if it's time to
get up. We turn our backs hoping he will get the idea, but he just
stands there tapping my shoulder until I scream at him. I don't
want to be nice to him or he will think he is supposed to awaken
us. We treated him for worms. He's intolerable. Please do something!"

These parents know it is "wrong" to hate their child; they want
us to sympathize at least or share the guilt of their feelings. It is
countertherapeutic to tell them they are bad for feeling this way;
they already know that—at least the ones who call.

The ones who *don't* call early but will take their child to the
hospital or doctor's office and give a spurious tale about a fall
down the steps are the ones who feel the child "had it coming."
How did it start? Surely most parents don't scream or spank
their six-month-old babies when they get sick or wet themselves
or wake up at night because of hunger. Did the child initiate his
own battering or deprivation? Was he something less than perfect in his parents' eyes and "asked for it" by awakening every
morning at 2 A.M.? Studies of battering parents reveal that they
are *not* psychotic, which we all used to believe and would still like
to. They are terribly lonely people who really felt the child was
somehow going to enrich their meager, loveless lives. They may
have wanted this child, or something like it, to love, but soon
found out the infant needed more love and care than it was able
to give in return. "She thinks we love her little brother more
than we love her. If she keeps this up, she may find it's true."

If the baby had laughed and smiled and cooed when it was
held and rocked and cuddled, the parents might have been able
to accept some of the drudgery of its care and even felt that the
child was giving enough love to balance things out. But these
parents frequently come from the ranks of the touchy, need-
to-win, unable-to-wait, hedonistic hyperactives who after a few
seconds of sexual fun find themselves saddled with a responsibil-

ity that their poor self-image is unable to cope with. They have little ego strength; everything has to go their way. Remember, they are the ones who have felt gypped by life. Their narcissistic child is just another reminder that their theme song is "Is That All There Is?"

If a child awakens at 2 A.M. because he wet the bed, has a headache or stomachache, or feels frightened and miserable because he had a nightmare, it is quite possible that his cortex is not functioning properly because of inadequate enzymes and chemical systems, and a low blood sugar. He might wander into his parents' bedroom seeking relief or comfort.

His parents at that time can not be expected to be operating optimally. They may not be functioning with full cerebral capacity at 2 A.M. either—oxygen, glucose, and cortisol are at minimal levels—and may respond a little heavily to the nuisance from the nursery. Don't rouse a hibernating bear.

At least they won't jump up and respond with, "Hi, there! How nice to see you. Let's cuddle a little bit." A more normal response would be a little more negative, "For God's sake, go back to bed!"

They may have heard of disregarding unacceptable behavior and turn away—the body English that is supposed to tell the nocturnal visitor that this is not the time for love. They usually try a little verbal discipline, which falls on the unhearing ears of the infant who has an earache or stomachache or nightmare or is restless in the middle of the night.

So these persistent pests just stand there tapping their parents on the shoulder. The next move might be a sudden slap across whatever was close enough to hit. These parents have usually been disciplined in the same way when they were children; it appears to be the only method of control that they know.

The child responds with an outburst which gives new impetus to "I'll teach you!" and a justification for further punishment. Somehow the contest terminates with no winner.

Frequently the participants are unable to remember the details of the encounter, probably because neither was using the cortical areas of their brains. The animal brain and/or limbic system were the only parts that were operating. The memory areas and the conscience part of the cortex were not available at that time because of faulty nutrition and low cortisone levels. It was animal growling at animal.

Of course children can get battered at any time of the day or night, but the incidents seem to cluster in the 1 to 5 A.M. time period. Late afternoon is another tough time for humans; car accidents driving home after a tiring, boring day, children irritable after school, feisty toddlers who are hungry and did not nap are into poisons. Many children are at least pushed around at this time if not actually battered.

Babies—especially the ones we are interested in here—will detect these not-so-subtle clues from the very people they must rely upon. As weeks and months pass, they will suspect they are not exactly favorite guests. We know children learn at a young age; can they learn a sense of less than one hundred percent acceptance? This inner fault of the nervous system usually leads to increased external pressure to conform. Parents, realizing that this child has to learn to control his animal impulses, try spanking, screaming, isolation, ignoring, withholding until finally the life style of the household is hostility punctuated by commands and questions: "What are you doing now?" "Get out of there!" "Go to bed." "Finish your supper." "Don't do that!" "Don't put toys in the toilet!" "Why did you goose your sister?" "Go to sleep, it's eleven o'clock!"

I remember my mother calling me "Gertrude" when I was glumping about the house or acting mean or irritable. (Gertrude was the mean little kid in *Polly and Her Pals*, a popular comic strip when I was small.) This did not have the reaction of immediately improving my disposition that Mother wanted. It might have even suggested an alter ego for me. And there was no way I could tell her that I did not feel right; I had never lived in anyone else's body so I could note the contrast. I had frequent earaches and a mastoid operation at age five, eye-straightening surgery at age six, and bed-wetting until age thirteen. Stress of some sort was eating at me, but no one put it all together. As time goes by it is difficult to determine what is a learned response to gain attention—albeit "bad" or negative attention—and what is strictly this poor connection in the nervous system.

His ability to sense that his loving caretakers are getting tired of, bored with, or angry at his constant sickness and/or fussiness, may promote the development of secondary psychological problems: depression, guilt, hypochondriasis, phobias, overdependence. Or he may play games because he has somehow learned that sickness is an attention-getter. The following story of Bill shows how a hyperactive child got into a battering situation because of his superactivity:

"It was an uneventful pregnancy. What I lost, the baby gained, so no weight difference for me. 'We have another boy,' were the first words I remember my husband saying to me as I awoke. 'He's fine! So don't worry.' Billy weighed eight pounds, ten and one half ounces, and his pediatrician assured me I had a good, husky, normal boy. He put him to the breast at six that evening. My milk had already come in and he ate well from the start.

"In December, when he was two months old, a niece called 'Hi!' from the front door, and Billy answered 'Hi!' from the kitchen. From then on one only had to leave the room and reenter to be greeted by Billy's cheery 'Hi.' On December 28 he sat up alone for the first time, playing with toys and watching TV. He didn't like the playpen at all. At this time he started sucking his thumb, a habit I have never been able to break. He weaned himself at eight months, he could walk from object to object at nine months, and by ten months he tried to run like his older brother. Once he got going too fast and hit his head, sustaining an inch-long cut above his eye. How he loved stairs. As the older children's rooms were up there it was hard to keep him down if the door was left open. He'd sit about halfway up and sing and jabber to himself. He loved to run the length of the front porch and in winter the living room and dining room.

"On Billy's second birthday that fall we bought him a second-hand trike. Three days later he went head first over the handlebars. He knocked out his left front incisor. He was without his front tooth for almost five years. He was very inventive and made up games and occupations; with rope and a tin can he'd be off 'selling gas and oil.'

"When he was three and one half I let him play out on the lawn and sidewalk. He'd take his red wagon and go from corner to corner, usually singing a happy tune. He had an uncanny sense of timing, and would watch for Daddy to come home around the corner.

"He had many falls and spills, but seemed to tolerate things well. At age four and one half years he fell in the cesspool. It took a team of men to get him out. He must have been standing on something as he only was in up to his armpits. We cleaned him up with a Lysol bath and the doctor gave him a typhoid shot. Billy never even had a reaction.

"It was about this time that we noticed odd things about the Zilches, who lived next door. Mrs. Z. would throw scalding dish-water over the fence directly on a spot that Billy had occupied just seconds before. Mr. Z. would scold Billy every time he saw him drive by in his red fire truck. I told Billy never to go into their yard, but once they hid his truck when he parked it on the strip of property that separated our driveways. We had to call the police. The Zilches were odd people; they never had friends that came to visit, not even to see their girls. We never heard those girls laugh or giggle in all the years we lived next to them. They never used their driveway, but would be furious if some-one else did.

"On July 14, Billy came to the front door making the same noise he had made when he fell in the cesspool. He was dirt and grease all over. The greasy spots on his head were a pretty good size. I gave him a bath. He couldn't seem to tell us what had happened to him. His eyes had a frightened look, but the pupils were equal. We bathed and dressed him and he went on to play. Almost immediately two policemen arrived. They said they had a warrant for Billy's arrest. We asked him if he knew how old Billy was. The officer said no. Then we brought in Billy. The Zilches next door had turned in a complaint that Billy was throw-ing rocks into their yard, and they had a paint can full of them to prove it. The next time Billy saw Mr. Z. he threw his arms about me crying, 'Don't let that man get me!' " Mr. Zilch, the neighbor, apparently a rigid, humorless misanthrope, must have felt that Billy needed more restrictions than he was getting and applied *his* method.

"As months went by the hair where the oil spots were turned

several shades lighter. In the next few months he became super-active. He'd swing too high on the swing. He developed an odd laugh. He didn't respond as formerly. In the house he ran and ran. He stopped talking to us.

"In 1963 brain injury was confirmed by a doctor. An encephalogram was ordered. A Nembutal® suppository was used so he would be quiet for the test, but he was awake and screaming all that night. The brain damage only served to accentuate his hyperactivity. What followed was a nightmare of strange, unpredictable, sometimes violent behavior, convulsions, attempts at control with Dilantin®, Dexedrine®, Mellaril®, and Thorazine®. He would suddenly throw his watch at his sister, or hit, pinch, or scratch me for no reason that we could see. It was the usual thing for my legs to be black and blue where he had hit me so hard. He was now having grand mal epilepsy, and to control the seizures, we had to use so much medicine that he was drunk all the time.

"We had to move a couple of times because Billy would break down doors and wreck the furniture. At a parade in Portland once he had one of his wild attacks, storming about and yelling. Someone called the police and they had to handcuff him to subdue him."

The moral of the story is don't let your neighbor batter your child. Somehow his mother has been able to hold this boy together through some terrible ordeals. She knew that his wild destructive behavior was not directed at her or because of her, but that he had suffered some hurt. She was strong enough to realize that she must not take his actions personally, and consequently she did not react directly to him. Another mother might have felt that severe discipline was called for; this mother applied love even when she had to restrain him.

These children *can* appear as impulse-ridden pests to some people. They are more likely to be approachers and test their parents, the school, the helping professions, and, as with Billy, their neighbors.

Benadryl®, Phenergan®, and other tranquilizers are helpful for these wild ones. They are safe and usually serve to give everyone a chance to relax and reload. But most everyone finds the improvement short-lived and before they pour the whole bottle down his stubborn throat, they call with the second notice, "We've had it." The standard no-sugar-and-protein-nibbling diet should be helpful in allowing these children—and adults —to be more comfortable in their environment.

No wonder these children are more likely to be battered, abandoned, or put up for adoption. This is especially true of children whose parents have a problem with their own self-concept; these parents have a low tolerance for children with dismal characteristics. They may demand or expect perfect behavior, but because these children are so distracted by their environment they cannot perform adequately, so they are punished, rejected, or ignored. They really cannot help control much of what they do; they act reflexively. And because they are disciplined—often severely and repeatedly—for something they cannot prevent from happening, they begin to get discouraged, depressed, and bitter. Hyperactive approachers—the very children who need a loving, structured home and school environment—are the ones who get hurt because they went too far, or because some adult did not understand, or because these children don't read the incoming clues from their environment.

Just one more stress for a person who already is unable to handle much. No wonder depressed people have a high incidence of sickness, real and imagined. How many children are subtly but nonetheless hurt by the psychological battering so that they have to be reared again in the psychiatrist's office?

13 · Handling the Impossible Child

The following behavior traits may be considered part of the syndrome and should disappear during the treatment for primary hyperactivity. They may, however, be the result of secondary emotional problems related to the development of the bad self-image because of the constant criticism from parents, teachers, and peer group. If they are observed and treatment is instituted before the age of ten years, they are usually reversible. After the age of thirteen years they are more likely to become fixed as a part of the adult personality, and treatment is possible but difficult and prolonged.

		0	1	2
148	Never satisfied; bored; "Is that all there is?"	occasionally	some	frequently
149	Disappointed in birthdays, holidays, Christmas	occasionally	some	often
150	Frustrated with delays and disappointments	occasionally	some	always
151	Blames others, denies wrongdoing	no	occasionally	yes
152	Sneaks out of fair share of chores	no	occasionally	always
153	Temper outbursts, chip on shoulder, breaks furniture	no	occasionally	yes
154	Lies, cheats, steals, lights fires	no	rare	yes

		0	1	2
155	World owes him a living, feels cheated, wants revenge	no	occasionally	yes
156	Wants to run things, can't play well with others, complaints from other parents, no friends	no	rare	yes
157	Overasserts, bullies, brags, sasses, mean, surly	no	rare	yes
158	Laughs at discipline; isolation and ignoring don't work	no	occasionally	yes
159	Loner, depressed, withdrawn—"I'm no good, you don't love me"	no	occasionally	yes
160	Does bad things, says "Sorry." Does it again	no	occasionally	frequent
161	Encopresis (BM in underwear)	no	twice	frequent
162	Abnormal sex interest	no	occasionally	frequent
163	Truancy, runaway, disappears over minor things	no	once	frequent

Psychotherapy is advised if the above observations do not disappear within a few weeks of the institution of treatment for the hyperactivity associated with them. Some of the clues above sound almost paranoid, which is a little frightening. Some of them sound as though a depression was going on.

The diagnosis is difficult to make by examination alone. But a checkup with the doctor would seem reasonable to assure adequate height, weight, and arrival at the proper developmental levels. Some reassurance is needed that the child has adequate vision, hearing, and speech. A blood test for anemia is wise, and if he has friends, maybe he ought to be dewormed. Does he have cavities? Is there evidence of allergies? If he has the tension-fatigue syndrome, improvement might take three weeks. We doctors may discover only slightly retracted eardrums behind the wax. There is no obvious clue like a blind eye or scissors gait or a tattoo on the forehead that says, "Trouble." We are at the mercy of the mother (usually), who may overstate the problem because she is a sensitive, tense type who notices the child more, or who is unwilling to admit that she may be the catalyst; she may not want to admit he is a problem because she has learned that this behavior is of her doing.

She may have made her mind up that it is all genetic—and all from the hated in-laws' side of the family. She may, however, not even mention the possibility of the syndrome, even though the doctor finds his office a shambles and that the child is exquisitely ticklish, goes wild over shots, and is accident, sickness, and allergy prone. Her acceptance is the first step in the treatment or he will surely face some psychic if not physical trauma when he gets to nursery school or kindergarten. But some parents need to have a crippled dependent child.

The doctor has an obligation to attempt to intervene; the professional knows the consequence of unbridled hyperactivity just as well as the dangers of an untreated strep throat. A key question in ferreting out cause from effect is, "Is he like this with you only, or is he worse in crowds and stimulating situations?" Remember that the global statement about these children is, "He is unable to disregard unimportant stimuli." Our suggested remedies may be effective for any child who has unacceptable behavior, but if he is worse with mother and/or father, the fault may be in *that* interaction, and psychological intervention would seem appropriate.

Our subject is better in a one-to-one situation, and by definition is worse in a crowd or stimulating environment.

We have always assumed the twos were supposed to be terrible: whining, crying, noncomplying (especially at bedtime), impulsively acting out, and eating little and strangely. Since we are examining all our old cherished beliefs, maybe we should start here.

"We knew before birth he was a little more active than our other child, so we took your advice and maintained a calm environment and eliminated all the allergens. I nursed him frequently, watched my diet (no sugar or additives), learned to take naps between feedings, gave him love in a gentle way, kept light and noise at a subexciting level, and thought I had it made. He got extra vitamins, especially C, but no sugar, white flour, or additives. He had a few infections but nothing prolonged. He sat and walked early, was curious and gregarious, but had no bad accidents or poisonings.

"But almost precisely at two years of age, he converted to a monster. It was mainly centered about eating and sleeping. His appetite dropped off as I expected, but he also refused to go to bed and/or sleep until 10 P.M. or so. Even then we weren't done with him; he tossed and turned or would cry out as if having a bad dream. Then he would be up at 5 A.M., wet, angry, and hungry. But then he would only eat a few bites and feed the rest to the dog (a nonallergenic poodle). No new stimuli, traumata, or deprivations occurred that would or could explain it; teething wouldn't last this long. My husband says he's spoiled rotten and thinks we ought to beat him until he responds to the rules. I think if he would eat better, he would feel better, and we could manage him with love and reinforcement of his occasional good behavior. Before I let myself go and really hurt him, tell me what to do. We've had it."

The two-year-old *is* characterized by whininess, a loss of appetite, and an almost constant runny nose. He is frequently stubborn and defiant, especially about toilet training, eating, and going to bed. Everything is "gimme"; he is a dog in the manger—a complete narcissist. Beating him and shouting at him only seem to fix him more surely into his noncompliant set. But usually he does just enough cute things to make us forgive his negativism. A rule might be this: If he laughs and smiles more than he cries and frowns, he is probably doing all right, although the percentages of these activities may be fifty-five to forty-five. After about a year of this, both parties become bored and go on to other, more subtle ways of getting on each other's nerves. But before this response becomes a life style or sets the whole ambience of the home, or before the child gets battered or gets a bad self-image, or the parents split because of a tense, uncomfortable home, parents should be aware of some alternate paths. They should not accept the usual pediatric platitude: "He'll outgrow it; it's a phase." Where do we draw the intervention line between expected, predictable, "normal" irritability and a pathological deviation?

Even though whininess seems to surface precisely on the second birthday, as if the child read the book, this is another one of the many human characteristics that may have a complicated origin. Maybe a twinge from a pushy three-year molar makes the child sigh, fuss, or groan. His parent says, "Oh, don't do that." The child is negatively retarded—but still rewarded—by this attention. He is virtually forced to repeat the noise and, although the tooth finally erupts and the original reason for his complaint has disappeared, he is locked into his behavior. This usually continues until he discovers no one is paying attention or until he stumbles on some other irritating or attention-getting form of communication, like repeating a swear word, hitting the new baby, or putting everything into the toilet bowl except his own BM. Maybe we should redefine the two-year-old: If he whines, has frequent colds, loss of appetite, and sleep resistance, he is abnormal, sick, or under stress. If his biochemistry could be reorganized, maybe he will outgrow this difficult phase more quickly.

What about the two-year-old who fights going to bed, has multiple allergies, repeated ear and chest infections, and won't eat, looks tired, whines all the time, and has circles under his eyes? The doctor finds nothing wrong. No sickness, no anemia, so he diagnoses parental mishandling or gives the standard, "That's the way they are." The parents are told that they are making him nervous, or if they would feed him properly he would get better, or that all two-year-olds are like that, or if they would turn their back on his bad behavior it would disappear.

How about assuming he does not feel well? Many parents relate that their child's irritability had its onset on his second birthday. Perhaps in our approacher enzymatic functioning was adequate until he arrived at a stress crisis at age two. A number of events may occur which may be stressful to him. He grows less rapidly and needs fewer calories and eats less, he cuts some molars, he gets a cold, he discovers sweets, an attempt is made to toilet train him, he is left with a sitter, and/or he goes to nursery school. Internal enzyme depletion coupled with the usual environmental stresses is enough to make him feel rotten. He has a headache and low blood sugar and he behaves accordingly.

"If he would just eat, he would feel better," is the usual maternal cry. Well, yes and no. We know the child at eighteen months to four years needs fewer calories than he did in the first year of life. If he kept up his rate comparable to that of his first few weeks of life, he would be twenty feet tall at age twenty, so obviously he needs fewer calories as he gets older. His brain and other organs are not growing as rapidly, but still they need amino acids, vitamins, and minerals to allow normal function. The tricky balance is to get enough of these essential nutriments into him without a caloric overload.

Even a minor stress like the flu or teething or an allergy could deplete his stores. This, coupled with the normal appetite reduction, could be sufficient to leave him in a negative balance for the nutriments that make the enzymes that pick up the nutriments in his diet that are absorbed and make the enzymes, etc. Then he feels so rotten that he won't eat—the very activity that he needs to break the cycle. The usual parental response to open defiance is open defiance. Deadlock.

We must firmly resolve to say something positive about our children twice as often as we put them down. If this seems impossible it may be because the children feel awful. They may feel awful because the body chemistry is askew. If we can make the person inside that overly sensitive body become more comfortable, he may get the idea that life is fun or at least an interesting challenge.

He might be anemic and/or have a milk allergy and/or an allergy to the pillow and the mattress or the cat he sleeps with. Clean out his room; have him sleep on foam rubber on the floor. Change his diet. Give him some iron drops and stop the milk, sugar, and white flour. Let him do the nibbling on protein and show acceptance. Never expect him to eat a big meal; let him nibble on little bits of old-fashioned peanut butter, fruit, and berries. Stop the artificially flavored vitamins and give him the vitamin B and C as described earlier.

The enzymes in the intestinal tract would appear to be the key linkage so the body may digest and absorb the essential amino acids, carbohydrate, and vitamins which allow the enzymes to make the chemicals that allow the brain to get the message that the world is not so bad after all. In any case, it is amazing how the behavior of these children can be turned around almost one hundred and eighty degrees by a vitamin B and C injection. Overnight they sleep better, begin to eat, and are more likely to adjust to the day-and-night cycles of the family. Sleep is quiet and restful and they are cheerful, calm, and cooperative during the day. The enzymes of the brain, liver, and in the lining cells of the intestinal tract are now provided with the catalysts they need to function. These cells are now able to provide the chemicals that make the body run smoothly. If the child feels better, he eats and sleeps better and the vicious cycle is broken. His environment can say, "You're a nice person; it's nice to have you around."

Billy's mother seems to feel it worked:

"In the last two years we have tried big doses of vitamins and more recently the no-sugar diet. Billy is a big help to me now. He can do most housework, keeps up his own room, washes dishes sometimes for me. He likes to run the washer and dryer—makes a game of it—and can fold and put away his own clothes. He also gets a meal once in a while when I'm sick or my legs won't hold me up. This fall he has started to learn to mow the lawn with a hand mower. This summer I finally got him to let me read aloud to him. When crime programs come on TV we now read.

"We tried decreasing the Dexedrine® and Mellaril® which had both been very helpful in controlling his activity and violence; he seemed calmer now that the no-sugar diet was working. Some of his sudden lashing out at me stopped when I stopped the Mebaral® (a type of barbiturate). If Billy gets too many sweets like a cookie or a piece of pie or pop he begins to have one of his fury spells. I can give him meat or peanut butter or nuts and he'll quiet right down."

The stress here might be more upsetting to the parent-caretaker than the child. Our basic premise is that these conditions are largely genetically produced; the parents, then, would be more than likely to be boggled by similar symptoms. If stress allows the problems to surface in *them*, the symptoms become an added stress.

If a child awakens his parents because of a cramp, he may find they are having the same problem (they are related) and sympathetic understanding may not be readily available. Then follows a rapid deterioration of what should be a joyful experience. It is suggested that the parents of such a child should follow the same diet and vitamin regime. Obviously calm, rested parents will be able to cope more easily. Before you request a prescription for Valium® from the doctor, a trial of protein nibbling and stress vitamins is appropriate.

Indeed, one of the main benefits of having parents is to learn what is right and wrong and how to suppress present impulsive pleasures in order to gain future satisfactions. These learned responses are programmed into the brain at the top or cortical level, and are supposed to keep us out of real trouble (or jail) all of our lives. But the calmest, most consistent, loving parent or teacher will find it impossible to teach love, reading, sense of right and wrong, or use behavior-modification techniques if the cortical functions are not operating optimally.

"He was pulling a knob off the TV set the other day and I said 'no.' I was firm but not frantic; insistent but not demanding, and I didn't shout. He immediately fell on the floor, screamed, and pounded his head, fists, and feet against the floor. I was hoping it was just a temper tantrum but it looked more like a convulsion. I threw a cup of water on him to cool him off but it didn't even interrupt his rhythm. I left the room thinking he would quit if he had no audience. I timed it; it lasted six and one half minutes. He stared into space for a while as if trying to remember what he was doing before he was so rudely interrupted, and went right back to the TV! Now he looks at me, smiles evilly, says 'no' and pulls at the taped-down knobs. He's as defiant and stubborn as his father. How do I teach him the rules of life and property?"

"Tommy has done it again! He's only six years old but he is already a crook and an arsonist. He lies, cheats, steals, and won't do a lick of work around the house. We've pleaded, bribed, and beaten him, but nothing works. He does something awful—like setting a wastebasket on fire. We catch him at it, he says he's sorry, and then turns around and does it again! Can this be treated? Should we have him locked up now? I'm sure a psychiatrist would just blame me for not teaching him self-control. A psychologist told us to use behavior modification and ignore this bad behavior. But how can we turn our backs on a burning garage or a drawer full of junk he's stolen from the local merchants?"

Lighting fires would be wrong in any age child if it occurs more than once or twice. It sounds to me as if Tommy has a conscience, but it gets bypassed. Tommy's conscience is filed away in his memory, but the connecting link is faulty. He is unable to profit from these internalized controls that his parents have built into his brain. His cortex cannot do what we want it to do because of too many incoming stimuli (approachers), or perception distortions (sight and hearing dysfunction), short circuits (epilepsy or epileptic equivalents), not enough nutrients (low blood sugar, calcium, B_6), or poorly functioning enzyme systems.

It's as if the stimulus that enters the nervous system pathway (see a match) goes right up to the response area in the motor cortex (light a fire); it did not check with the area that stores the information that some actions are not socially acceptable. When the deed is done, of course, the approacher can recognize that he has done something wrong and may even admit the transgression, vowing it will not happen again. But it does. Similarly, a person suffering from tunnel vision often drives through stop lights. This "lawbreaker" would stop if he saw the sign, because he obeys signs—but he didn't see it.

A few Saturdays ago the mother of a patient of mine called frantically because her son had burned down another garage. Somehow she felt I could help, but I'm not very good with fires.

Her son, Eddie, is hyperactive, tearing about, staying up late. See a toilet, flush it. See a match, light it. Respond, approach, do something. Being a good mother, she punished him for setting the waste basket afire six years ago, and also took him to the local fire station, where he was to be impressed by the horrors of fire. The attention may have only rewarded him for his transgression. She tried burning his fingers. ("The burnt child dreads fire.")

Nothing worked. He graduated at six to burning comics

under a porch, and then a local garage, which was more exciting because of the gas and oil. The parents thought, "Don't fight him; join him." They had him light socially acceptable fires: candles, fires in the fireplace, and garbage in the back yard. Get it out of his system. It only served to make him a more efficient fire starter. They tried to watch him like a hawk, but he is so quick and sneaky he was able to elude them.

Because of his disruptive school behavior, amphetamines were tried. He settled down, finished his work, and stopped bugging his classmates. His parents were able to say something complimentary about his work instead of the usual, "Where are you? You could do better if you tried. What are you doing? Are you into the matches again?" He began to like himself, and he took less interest in fires. They had almost forgotten about his little "sickness." Five years went by.

On that Saturday, however, the mother was awakened at about 10 A.M. by the unmistakable scream of the fire engine siren coming down her street. She knew, somehow, it was her problem. She leapt reflexly out of bed, donned her robe, grabbed his medicine, and charged out into the street. Sure enough, a garage was engulfed in flame and Eddie was nearby, watching excitedly.

"He forgot his pill; he forgot his pill," was all she could think of to say in his defense.

"Get out of here, lady; we've got a fire to put out," was the fireman's response. She really couldn't get the busy man to understand that Eddie's brain center in his conscience for the control of fire-starting was not chemically connected to the rest of his nervous system.

"The doctor says . . . " fell on deaf ears. Later that week at the juvenile detention home hearing she was asked if she would seek psychiatric help for Eddie. She said she had this pediatrician who was helping Eddie with his problem. "Well, OK," said the court, not completely convinced.

We aren't done with him yet and I'm not that sure that I'm providing the right kind of psychiatric care, but she sets her alarm for *every* morning now.

We are biding our time until maturation of the nervous system somehow allows this impulse control center to become a part of his total reflex pattern.

If we doctors confront the harassed parents with "you must apply more discipline; these impulsive children need more rules and limits must be set for their behavior," it *sometimes* works. Many children are tense, anxious, and hyperactive because they have no consistent built-in guidelines (conscience), as if they were on a limitless plain with no familiar object in view. We don't use the handrails when we drive over the bridge, but we feel more secure and comfortable knowing that they are there.

The alternate advice of "ignore bad behavior and it will go away" may have the disquieting effect of extinguishing the child along with the bad behavior. Babies afflicted with any or all of these problems are a menace to themselves as well as to their caretakers. One of these approachers discovered that if he opened the second-story window to get a better look at the cherry blossoms, his mother screamed and pulled him back in; he got attention for climbing out, but *he* started it. His parents didn't climb out first to show him how. Now they nail the windows shut during blossom time.

But this technique can work in sublethal situations. A couple I know were able to control intramural fighting among their three aggression-prone sons by wearing stereo headphones and listening to Tchaikovsky's *1812 Overture* to block out the noise.

Previous to this deconditioning the boys had learned that their parents would always stop the melee, so there was no need to worry about getting hurt and they did get some attention. It took a great deal of explaining by their psychologist that the boys would not kill each other (he wasn't completely sure himself).

Now as they fought, the only reward was pain, which is a well-recognized motivational device for discontinuing whatever causes it. Each new fight then triggered a response by the parents to make a mark on graph paper and start the record. It took two weeks and a few black eyes and bloody noses, but the two-a-day fights were down to but once a week.

We all need to hear an encouraging word or feel accepted by family and peer group. But consider the constant put-downs these kids receive from the disappointed, depressed parents.

"But," the parents say defensively, "he doesn't do *anything* we can reward him for." What *can* parents say to these terrors? "I love the way you run from one room to the other!" "You certainly stay up late; you must have a lot to think about." "Thanks for fixing breakfast; I'd like my eggs a little less black and with fewer shells." There just doesn't seem to be any acceptable behavior to reward.

Steps to family fun:

1. Have a clipboard with ruled paper handy. List the behavior most upsetting to the adults in the house (e.g., whining, crying, noncompliance, temper outbursts, bad words, etc.) leaving space after the items to total daily frequency. Just establishing the magnitude of the problem is half the treatment. Turning your back on the unacceptable behavior gives you something different to do rather then just confronting the miscreant. The child is supposed to suspect that he is getting no response; the reward or reinforcement is gone. He tries something else. The adults are to make an effort to comment on some neutral or pleasant aspect of the child's body or behavior. (E.g., "I like the way your right arm is attached to your right shoulder." "When you walk, you put one foot in front of the other." "Your nose is exactly between your eyes.")

You should notice that the totals on the clipboard are reduced by fifty percent in two weeks. Remember you want improvement, not perfection. You should find you are saying nice, positive things twice as often as you are giving commands or asking questions. These latter two forms of communication are considered by children as put-downs. (E.g., "Come here." "What are you doing now?" "Did you spill that?") If he is better, you should be better; if you are better, then he gets better.

This sounds ideal as a home therapy, but many conscientious parents are unable to make it work. For behavior modification to be effective, the child's cortex—the repository of learned acts—must be receptive to the message from the environment. If the enzyme function is below par and the supply of energy is inconsistent, the cortical nerves are not responsive and the message is lost or garbled. The child who slips in and out of bad behavior must be operating at his lower animal or limbic level; if his cortex isn't able to operate, he can only use the next best circuit. This limbic system is not programmed for the Ten Commandments, logic, or behavior modification.

2. The mean child who is lying, cheating, lighting fires, and constantly fighting or "borrowing" things may have a conscience but cannot use it because of faulty cerebral connections, low blood sugar, or an odd EEG. He must be helped nutritionally and medically before he is labeled a delinquent. With the help of neighbors, relatives, friends, teachers, and counselors, observe the child's behavior, especially the response to sugar ingestion. Notice how an insignificant stress (saying "no" to a demand) will put the child on the floor if timed two hours after a doughnut, a dish of ice cream, or even a piece of gum. The same stress or demand two hours after an ounce of protein will be met with calmness or a shrug—"I don't care anyway." It is a joy to watch both child and parents improve in their interpersonal relationships because they "like" each other after the diet change. We seem to be overly programmed to the psychological etiology of deviant behavior. The relief of guilt that parents feel when they realize that not *all* of the awful behavior is their fault is the first step in therapy.

3. A trial of medicine may be the next worthwhile step. It allows a respite from the child's antics so that the parents may be able to give more consistent attention to socially acceptable behavior. A calming, not sedating, dose is tried. (Benadryl®, Phenergan®, Thorazine®, Stelazine®, Atarax®, or Mellaril® may provide the atmosphere of ease so that environmental manipulation can be effective.) Barbiturates are almost never used; they usually have an adverse effect on these children. Indeed, if a child is given phenobarbital and he is stimulated, it almost always means that he is one of the approachers.

Calcium and magnesium, either separately or combined as in dolomite, are helpful at bedtime or every few hours all day. Extra B vitamins, along with C, have already been mentioned. If you don't get through to him, an EEG might help. But once he is cheerful and eager, his caretakers would have some positive social action to reward and this touchy child might just grow up to be a reasonably normal adult.

14 · School and Learning Problems

The three-year-old loves to use his big muscles, he is ready for "parallel" play, he has a better attention span than the two-year-old, but may still blow his top when frustrated. Toilet use is usually accomplished without much adult help. He loves stories. Nursery school is usually tried and is successful by age three years. *Usually*. The minimal stress of the separation from the home plus the stimulation of the nursery school or kindergarten is helpful to parents, teachers, and doctors in revealing who is at risk.

"The nursery school is about to throw him out. He screams, hits the others, constantly interrupts story time, will not take a nap or even put his head down for quiet time. He acts as if he's got a hot poker in his rear; he's so touchy. He talks loudly. Finger painting is completely off the paper and onto the other children. I have a job and need him in the school; please slow him down with something."

It happens to about twenty percent of every class. About that many children have behavior traits that suggest they need help. The whole purpose of this book is to identify those at risk and to help change the course of their personal history early, before "bad" behavior becomes fixed as a way of life.

Enough studies have now been done to arrive at a few conclusions as to what group of children is more likely to suffer permanent scars in its growth to a reasonably satisfactory adulthood.

Until recently it was not felt important to identify these children prone for school failure because there were no methods

142

available to help them. Now clever teachers, physiotherapists, opticians, neurologists, and psychologists have devised scores of exercises, devices, programs (massage and hypnosis included), or new approaches to get information into a sub-optimal nervous system.

"She is accident prone. They recognize us at the local hospital E.R.; we made three trips in the last six months. Two eyebrow cuts from falling against the coffee table; it's edged in foam rubber now. Then she fell on a milk bottle she was 'helpfully' bringing in. She's a klutz; she just doesn't watch where she's going."

Many learning disabilities are associated with soft neurological signs. These signs enable the physician and parents to deemphasize the emotional component of the learning disorder. Fifty percent of children with soft neurological signs have reading problems. Neurological items most often found in the child guidance population: poor gross motor coordination (balance, hopping, throwing), perceptual-motor difficulties, defect in fine coordination (speed, dexterity, graphic skills), strabismus (crossed eye), mixed laterality, some ambidexterity, and history or presence of speech defect. A child adequately exposed to reading should learn to read normally just as he matures to the point of walking normally. Some doctors and most teachers do some perceptual-motor tests to see if the child is up to his age level in development. The Denver Developmental Test, the draw-a-person test (or complete-a-man test), and a variety of reading readiness tests are available to all to identify the slow, the unsure, the culturally deprived, the dyslexic, the brain-damaged, and the maladroit.

The doctor assumes that the parent will reveal all the domestic stresses that may be preoccupying the child, and the parent assumes that the doctor will discover any possible impediment to normal school functioning. Both are naive.

It is unfortunate that the teacher has to be the nutritionist, doctor, parent, and psychiatrist for her class, but if she wants to communicate with the children's cerebral cortices, she must make sure that gray matter is functioning or at least minimally receptive. The doctor does a reasonably thorough physical examination before school to detect anomalies of growth, vision, hearing, and organ function that might interfere with the child's functioning in a new and challenging social situation.

But the teacher's evaluation is the key as she (or he) is where the buck stops; she is the supervisor of the stress situation and must be able to intuit the child's overall acceptance of his place in her class. His eye movements, his body English, his interaction with his peer group, and his enthusiasm toward learning are observations she should be able to make. She knows about the short attention span and makes allowances for it. She knows how overly excited the three-year-old can get—how poor is his self-control. It is an ideal situation to make comparisons.

Pediatricians are especially responsive to the observations of nursery school and kindergarten teachers. We rely heavily on nursery school teachers to finger the disturbing or disturbed child.

Information from the teacher and/or the school:

Obviously some of the statements are age-related. Remember, these children have to be worse in a stressful situation or when they cannot cope with too many incoming stimuli. They should have *more* symptoms in the classroom. They may have no symptoms or problems until a tough, rigid teacher comes along, when extra homework is assigned, or if placed in an open, noisy classroom.

		0	1	2
164	*Activity*: trips to toilet, fountain, pencil sharpener. Restless, fidgets, out of seat	no	some	excessive
165	*Distractibility*: disturbed by small noises or movements, confused by group activity or open classroom. Better in one-to-one relationship. Unable to cope with new situations	no	some	true

	0	1	2
166 *Social*: talks, disturbs, touches, pushes, fights. No friends; class clown	no	some	a lot
167 *Work*: goofs-off, unfinished work, asks questions. No responsibility for own work	never	some	frequent
Perception-motor Skills			
168 At grade level for reading	yes		no
At grade level for spelling	yes		no
At grade level for writing	yes		no
At grade level for arithmetic	yes		no
169 Fine motor skills	adequate		poor
Gross motor skills	adequate		poor
170 Comprehends spoken instructions, hearing	adequate		problem
171 Difficulty with grammar, uses incomplete sentences	no		yes
172 Difficulty with relative values (tall, heavy, far, etc.)	no		yes
173 Difficulty with spatial relation (right, up, over, etc.)	no		yes
174 General assessment of native intellectual potential	average or above		less than adequate

Teachers quickly report aggressive acts and general hell raising because they disrupt the classroom routine more than the minimal compliance of the scared loner. The squeaky wheel gets the oil; so the mischievous child gets the tranquilizer. The teacher might assume that this impulsive child did not get enough discipline at home where, in fact, he might have gotten *more* than the average because his supernormal gregariousness has elicited supernormal—but ineffective—punishment.

When the school calls the parents to arrange a conference because something is wrong, the parents may become guilty and/or angry. So it's better for the teacher to make observations, not conclusions. The wise observer-teacher should list only the behavior that she feels is deviant from the norm for her class. Value judgments such as "evil," "spiteful," "criminal type," "emotionally disturbed," "insecure," "neurotic," "stupid," or "afraid" are to be avoided at all costs. Never mention the diagnosis, as that is reserved for the doctor who requires this prerogative. (The wise parent never mentions mono to the doctor, but only says, "He has a sore throat, temp of 101, swollen glands, and a heaviness in his spleen area. What do you think?" This technique, Winning Without Actually Cheating, is a Stephen Potter (British satirist) ploy, and useful in all fields of human interaction; everyone is allowed to feel worthwhile if not important.) Since hyperactivity is a medical entity for which doctors are not yet sufficiently programmed, she may have to overstate the classroom findings in order to get the message over. "More active than others," "noisier than others," "looks around a lot," "knocks things over," "hits," "pokes," "shoves," would be examples of what she might report.

Some wise teachers will cheat just a little and list the criteria for the hyperactive child. She lists neatly on a piece of ruled paper:

1) Short attention span
2) Distractible
3) Unfinished work
4) More active than others; moves about room

The doctor is forced to make the diagnosis. "He sounds hyperactive to me." He may prescribe medicine, if that's what she wanted.

For another education problem, the teacher may have to fudge a bit again. She seals the following note in an envelope and marks it "personal": "Dear Sir, I am worried about John. He is such a nice boy, but he occasionally seems withdrawn and out of touch. He will occasionally do inappropriate things or stare blankly into space. He may lash out in anger at someone for no good reason. He may stop in midsentence. Please help. Sincerely, Teacher." Note that no mention is made of epilepsy, a diagnostic term.

The doctor, who likes to help, says to the parents, "I'm sure it's nothing, but let's get the brain-wave test; he might have some dysrhythmia that makes him do these odd things."

Education journals inform teachers how to recognize hyperactivity, anemia, low blood sugar, epilepsy, and drug abuse, so they try to make behavioral assessments to help the doctor, who cannot sit next to the child in the classroom. "Sits in the corner sucking his thumb," is factual, but not "acts depressed, insecure, and withdrawn," although that may be true.

Hyperactivity may be caused by a number of genetic, toxic, chemical, and environmental factors and in itself may lead to a number of well-recognized psychiatric syndromes. So we're back to the pediatrician, who is supposed to feel the ambiance of the family in the infant's first few visits to his office.

Observers of the growing child are now aware that poor parenting, maternal depression, family stress, and inadequate nutrition can have a deleterious and permanent effect on the developing brain. Lack of interaction and stimulation in the first two or three critical years may create a lifetime of withdrawal and apathy. As with the lazy eye that leads to disuse blindness, so the nerves, if inadequately stimulated, will actually atrophy. If an infant is not exposed to a variety of sights, sounds, and "feels," he can forever lose the ability to discriminate different modalities of sensation.

If parents are apathetic, preoccupied with poverty, and/or nonreaders, they would be less than enthusiastic about stimulating their child. The child is now doubly hurt; first by genetic weaknesses and then by an unsatisfactory environment. Then the unfamiliar, frightening overload that rushes at his nervous system when he arrives at school jams the circuits. The disturbed, noninteracting infant produced by these turned-off families responds just as if he had been hurt by prematurity or pregnancy insults. He feels threatened and reacts with apathetic, thumb-sucking withdrawal or with random, nondirective hyperactivity.

Our approacher may not have suffered this infancy deprivation. He may have been cheerful and enthusiastic for living because he was wanted, accepted, and loved. But when he faces the
rules of first grade ("Sit still, learn, and achieve"), he may develop doubts about his capabilities, and depression clouds his
view —discouraged by his failures, mad at the world that put
him in a losing situation. He will respond with any one of a
variety of symptoms, again suggesting a psychiatric problem:
school phobia, stomachaches and headaches, impulsive acting-
out, and sullen noncompliance.

It is not unusual for these stress-prone children to get sick just
after the mother has paid the nursery school fee and started a
self-fulfilling job. Then she has to stay home because he has a
fever, a stomachache, or he threw up. The calmer one-to-one
mother-nurse-nurturing relationship with the sick-dependent
child is, of course, rewarding to the child. The absence of anxiety is comforting; his ability to control his mother makes him feel
masterful. He may even learn to continue his illness or notice the
slightest hangnail as a valid reason for staying home. He learns
that hypochondriasis is an effective avoidance tool.

Teacher and principal see most of the children performing
well, so if a few don't fit in and they have an average IQ, then it
must be some other factor. There's nothing else but the home, so
the parents are the villains. They must be doing something
wrong. This attitude forces guilt and anger upon the parents,
who may respond by leaning on our hero (or victim), who now
feels totally abandoned.

Children (and adults) in any group situation set up their own
pecking order, either overtly or covertly. This happens very
quickly in the classroom. Go into almost any schoolroom above
the third grade and ask who is the jerk, the slob, the class points
at our loser, who is snarling and glaring back. When other children discover that Charlie is touchy or flies into a rage over the
slightest insult, they are "rewarded" for taunting him. Charlie is
unable to disregard the heckling and responds with violence. It's
the learning theory in action—bug Charlie; Charlie overreacts.
The others are rewarded and programmed to try it again and
again. Like any ingrained reflex, they find it almost impossible

to stop. He usually leaves his jacket on in the classroom on the assumption, I imagine, that he will be able to split more quickly if things get any worse.

These children are more likely to grow up having serious doubts about their self-image. Because they know they are at the bottom of the class pecking order, they act badly. It is axiomatic that if a window in school is broken, the principal knows which boy in each class might have done it. They are told they are bad; they become bad. These losers feel that school is the villain and are paying "it" back for putting them down. They are signaling the world that somebody should do something for them.

Observations of the disturbing child's actions usually come as no surprise to the parents, who knew he was a little hyper, but after all, aren't all children somewhat active at that age, and why doesn't the teacher sit on him a little or enforce the rules? But remember, our definition of this sensitive child reads: "unable to disregard unimportant stimuli." He might do well or seem calm with one parent in a quiet room where there is little incoming stimuli. Indeed, one of the key questions in making the diagnosis of the condition is, "Is he better at home in a one-to-one situation and worse at school?"

Most of us find ourselves in stress situations every day. (What to have for breakfast, do I have enough gas to get where I'm going, can I get a little more toothpaste out of the old tube for one more brushing, can I diagnose the fever, should I pick the pimple now or tonight, etc.) But because we are older and have coping skills, the stress is short lived and we "survive" and even feel a small sense of victory because we could handle a tough problem.

But for a child, the stress clues are there for parent and teacher to read. A noisy classroom with many sights and sounds will challenge a feeble screening system, and too many messages arrive at the child's cortical level—too many for him to handle or ignore. The nervous system responds by conforming to demands with acceptance and compliance, or feels a threat and shows withdrawal, somatic symptoms, or aggressive acting-out. The cortex responds by the release of energy to the nerves to the muscles—wiggle, run, climb. Thus most sensitive children will respond physically: They run, scream, knock things over, and become generally obnoxious.

But what of the quiet, withdrawn child—most often a girl? Her sitting in the corner staring into space or looking down at her hands does not have to mean stubbornness or depression. Her dreamy withdrawal may also signify too much sensory input. Some hyperactives display *hypo*activity.

This seeming contradiction is resolved by rephrasing it: Both hyperactivity and hypoactivity may be created by the same basic flaw—the screening device in the limbic system has allowed too much electrical activity to ascend to and stimulate the sensory cortex. Sensitive children surrounded by too much incoming stimuli are uncomfortable; the response may go to the autonomic nervous system; rapid heartbeat, dilated pupils, sweaty palms, and queasy stomach will result. These new responses signal the brain that something awful is about to happen (i.e., be eaten by tiger or have root-canal work), and to feel safer and avoid uncomfortable anxiety, the victim withdraws—like pushing yourself back into the chair when the dentist points the drill at your mouth. The hyperactive's nervous system is acting as if flight is appropriate, and the cognitive part of the brain says, "I feel as if I'm scared; it must be this school. I hate it. Let's run."

"Your child seems nervous and afraid," says the teacher. Another judgment.

It is difficult for us adults to imagine that a healthy child could be so touchy in a fun-filled, nonthreatening nursery school or kindergarten. But once the adrenaline starts to flow, there is no technique available to turn the panic button off. We must resist the temptation to drag the reluctant one into the circle of activity, saying, "See what fun we're having." Panic and resistance will only mount. The wise teacher tries to ignore the child but lets her know that the situation she is missing is rewarding if she would just join in. Usually after a few days the child moves closer to test how much anxiety surges through her body by the new proximity. If symptoms recur, she retreats. Teachers are assailed with a wide variety of therapeutic methods that are frequently successful for the inventors, but may not work for the imitators. Psychologists know that behavior modification is successful if the teacher would believe in it and try it. If the teacher fails, then she didn't try hard enough. The oracle speaks. "Something's wrong with the teacher."

This, the only so-called psychiatric condition seen more frequently in girls than boys is fear of going to school, or school phobia. It is most common at age five or six and is assumed to be related, not so much to the dangers of school per se, but to the fear the home will break up when her back is turned. Associated difficulties of an unresolved Oedipal conflict add up to a panic situation every morning: rapid heartbeat, sweaty palms, dilated pupils, screaming, running away, hiding, bracing her feet against the door jamb, etc.

The doctor, if need be, and the parents have to hogtie the child and forcibly drag her unwilling body and dump it on the principal's desk. This confused official must decide to be tough and demanding or work out some compromise.

School attendance must coincide with psychiatric treatment. School, parents, and counseling services are supposed to be supportive enough to allay the anxiety so obviously written all over the child's body.

Here is another good example of how a latent genetic fault can be activated by a stressful environment. The therapeutic approach, obviously, is to eliminate the stress (get him out of school?) or to help him stand the stress. But the noncompliant or pouty, stubborn child is upsetting to the adult who prefers to have everyone join in; it makes it more fun for the teacher if all are eager and attentive.

One should *not* assume these children are neurotic, although we have been trained to label them as such. The environment, home or school, is perceived by the cortex as threatening. It does not *have* to mean that the home is breaking up, although that may be part of the problem.

Serious thought is now directed to the discovery of some unrecognized source of stress at home or the school. If one searches hard enough, some psychic stress can be found in everyone's life. Since many schools feel the behavior is due to an unsupportive home, perhaps a review of environmental, social, and emotional pressures at home would be worthwhile. Does the early morning sun glide through the venetian blinds in an irritating way? The parents may not suspect in their efforts to provide a "structured" home that this is more than the child can handle, and he may carry his concerns to the classroom. Many of these children have rigid, tough fathers who might have suffered similar feelings when they were small (remember, some of this is genetic) and, because they were told they were lazy goof-offs, they ride their children, especially the boys. I saw a boy, aged four years, who is now a busy, cheerful approacher and difficult to manage. But his mother prefers this to the depressed, hostile, seething demeanor he displayed before she divorced her strict, unaccepting, punitive husband. The boy still will be faced with a host of problems before he grows up, but "at least he's cheerful." My mother knew I was a goosy kid and kept me home until I was six and one-half before letting me tackle the first grade. It was still scary.

What's the school like?

Open, noisy classrooms may be a big distraction this child cannot disregard. Dr. Ott has found that children in classrooms lit by fluorescent tubes are more likely to become hyperactive. The subliminal flicker must set up a stressful pulsation in the cerebral cortex of the susceptible. Some children watching TV in Europe years ago would be subject to convulsions because the phase bar moving across the screen triggered an irritable focus in the cortices of certain children; a weak filtering system in the pathway to the brain did not dampen this incoming stimulus.

The teacher is the key person because she is standing in the middle of the child's stressful environment, or she *is* the stressful environment without really being aware of it. The child may love the teacher and want to please her, but cannot quite work up to his exaggerated idea of her standards, so he does nothing, assuming this is a safer method. At least he cannot be graded down. Some have terrific consciences, but their immature nervous systems will not permit a performance commensurate with this ideal.

What works for one may be invalid for another. The common motivation seems to be that it is important to do *something*. People, including children, should be happy social animals. The chief value to the child is that someone cares; there is hope. He is not such a bad person after all. The message is teach the child to have some self-respect—"You are worthwhile." Obviously, intervention must be accomplished early—age three to eight years—before patterns and attitudes become fixed responses.

Are We Bad If We Can't Read? The nonreader is not just a stubborn brat, but may be unable to decode the ink spots on the page. I've heard of businessmen who carry on quite successfully with a limited ability to read and write. They are bright and have been able to fake their way through whatever schooling they needed by their acute auditory perception and speech facility. They may have no trouble with numbers and mathematical problems, but letters and words are frequently a jumble of chicken tracks across the page. It's as if someone had reamed out the center in their brains for programming and recognizing word symbols.

The adult so afflicted will dictate any letters or orders to a secretary, usually a girl (girls almost never have the problem). She types it up, and he, without reading it except for any numbers in the text, signs it (often misspelling his own name). His correspondent may have the same problem, but his female secretary reads the letter, fills the order, or types another letter dictated by her boss.

These people do not like to read books or magazines; it's too much of a struggle. They may read a paragraph and find it makes no sense. Upon rereading, they find they missed a *not* which obviously changes the whole meaning. This discourages their interest and they turn to TV, movies, or sports for recreation.

These boys cannot seem to remember the sound that is associated with the symbol. It is called dyslexia. A child with a dysperception for word symbols hasn't a clue for handling the page in front of him. The letter *d, b, p,* or *q* is just a circle and a line; his right-left and/or up-down analyzing methods are not functioning. *Was* comes in all at once and frequently is perceived as *saw.* A *3* and an *E* are mirror images with no inherent difference that allows discrimination.

Once it had been felt that poor reading skill was due to lack of books and reading aloud in the family. The child reared in such a family had never seen an adult absorbed in a book nor shared some exciting paragraph. The child would then assume that reading was a boring drag. Some environmental stimulation must be a factor, but now we also know that the discouraging condition, dyslexia, is frequently found in all the males in some families. Tests show that word reversals, confusion of b and d and p and q are found to be identical in many fathers and their sons. It's obviously a genetic trait.

It has been known for some time that Orientals in general and the Chinese in particular have little or none of these deviant children. Besides heredity, social pressures or some subtle difference in parenting could explain some of this. Educators felt that education is simplified in China because there is a different written character for each spoken sound. The English language, for instance, has several different sounds for the vowels and even some consonants; thus reading for even the brightest first grader can be very confusing.

Children (and adults) have a fear of failure, and will refuse to expose their ignorance by asking a question. They don't want their peer group to suspect. Also, they don't know what to say; they cannot diagnose themselves. A few children (usually boys) who are unable to read at grade level but have good auditory perception will "read" aloud to the class from a familiar book completely by memory. The words are a bunch of incomprehensible tracks across the page, but they recite the story accurately—even turning the pages appropriately! But they cannot write down dictation or copy from the board. They may ask to have some instruction repeated, and still not understand it. Sequencing is almost impossible; repeating a few digits or unrelated words is poorly done. They may retain a few principles of pronunciation and then, when asked to perform, the whole hard-learned deciphering ability is just gone. The children so touched have been—and still are—labeled lazy, stupid, noncompliant, and/or stubborn. If a child finds himself lost in the world of words he becomes anxious, and depending upon his personality he becomes hyperactive (usually) but he may become sullen, angry, mean, or hostile. Some are depressed and cry. They develop psychosomatic symptoms such as school phobia, headaches, allergies, stomachaches. All these familiar symptoms could be grouped into a classification of reaction to stress. Without remediation, this genetic factor would lead to school failure and the label of stupid at worst or nonmotivated at best. Most authorities are convinced that early detection (age three to four) is possible and remedial training will preclude the first-grade frustrations. Teachers and parents must recognize this problem at its earliest stage, before the depression of failure becomes established and restricts all academic performance.

Doctors—and especially pediatricians—must be alert to clues that indicate the presence of a perception or motor dysfunction and refer the child for further testing or remediation.

In general, there are four forms of perception-motor disability or difficulty in using symbols in communicating:

(1) *Hereditary.* This type, passed from father to son, is not as discouraging as it once was as the newer methods of multisensory learning have improved the outlook. Hyperactivity, distractibility, and disruptiveness are usually secondary to the frustrations of "not getting it."

(2) *Minimal cerebral dysfunction.* Prematurity and the complications of pregnancy may have hurt the areas of the brain specifically associated with symbol deciphering. Usually some maladroitness and left-right confusion are associated. These children are more likely to have EEG abnormalities.

(3) *Developmental lag.* These children will eventually arrive at a satisfactory reading level, but consistently run two years behind their classmates. There is no way to predict this, so tutoring must be initiated early, before discouragement gets a foothold and stops further progress.

(4) *Hyperactive-Distractible Approacher.*

The etiology of the condition is important only if the doctor is looking at the patient; he likes to know because he is the labeler. New methods using other pathways to the brain have only been developed in the last three decades. (Supposedly Nelson Rockefeller had this condition —which only goes to prove that one's environment can help.)

The remedial tutor is concerned with doing something; he

must first get the child's attention and then start the step-by-step processing of usable information into the brain of the student at his side. The cause is not so important as induced responses are stimulus-determined and are mediated through the nervous system. First the cortex (where these cognitive skills are centered) must be made alert and receptive by diet, vitamins, medicine, alpha awareness, motivation, and/or love. Then the teacher is able to get through to and work with the potential lying dormant.

15 · Treatment for School Problems

Now comes the big question: Should the child have medication? Traditionally, the doctor who finds no physical reason (ear infection, sensory defect, anemia, worms) or unsupportive or unaccepting parents, will prescribe a tranquilizer which prevents the child's cortex from getting the anxiety message or calms down the limbic system so noxious stimuli are not transmitted. Frequently this works. It allows the child to be exposed to the school environment without suffering anxiety. If the child can participate in the activities without feeling uncomfortable, he might get the message that it *is* fun, and forget his previous fear. The medicine may be reduced until a new threat appears.

Occasionally some combination of medicine (Dexedrine® and Mellaril®) is very calming and effective so that therapy (whether home, school counseling, or psychiatric) can be instituted.

Many parents are frightened by the prospect of drug use, and envision the child shooting heroin by age eleven. We all feel squeamish about our drug-oriented society, and "pushing" drugs promotes the idea that there is a pill for every human complaint. I subscribe to this with some reservation and am happy that we have a few alternate paths to successful maturity.

The hyperactive child has the skills, but can respond only if he is in a structured classroom, is on a protein diet, and is in a small classroom with carpeting, incandescent lights, and a sympathetic teacher.

"I know he would feel better and be able to cope with his world if he would eat a more substantial breakfast. But he's already so uptight in the A.M. that he gags on the cereal. If I push an egg down him, he throws up."

Many of these children are so keyed up the night before, assuming they are going to be put to death the next day at school, that they cannot relax and go to sleep. Preventive measures have to be begun early.

Helpful: protein for supper. No dessert or sugar at all. At bedtime a mouthful of cheese, peanut butter, bean soup, or meat prevents the blood-sugar level from dropping so low that there is not enough energy available for the cortex to do its job: to make the child a social human being or at least to allow him to operate a little above his animal limbic system.

"He is seven and loves school once he gets there. But I have to drag him out of bed, forcibly dress him, and spank him before he'll eat. He throws up. We drive him to school, turn him over to the principal who gets him to the class. He participates, does his work, and seems none the worse for all this wear and tear. I take a Valium®, two aspirins, and have a cup of coffee. I am recovered by the time he gets home cheerfully at 3 P.M. Is there a better way to live?"

After some detective work, this mother and I figured out why her son seemed to be almost in a coma in the mornings. He loved to eat sherbet at bedtime—not one cupful, but five. When he ate some protein at bedtime he could jump out of bed in the morning. He wasn't goody-goody enough to say, "Good morning, mother. What can I do to help around the house?" But he was able to function on a human level, at least.

If he feels awake in the A.M., he might be more receptive to breakfast suggestions. If he is still reluctant, his parent might be able to at least get a gob of old-fashioned peanut butter (no sugar) on a quarter of a piece of whole-wheat toast down him.

Some children refuse to eat breakfast because they somehow suspect that they do feel worse if they get dry cereal with milk and sugar. Some cannot eat and are very nauseated in the A.M. because of the sugar they ate the night before; they have slipped into acidosis because the body often burns up fat in the absence of other fuel. Acidosis can cause nausea and vomiting (see Chapter 10).

Recently, the concerned parents of a thirteen-year-old, attractive, intelligent, blue-eyed blonde girl asked me for help. The girl loves school (she says), has always done well academically, and has a host of supportive friends. Right after Christmas vacation, however, she began to suffer severe stomachaches the moment she stepped over the school threshold at 8:45 A.M.

A visit to her doctor ruled out pinworms, appendicitis, constipation, and gastroenteritis. An X-ray showed only an irritable duodenum (increased activity of the small bowel just beyond the stomach), but no obvious ulcer or serious intestinal pathology.

The next stop, of course, was at the psychiatrist's office. This doctor assumed that since medical pains had been found absent, her distress must be psychosomatic. He felt she had a serious problem deeply buried under her symptoms, as there was no easily detected cause-and-effect mechanism such as dyslexia, broken home, mean teacher, or restroom shakedowns.

She would be driven to school, escorted into the office despite her distress, allowed to sit for a minute or two, then pushed into her first period class by the firm but sympathetic principal. She would somehow survive the day, the stomachache would slowly dissipate, and by evening she would appear quite normal again. The family would try not to pay attention to the symptom but show interest in academic and athletic progress. "Maybe tomorrow she'll have a good day," the guilty parents thought, always wondering where they had gone wrong. And every once in a while she would walk through the school doors without a single twinge.

Three months of this was enough. The parents tried a new tack. Beginning one Friday P.M., she was forbidden to eat any products with sugar or white flour. She was encouraged to nibble on protein and on Sunday evening was given a big gob of peanut butter. Monday morning she had a piece of whole-wheat toast with melted cheese and an orange, and sailed through the day—but not without some anxiety, wondering when the old familiar pain would strike. I can picture her with her head cocked toward her stomach (like a robin looking for a worm) in anticipation (navel gazing) trying to read her body.

On Tuesday night some friend gave her a couple of brownies,

and Wednesday A.M. the stomachache hit her as soon as the first period bell rang. This attack was short-lived, but at least everyone had renewed hope for ultimate success. Each symptom-free day indicated that they were on the right treatment. Perhaps the diet would not have been successful without psychiatric intervention, but it would have been interesting to see if nutrition therapy as the initial technique would have been sufficient. Did the Christmas stress and goodies destroy her cerebral and adrenal enzymes so that the minor stress of school became the major factor?

The psychiatrist assumed it was school phobia because of the time of onset, and had worked out a neat theory of the psychodynamics. He made a judgment because his training had been geared to accept no other causal relationship. He was right, though—the stress was there, but the reason she could not handle it was her ineffective biochemistries.

Her body could handle Saturday and Sunday, but not Monday through Friday. It takes at least two factors operating coincidentally: Some environmental stress acts upon a genetic proclivity made manifest by a nutritional flaw.

The intensity of the response would be determined by the severity and the duration of the stress plus the resiliency of the nervous system and its biochemical integrity.

A violent temper is frequently seen in both father and son. Is there a gene for violence? Or does a fluctuating blood-sugar level make some people so mean that they don't care what they say or do? Under the influence of a carbohydrate breakfast, the child might experience a falling blood sugar at about the minute class is beginning. The flow of adrenaline is stimulated when this drop occurs. The brain senses the somatic aspects of anxiety when adrenaline is flowing, and assumes that the particular environment present and being observed is dangerous. Flight seems appropriate.

Two mechanisms are operative: The limbic screening system allows too much sensory stimuli to overwhelm the cortex; the cortex feels threatened, as if a tiger is nearby. It initiates the cortico-thalamic-pituitary-adrenal mechanism that we all have to get ready for flight or fight. This doesn't happen to all children, obviously, just to these sensitive ones who have a genetic filtering weakness or some form of minimal cerebral dysfunction. If it happened to all children, no one would go to nursery school.

The second related mechanism—and it seems to be most likely found in these same children—is the hypoglycemic response that follows carbohydrate consumption. Hypoglycemia and tension-fatigue syndrome may exist separately but are frequently found together. This magnifies the blood-sugar drop already initiated by the first mechanism. When the sugar in the blood drops rapidly and/or it arrives at a low level, the cortex is not receiving nourishment and, depending on the individual, a variety of limbic system (animal) behaviors might be activated: crying, depression, paranoia, meanness, headache, stomachache, and noncompliance. Many parents report their child is a "regular Jekyll and Hyde." They *can* be cheerful, cooperative, and good for twenty minutes, then slip into a screaming, kicking fit the next.

The hyperactive boy who is cheerful and busy at home and at grandmother's where he runs with the dog finds he cannot sit still at school. He seems bright but cannot put anything on paper. He is distractible and disrupts the class. He is called bad and his parents are told to discipline him and provide a structured environment.

Is it too much to assume that he doesn't have enough norepinephrine in his limbic system, that he notices stimuli too acutely, and that he has an abnormal response to carbohydrate?

If the child's potential is adequate for the grade, and reading is not too great a struggle, then the fault may be his inadequate limbic system and/or a low blood sugar. It is too late to go back and feed the mother an adequate protein diet so her unborn baby can be assured his normal brain potential; we have to work with what we have. But the brain cells he comes to school with must be supplied with protein and vitamins so he can use what he has.

It might be as simple as getting a better breakfast.

I am appalled by what passes for breakfast in some homes in the name of good nutrition.

Nutritionists tell us of school breakfast programs that improve the attention span and learning capacity of the students by fifty to ninety percent. The chief difficulty is that help from the government's agricultural surplus program comes in the form of flour, sugar, and milk—the very things we are trying to eliminate from these children's diets. Allowing free access for all children in the classroom to nuts, cheese, and other bits of protein snacks can calm down the wildest, most noncompliant, and most distractible children.

Teachers and child psychiatrists in Norway deny that they have a problem, which seems incredible when we realize the large numbers of blue-eyed blonds in their schools. The government, however, wisely provides fish and cheese to school children shortly after they get to school.

Teachers tell me how they have been successful in activating their pupils' brains by merely providing a can of mixed nuts that the children may nibble on as needed. They acted upon the information that a child's brain has two to three times the energy requirements of an adult's; it is impossible for them to function from breakfast to lunch without nibbling on some protein.

Add vitamins as a catalyst, vitamin C and B complex. No sugar, additives, food colorings, aspirin, aspirin-related foods or drugs, white flour, or dairy products; he is to nibble on protein. Talk the teacher into having protein snacks available in the classroom and the principal into eliminating sugars and desserts from the lunchroom and candy from the machine in the hall.

Extra calcium (dolomite) may have enough of a calming effect that tranquilizers may not be necessary. Also use calcium and magnesium for evening calmness and wait for the enthusiastic response from the teacher. If he is fair, ticklish, loves sugar, and has sleep problems, he should respond immediately to stimulants and a protein diet plus added vitamins. After the usual medical check, anemia test, and worm therapy, the methods outlined previously should produce a ten to one hundred percent improvement within three weeks.

The previously mentioned vitamin supplements may also help the debilitated enzyme systems become more efficient and produce the hold-the-body-together chemicals.

Teacher's note: "He has deep circles under his eyes, and

seems washed out and lackluster. He often complains to me about being tired or having stomachaches and headaches. He snorts and zonks frequently, as if his nose is plugged. He is irritable and ready to fight if teased. His hands are occasionally cold and clammy. He drifts off in another world. I noticed at lunch how he gulps down the chocolate milk and dessert, but won't touch the protein and vegetables on his plate." If pallor, circles under the eyes, and stomachache are prominent parts of the picture, milk, eggs, and wheat should be eliminated. Allergies are an exhausting problem to many people. If the parents have followed through on diet and home support and the child seems to have the IQ and perceptual potential and he can finish his work and seems happy sixty to seventy percent of the time, he can survive the stress of school and growing up in his society.

If the complaints are still present, maybe a stimulant and/or a little thyroid might settle him so the teacher and the parents can say something nice about him.

If all has been done at home and school to get him out of the lower slot in the class pecking order and he is still unable to hack it because his behavior gives him away, a trial of Ritalin®, Dexedrine®, Desoxyn®, Biphetamine®, or Cylert® must be tried. The key to drug use is the answer to the question. "Is he worse in a crowd, class, circus, or supermarket?" An affirmative answer has to mean that the main problem is his poor nervous system filtering mechanisms. (It helps, of course, for the parents to take their child to a blue-eyed doctor who has a hyperactive child of his own. "Let's try some medicine and see if it works. If he settles down, then he's hyperactive.")

The rationale of medication is based on the theory that these children have a chemical lack of norepinephrine (a stimulant) in their limbic system (or reticular activating system or arousal centers and/or related connections). It is as specific as penicillin for a strep throat or insulin for a diabetic. If we tell a diabetic he ought to make more insulin and he doesn't, he may take that as a moral judgment and think he is evil. Do we have a right to judge these children bad because they notice their environment more acutely? Some authorities believe that the medicine is so specific for this problem of disruptive approachers that it should be tried first. If the child responds favorably—calmness, longer attention span, finished work, better handwriting, improved peer relations, decreased impulsiveness—then the child does have the problem, and continued control with the drug on a daily basis is all that is required.

It is sometimes amazing how a writing or reading dysfunction can be controlled with medication as if the brain were not hooked up properly. The chemical synapses are reinforced by the medication; they were always there, but not optimally operative. Articulation and writing are frequently easier and smoother.

Many children who appear to have a specific reading disability (cannot program the incoming letters into meaningful words) can make sense out of the printed word within one hour of swallowing one of these stimulants. Even if such a dramatic result is not apparent, remedial reading teachers tell us the child at least has a better attention span and a better attitude.

One good reason why doctors treating these children have rarely seen dependence or habituation develop from the use of these drugs is the paradox of these stimulants acting as "downers" to them. My daughter refused to take her amphetamine on volleyball days because she felt it *slowed* her responses, although it provided her with the necessary attention span and concentration ability to succeed academically.

The dose in milligrams is not based on weight like aspirin or antibiotics; it is based on response. Some need a lot, depending on age, stress, teacher, etc. I have a patient who needed six pills for the third grade, none for the fourth, and only two for the fifth. His third grade teacher was a Prussian martinet: "Anyone who moves his eyebrows goes to the principal!" Charley, of course, moved his eyebrows.

About ten percent of these children develop a tolerance to the medicine.

January call from mother: "I'm so discouraged. He's been on this since September and has been fabulous. But at the conference yesterday the teacher said he's right back where we started."

"How's his appetite for lunch?"

"Oh, great. He eats everything in sight."

"Then he needs a bigger dose."

The appetite loss is one clue to the proper dosage; it is a side effect and means *that* particular number of milligrams of *that* particular medicine is doing something to the nervous system and should be having a beneficial effect on the rest of the norepinephrine-activated nervous system also. Within a week of increasing the dose daily until some loss of appetite for lunch is noted, the teacher should be enthusiastically aware that our hero loves school, stays in his seat, finishes his work, and can read and write without such a monumental struggle.

Usually the dose is merely increased until the initial beneficial effects are observed again. But if a high tolerance develops, it has to be discontinued for a week or two. If it worked before, it will work again. "We should be able to stop it in the summer and when next fall comes, if he needs it, we can probably go back to the lower dose."

Usually if the medicine can be avoided on the weekends, this tolerance is not a problem. But some of these touchy children need something on weekends because of family gatherings, Sunday school, grandmother's candy treats, etc.

If the morning is satisfactory but the afternoon is a disappointment, a noon dose—often only half the breakfast dose—is usually effective. All of these drugs except Ritalin® have a time-release form, so a useful alternative is to try one of these long-acting tablets or capsules at breakfast. There is often a smoother action all day, and the child avoids the embarrassment of the teacher calling him out at lunch with, "Here's your pill, Charley." The major disadvantage of this form is the insomnia it may produce, but these people frequently go to bed at 11 or 12 P.M. so it may not make that much difference. With many it has the paradoxical effect of making them drowsy.

It may be best to be imprecise in cluing the teacher as to the exact time of beginning medication. She may destroy the experiment by making it work if she approves of medication or making it *not* work by applying more stress if she disapproves of "drugging" children. If the mother can discover what day her child had a loss of appetite for lunch, she then calls the teacher that afternoon to ask how he acted. The teacher should be in the office looking up the home number to report to the parent how beautifully the day went. Both should shed tears of joy. "By George, we've done it!"

If the mother and the teacher can communicate, a satisfactory dose can be worked out that allows the child to function comfortably in the classroom.

A fifteen-year-old boy was benefited by the medicine, but due to parental oversight or personal reluctance he got it inconsistently. His first teacher of the day would have him write his name when he arrived. If it was legible, he stayed and had a successful day. If it was a scribbly line, he was sent home. The latter situation occurred on medicineless days and school was pointless, for him as well as the rest of the class.

The medicine usually has worn out by the time he gets home in the afternoon, and if he acts up then, his mother may feel the medicine is making him worse. Some of this may be a rebound phenomenon, but part of this peevishness may be explained by a falling blood sugar from an inadequate or carbohydrate-high lunch. The mother should shove a dollop of peanut butter, egg, meat, or cheese into him, turn her back for thirty minutes, and then ask, "How was school?" His response should be a simple "OK," and not a screaming tantrum. Even if the afternoon is less than perfect, the mother should be reassured by the teacher's "He is one hundred percent better," and be able to tolerate his P.M. mischief, comforted in the knowledge that he likes himself because he is achieving in school. When he gets home, a half dose might be appropriate to hold him together until bedtime.

No cure is promised nor should be expected, only control. It is a holding action while we await maturation. Adolescence has some stabilizing influence on these people. If the medicine allows for the development of the good self-image, then the slight risk of medicine dependence has been worth taking. Most patients hate to take medicine, especially after the age of ten years, as they feel this makes them different from their peers. They wonder if it means they are sick, crazy, or stupid, especially if a psychiatrist is in charge. They know psychiatrists treat crazy people; this is a good reason for a family practitioner or pediatrician to be in general charge of these cases. The medicine is supposed to make the child feel comfortable with himself so he may be complimented instead of blamed.

If a loss of appetite occurs, and the teacher notices little or no change in social or academic performance, there is a mistake in the diagnosis or another drug must be tried. If he doesn't turn on to the academic world right away with the protein diet and some stimulant medicine, he needs the help of a reading therapist. It's almost an emergency.

If he is worse at home, the stress is usually there, and perhaps family counseling would be wise. If he is worse at home, and *better* in a crowded noisy classroom, then he is *not* an approacher and some other cause of the misbehavior must be sought. Again, some search for anemia or hearing and visual problems must be made.

If little or no response has been achieved, get a perceptual-motor test for auditory and visual difficulties which interfere with the child's ability in processing input. Psychological testing might be worthwhile at this point, although reading readiness and draw-a-person tests may be adequate. If the results are still equivocal, a brain-wave test should be considered, as he may be suffering from some psychomotor or temporal lobe seizure.

An EEG test (electroencephalogram or brain-wave test) might be worthwhile at this juncture, especially if he has good and bad days unrelated to sugar or carbohydrate ingestion. All of us have been disappointed in the benefits of this diagnostic tool; twenty to forty percent of the tests on these children are read as abnormal, but the abnormalities do not seem related to any sympton or sign that the child may display. Still there is a higher than normal correlation of abnormal waves in the EEG with inappropriate staring into space and wild destructive behavior triggered by some slight environmental stimulus. (Mother says "No, you may not watch the TV anymore." The child falls on the floor and has a violent temper tantrum and puts his foot through a door.) Educational, social, psychiatric, and/or chemical intervention is absolutely necessary while the psyche is pliable. That's why I'm writing this, for heaven's sake.

16 · About Electroencephalograms

octors are curious people, so it came as no surprise to the world a few decades ago that the brain-wave test, or electroencephalogram, was devised to aid in the diagnosis of a variety of brain problems. Electrodes are attached to the scalp and the electrical energy from the cortical surfaces of the brain is amplified and recorded.

Diagnostic accuracy forces one into the position of having the test done; one would not want to overlook a surgical lesion. This graph can be compared to normal ones and an interpretation can be made as to whether the patient has some interruption of cortical function—blood clots, tumors, or epilepsy—which would alter the rhythmical, symmetrical pattern of waves coming from the surface of the brain. These odd waves would be helpful in corroborating the findings from the history taking and the physical examination.

It was hoped that this test would provide some helpful clues in the diagnosis of the hyperactive approacher; if the phrase "minimal cerebral dysfunction" has any meaning, all these children should have peculiar brain waves. Actually, only about twenty to forty percent of diagnosed hyperactives have an abnormal EEG, and these don't correlate with any symptom that the patient displays. If a patient *does* have some episodic motor movement or alteration of consciousness, he is more likely to have some deviation from the normal in his EEG. Perhaps, then, there is no point in ordering the EEG if one suspects it will be abnormal.

The real dilemma occurs when a patient has been labeled hyperactive and is placed on appropriate medication, but he refuses to improve. He might be calmer, but his wild outbursts of inappropriate aggression could almost be labeled periodic attacks, like seizures.

The following story of Teddy might illustrate this. He was obviously hyperactive:

"Usually Teddy felt the slightest scratch or pain and built it up to a major disaster. I felt that he just wanted more attention and that was a way to get it. Yet, again, I saw him bang his head against the wall time after time, and it didn't bother him.

"Sometimes he felt the cold too, so much that if it was sixty degrees outside, he would bundle up like it was ten below zero. He would sleep under two wool blankets in eighty-five-degree heat sometimes. Again it could be thirty degrees and he wanted both his windows wide open and no covers, sleeping in only his underpants. He would walk to school one morning bundled up so that only his eyes showed, and again in the same cold weather, go in his shirt sleeves. He would go on little or no food at times, and at others would eat and eat until he couldn't swallow another bite, but he would still eat.

"Teddy also talks, talks, and talks, and talks to anyone who will listen to him, and then again sometimes he is withdrawn and thinks everyone is talking about him.

"He does have abnormal hearing power. He always felt that people were watching and talking about him, yet in times of anger would protest that he 'didn't care what people said' about him. He is very crafty and stealthy—you don't see him or hear him if he doesn't want you to. If he got into trouble at school, he would run away. He was suspended from school for fighting in the halls. He didn't go back to school the first day after the suspension. That was his way of getting back at the assistant principal for suspending him. He broke quite a few school windows in company with several other boys because some of the teachers told him that he was failing.

"Teddy doesn't want anyone to have power over him. He does what he pleases and knows that no one can stop him because he won't let them. He runs with younger boys so that he can lead and they do as he says. If he said something to someone and they didn't answer him, he took it as a personal insult and would become angry and abusive. If an older boy crosses him or annoys him, he is so strong that he almost kills the boy before the fight can be broken up. He would start a fight and not be able to understand why anyone would fight back. He would be so angry that he was ready to kill. He would scream, 'I'll kill him! I'll hunt him down and I'll kill him!' even though it was Teddy who started the fight.

"At times Teddy was such a wonderful boy, and then all of a sudden would turn on us like an enraged bull. Like last summer when sometimes I would start to dig in the garden or to plant a tree, he would take the shovel and would say gently, 'Here, Mom, let me do that. It's too heavy work for you.'

"Then sometimes if I asked him to do something, he would say, 'Do it yourself. That's not my job and I'm not a slave around here.' If I got after him, he would leave home and be gone for hours or overnight."

This Jekyll-Hyde syndrome is slightly excessive for even a hyperactive. But no one thought of epilepsy until he had a seizure. Other parents might well ask after adding an antiseizure medication, "Why didn't we do this before? He's easier to handle now." But with Teddy, the damage was already done.

"His natural father had a violent temper. Teddy inherited it. He has no common-sense reasoning power. He doesn't understand why he can't take what he wants or do as he wants. He kept telling me he couldn't help it and he didn't know why he did what he did. If I pressured him, he would say, 'Because I wanted to' or 'Because it was just there,' 'To get back at you for punishing me,' 'I just wanted it,' 'I thought we could use them.' (This one was when he took some small tools from the auto store.) When I tried to explain that we don't take things that belong to someone else, he didn't understand why. Explanations make no sense to him. Or if I tried to explain why he couldn't do things to other people, it made no sense.

"Teddy thinks that if he wants something he can take it, and it is all right. I punished him for this so much, yet he could never understand why and hated me for it. If I punished him at home he would run away or strike back physically. Then it got to the point where if I scolded him or got upset with him he would either knock me down or threaten to kill me. Now he still feels that he can take some things he wants. He told us that he got some gas from a station in a small town one night when no one was around. 'If you will excuse me for saying so, Uncle Joe and Aunt Sarah's kids act up like hell and they don't get after them.' The children were three and four years of age.

"Was he trying to tell me that he realized that this was as far advanced in behavior that he was capable of and yet not realizing it but 'feeling it'? (A doctor told us that his emotional growth stopped at four and a half years.) Was Teddy trying to let me know that he was incapable of acting any older?

"I believe that Teddy was unable to accept and rise above any unpleasant happenings in day-to-day family life as his sister has. Something within him keeps him from doing so. For instance, I was very ill when he was two and a half years old and was in the hospital for about ten days. He has never forgotten it. 'You went away and left me!' he has shouted at me. And he has always had a fear of me going off and leaving him. Teddy was never able to absorb enough love. He felt rejected if I was cross with him or punished him. He felt that I should not do so because, as he said, 'I do what I want to and you or anyone else can't stop me.' He could not be reasoned with. Once he called his sister and very happily said, 'Mom's gone off and left you too, hasn't she?' (He had called the boy across the street first and been told that our car was not in the driveway—it was in the garage, but the boy couldn't see it.) When Donna told him that I was at home, he said 'Prove it!' I took the phone and talked to him for a few minutes. He feels that I love Donna more. You can't convince him that I don't, that I love each of them in a different way. He is gifted with his hands and did so very well in industrial arts at school. He did very well in anything he liked, but couldn't care less about the courses that he didn't like or when he didn't like the teachers.

"Six years ago Teddy came home one cold, dreary January night. He was AWOL from the Navy and had been for the previous seven months. He saw nothing wrong with it as far as he was concerned, but in a roundabout way he conveyed the idea that because of me, he was giving himself up. 'I know that most of what has happened to me has been my own fault. I still remember the things you taught me and I'm going to try harder now.'

"Three days later he turned himself in and served a few weeks in the brig down in Virginia, not too far from us. I went to see him several times, because I felt that he needed to know that I love him in spite of everything that had happened. He got a medical discharge from the Navy because they learned of the epilepsy (he had several seizures while on board ship, but was able, at the time, to cover up the fact).

"He still has a long way to go, but he is no longer the angry, rebellious person that he was. He married a girl who was the same type of person he is, but what could we say? We were afraid to try to talk him out of it, in fact, to offer any kind of resistance to it at all. It lasted a month.

"Because Teddy is so gifted with the use of his hands, he will become an expert craftsman or something of that nature. He does not read well because he can't concentrate that long. He lives in New Jersey now—works a steady job and is earning enough money to take care of himself. He comes to see us about once a year and writes occasionally. He drives a car, too. It is an absolute mania with him—cars are his passion, probably because I told him once that he would not be able to drive a car (a law in this area) until he had been seizure-free for two years. He was bound and determined to do it anyway. I made several goof-ups like that, but I didn't know any better. He still has a seizure occasionally, but is not on medication. The last episode that I know of was two years ago when he had several within a few weeks' time.

"He knows that he is 'different' and fights so hard not to be different, but acts so different and is so dirty at times and overly clean at other times. I understand that this is his way of fighting against his illness. I wonder if you are saying 'Ah-hah! Here are the clinging parents—not willing to let go of their son.' No, I felt that he needs to think and feel and know that we love him and trust him. Besides, he is grown now and we can not live his life for him nor make his mistakes for him. Actually, parents have to start 'letting go' from the time a child is born if we want children to grow up to be able to make their own decisions. I didn't say 'right decisions' because what may be right for me may not necessarily be right for them. When I make the wrong decision I have to work it out in my own way and they do too. I still worry about them when I know that they are having problems, but I can't interfere or offer advice. It is not right, nor respecting them as another human being. It's no wonder I made so many mistakes with our children, but today they both feel secure in my love. 'Ole Mom' is always here when they need her. That means so much to me—not because I wanted to be right while they were growing up, but because I wanted them to learn how to live as happily, as honestly, and as peacefully in this world as it is possible for anyone to live today. And I feel that children should be taught self-discipline or self-control while they are growing up. It would sure save a lot of grief on their part and on the part of those with whom they come in contact.

"It's taken me a long time to really understand that I had done my best with and for Teddy, and that is all anyone can do."

It is almost impossible to differentiate the several factors that made this boy difficult. What the environment does to the body and what the body does to the environment must both be considered: low blood sugar, a dysrhythmia of the cortex which would permit a distorted perception of his environment, schizoid tendencies (paranoia and seclusiveness), an inadequate screening system which would permit too many stimuli to overwhelm his tender cerebral cortex, a secondary bad self-image, genetic factors, and/or some dyslexia and related school problems.

But the clues were there early. A more all-encompassing effort should have been made involving diet, vitamins, amphetamines, Dilantin®, tutoring, and psychiatric counseling.

Teddy's mother commented that she believed children should learn self-control while they are growing up. Indeed, that's one of the purposes of parents. A conscience, a sense of right and wrong, are cortical functions. The child learns that his asocial behavior is not acceptable so he abandons it. But he cannot learn these lessons of life if his cortex doesn't work either through poor perception or poor memory. These two abnormalities may be due to faulty nourishment and/or crippling dysrhythmia.

If you are living with one of these Jekyll-and-Hyde types, take heart. Because if there is an occasional flash of normal, cute, helpful, cheerful human response, then you know his psyche is salvageable. Again, we must be sure that all of his systems are operative: enough amino acids to form the chemicals and enough glucose in his cortex to provide the energy. Do the no-sugar, no-white-flour, no-milk routine. If nothing happens after two to three weeks and he has had some nervous system hurt in his life (prematurity, anoxia, high fevers and convulsions, head injury and concussion), consider the possibility of the EEG.

I have observed a phenomenon which I don't understand in some children who seem to be suffering from the hyperactive-restless-allergic-ticklish syndrome. In order to determine if they are candidates for the vitamin program, I administer a vitamin B and C combination shot. When I call in a day or so the mother reports that the child seems worse! One mother reported her child came home, ran about the house, pulled all the curtains from the windows, jumped into the toilet, then tried to leap out of a window. It's as if I turned on the wrong system. Further investigation (EEG) revealed abnormal brain waves and benefit when placed on Dilantin®. I am assuming that some enzyme imbalance must account for this odd response.

Dilantin® is the usual drug for abnormal brain waves associated with odd behavior. (Phenobarbital is cheaper and safer and probably should be tried first although it usually stimulates the hyperactive person.) But swollen gums, fevers, skin rashes, extra body hair, and a very rare suppression of the blood count put Dilantin® down the list of the things to do. Four hundred to five hundred milligrams of B6 and one to three grams of calcium might be appropriate as the first choice. If this and protein allow an increased frequency of calmness and socially acceptable behavior, then you are on the right track. At least you have some behavior to reward positively. Openness, friendliness—that's what our neocortex does for us. It stores memory, has a conscience, and prefers human company. It controls, modulates, and suppresses the constant urgings of the lower animal in all of us that wants to get what it can, to dominate, to attack, to have sex whenever these forces try to surface. It is hoped with practice that the tenuous connection between the cortex and the MFB will become an automatic, albeit learned, more permanent part of his personality.

17 · Dropouts and Delinquents

Anyone who has had an operation is an expert in surgery and what should be done to improve nursing care. Anyone who has been to school is an education expert. Our democratic (?) society provides equal opportunity to all who can get to school to become educated. Perhaps we are expecting too much from the education process. Perhaps when our children appear to be social misfits when they mature, we have a handy scapegoat, the schools. We cannot, or will not, blame ourselves.

School administrators know that seventy-five percent of the children will move through the school system and end up with most of the basic skills to survive in our complex society. Is there a chance of improving the statistics? Should we dump the whole system and begin again? What are we educating our children for? Business success? Making a living without cheating too many people?

I still see too many children discouraged and depressed by school. They don't see the point; the global view of "study hard, and you'll grow up to be anything you want," is patent propaganda to them. If we force a rabbit to swim because we think he should have this basic skill, we will drown him or at least overwhelm him with anxiety. If we force a child, we might even make him mad enough to throw a rock through the school window.

Dr. Robins did not dig into the reasons for truancy. But pediatricians, psychologists, educators, and counselors know that children quit school because they hate it. It is not a sudden, last-minute decision, but a buildup of hate, frustration, and peer group scorn from kindergarten to seventh through ninth grade.

If he cannot read or unscramble the letters into something meaningful, and is all left-footed on the baseball diamond, *and* his parents take the school's side ("You could do it if you'd try!"), he should develop the above (Chapter 13) symptoms and/or give up, just sitting with arms folded, jacket on, defying the world. He has shifted into neutral with the motor running. If we don't do something, he'll turn that off. Perhaps the final straw of boredom plus the stress of pubertal hormones leads the kid —usually a boy—to say to the vice-principal in charge of discipline, "Up yours!" The youth is suspended.

The seething hostility that builds up from age five to age twelve years in this child finally culminates in his being expelled from the seventh or eighth grade after he calls the vice-principal in charge of discipline a dirty word. He was hoping he would be thrown out because the anxiety and embarrassment of being put down constantly got to be too much. It is comparable to the worker who is told by the boss that he is a lousy worker: "You make too many mistakes, you take too many coffee breaks, you talk and interrupt too much and are frequently tardy." If the worker cannot improve, he quits.

The scenario was written for him years ago when his parents told him he was bad. The school reconfirmed it by saying he is lazy or he could do better if he tried, and his "friends" mocked him because he was clumsy, odd, and cried when taunted. He gets the message that he is no good because he does not fit in. He feels unwanted, unneeded, gypped, and develops a bad self-image. If one is told he is bad long enough and loud enough, he will believe it and do bad things—a self-fulfilling prophecy.

A child may not be able to get better. He may not be able to learn to read, or he cannot help moving about, or the class may have determined to keep him in the bottom spot in the class order. Therefore he has to quit. He feels gypped; the world has cheated him, so he feels he must pay someone back. (Kids, regardless of background, share a very elementary eye-for-an-eye morality.) It is an easy step to fights, vandalism, thievery, crime, or at least misanthropy.

We have already noted that school dropouts who steal may become criminals, but only a small percent of criminals give a history of truancy. Truancy and stealing, linked to criminality or alcoholism in the father, increase the risk for an antisocial adult-hood. Families who have a high incidence of pain, sickness, and suffering produce a higher incidence of criminals. Battering parents are more likely to be isolated, unsocial strangers who rear children more likely to become hostile themselves. A study indicated that a high percentage of antisocial types gave a history of bed-wetting. Teachers tell us that nonreaders are more likely to drop out of school (obviously) and would conceivably swell the ranks of the malcontents. Psychological studies usually blame crime on the non-nurturing family or to the feeling of depres-sion and desertion if a loved parent was lost when the child was an infant. We throw the poor kid into the water and if he can't swim, we blame the teacher, society, the mother, TV, or any-thing else handy.

But we all know, or have been in, families where all or some of these antecedents have been strong and the children grew up to be strong, independent, and satisfied or at least reasonably non-neurotic adults. Is there some subtle, nonpalpable influ-ence, either genetic or environmental, that bends the psyche to good or evil? What causes crime and juvenile delinquency? We all recognize that it is multifactoral; can we identify those factors more consistently involved in the roots of crime? And if we were able to, could we eliminate them or at least control them enough so society would not have to waste so much time, money, and heartbreak on this open sore?

We don't have all the answers, but there are enough facts to indicate which children are more likely to become involved with sociopathy. Some are only touched with it or just flirt with crime; some have a total commitment, and cajoling and punishment seem to only reinforce their dedication. Police tell me that the game of cops and robbers is frequently played by people with the same personality traits. Those choosing the crime side are just a little bit more restless and inventive, while the law may attract those who need rules to feel more secure. Both groups know their chances of a violent death are great. They all know they cannot win. The police cannot catch them all, and the crooks know they eventually will leave some clue that will lead to their capture.

We are aware of the child's desire to be loved and accepted. If

he can be accepted and feel good about himself, and the behavior he is displaying happens to be socially acceptable, he
would be likely to repeat the performance. It is hoped that the
behavior he shows fits the standard customs, laws, and mores of
the society in which he finds himself when he is an adult. If he
discovers his society's leaders are mouthing law and order but
lying, cheating, and stealing, he will easily begin to disbelieve his
own internalized conscience and turn to drugs or crime because
of confusion, anxiety, or a sense of having been hoodwinked.

Some children, then, are driven out of the home or school and
into the arms of the accepting peer group. Acceptance by the
peer group is so important to children (and adults) that they will
do almost anything to show their classmates they are worthy of
their friendship.

I know a lawyer who works long and frustrating hours as a
public defender for youths who must remind him of his own
adolescence as a self-admitted hood—jacket, sneer, and duck-tail
haircut. I also met a medical student a few years back who admitted having been a juvenile delinquent in one neighborhood, but
was decent and law-abiding once the family had moved. His
behavior and attitude weren't influenced by parents, church, or
school. He felt his desire to be accepted by the local peer group
was what determined whether he shot out street lights and
taunted old ladies or whether he studied his lessons and observed curfew.

If one thinks he is a "bad" person, he is more likely to fall in
with "bad" people. "His friends are the worst kids in the neighborhood." If we ask him why he goes with such an awful crowd,
he answers, "They are my friends." It's as if we picked out his
eighth grade friends when he was two years old by telling him
how awful he was at two. He internalizes that domestic message,
so he is forced to relate to others with the same antisocial tendencies.

All this is a plea for therapy, help, readjustment, or understanding. My observations of growing children and adolescents
lead me to believe that the following attributes enhance "survival" in the first fourteen to eighteen years: parents, especially
the mother, who somehow maintain the concept of goodness or

worthwhileness in the child, and the child who has a basic cheer-fulness or sense of humor or at least a lack of deep, overwhelm-ing depression and/or withdrawal. I have found that the losers who eventually win have these supports: a sympathetic mother who takes the child's side against the school (less often the father; many fathers feel the "kid is spoiled and ought to be smacked"), a sense of humor so he can laugh at a few of his shortcomings, a couple of accepting friends, and some ability to read or the hope that "this too shall pass."

The ones I really worry about are those who appear angry, depressed, and/or bitter. They frequently comment that they are "no good," "I can't do anything," "Nobody likes me." And it's true. Humans like cheerfulness. The school is supposed to get them into a winning situation so they can enjoy success for a change.

A headmaster of a private school impressed me with his edu-cation insight. He has a sign above his desk: "First we teach everyone that he/she is worthwhile; second we expose them to an academic education." I am amazed by the different attitudes and feelings displayed by different teachers and principals; indeed, a whole school can become glum and up-tight when a new princi-pal with new policies takes over. Our sensitive children feel those vibrations, and if their control was subliminal before, it becomes manifest in maybe one hour. They can be motivated for one teacher and be a complete dud for another.

The doctor has learned that dedication and hard work got him *his* diploma, so his philosophy may be, "You can do it if you try, son." But I write letters to help move children from one school to another; sometimes this works: "For a variety of physiological and psychological reasons, this boy should be transferred to X school."

This thinly disguised plot to move a child out of a stressful situation usually triggers a call from the principal, who feels discouraged and/or angry at the suggestion that his school is not doing enough for my patient. I try to be cheerful with, "Charlie is touchy and hyperactive; something there has made it impossi-ble for him to concentrate. He is discouraged and disruptive."

Principal: "Well, he has to learn to deal with those stresses; he might as well learn now in a controlled environment. If you move him, you teach him that he can weasel out of any tough situation in his life. Also, if we let him go, every fringy kid in school is going to want to change."

Kind doctor thinks maybe they should *all* get out of that school, but says, "My feeling is this boy has some problems that he can't handle. He's getting to hate school and himself. I'll try diet, medicine, and supportive methods from here if you will get some counseling there. I believe these people cannot 'learn' to cope because of a touchy nervous system, poor enzymes, or inadequate brain chemicals. It's as if you were telling a diabetic to make more insulin."

"Huh?"

Deadlock. We are challenging a built-in, self-reinforcing philosophy that somehow refuses to admit that each child is different and must have a separate prescription for his education. If a child hates school or swimming and piano lessons, does it follow that a lecture or a scolding will improve his attitude or performance?

We must make growing up more fun. If it isn't fun, what's the point? If they hate school, they will quit. If they quit they are called bad. If they are called bad, they will do bad things. We don't have much time.

I am impressed with the work of the late Dr. Charles Shedd in Alabama and Kentucky. His multisensory, modified phonics, parental involvement, protein-diet approach has given not just hope but results. Success has bred success. I believe that few, if any, of the children that I saw in a school for perception-motor children in Louisville are on any kind of medicine.

But there is a dilemma here. I believe we should not give up on these children, and the work of various associations for children with learning disorders and the Kentucky Association for Specific Perceptual-Motor Disabilities indicate that the problem is remedial. But there are still children who fall through the slots because nothing is one hundred percent. What do we do with them?

In the not-too-distant past, the choice of life work was simplified for most children. If father was a farmer, the boys grew up to become farmers and the girls farmers' wives. Now the options are so varied that there should be enough different occupations to satisfy all the different personalities of the growing children.

If some children cannot read easily, it does not mean they are purposely noncompliant. The teacher must not take it personally when the disruptive boy does not finish his work. She must, however, be provided with some alternate methods of hooking the nonstudents into enjoying the education process.

School is supposed to release the child's potential for intellectual development, not suppress it. Children, if properly nourished, have basic drives to be curious, but each in his own way.

We must present conditions most likely to encourage the child to discover for himself the physical properties of objects in his environment and how they relate to him and to each other. He has to construct the theories about the world; this takes time. We provide opportunities; he explores and makes the discoveries. My feeling is to concentrate on some skill or talent that the child brings to the school. Remember, these children need to win, and by age five to seven they have settled on some adaptive behavior that allows them to handle the stress of their dysperception or motoric inadequacies. Their behavior may conflict with academic achievement, but it must be accomodated; however, our change-resistant institutions become uncomfortable with innovation. Parents and teachers must agitate and even storm about a bit to get the schools to become flexible and individualize instruction. The children's interests and their different learning styles should dictate some of the teaching techniques: i.e., teaching mathematics through building projects or using the Jungle Gym for solid-geometry concepts, a class newspaper with the class clown as the joke editor, half days for the restless ones, tape recorders for the auditory-perception students who are nonreaders.

I was made the joke editor of our class newspaper. I think my research in humor books at the library helped me learn to read better. I was the only one who laughed on publication day, however. There were a bunch of squares in my class.

Schools tend to assume that each age is homogeneous and can

be approached with only one educational method. We are all as different as snowflakes and need to have options within the general rules of eating, sleeping, and being nice to one another. Why should a child have to stay in school all day if he is bored and disruptive? Do we *have* to medicate him? If he is learning something, isn't that good enough? We know they learn better on a one-to-one basis. Can't we provide a student assistant to work with him alone? How about booths so they won't be distracted? If they get the message with their ears, how about a cassette with a lesson or story and let them run around the block and report back and give an oral report on what they heard?

We have to give options. Knowing that they need to be busy and successful, some sports like swimming, hockey, basketball, and bike riding are useful as there is less close competition as there is in running a race. Many of these boys love mechanical things and can strip cars and cycles and put them back together at age eight years. One mother told me that her five-year-old could not draw a man, but drew a motorcycle with so much detail she thought her husband had done it.

How about a work-release program? He could go to school for a couple of hours and then become involved with some project, sport, play, or working with mother or father. The dyslectic ones often do beautifully with mechanical pursuits. Why make them suffer in the classroom where all they learn is that they are failures? The teacher is where the action is; she is the agent of change and must be innovative in her approach to each child. She may find the barriers that separate her pupils from the fun of education are too great for her coping skills: class too large, active children, and too wide a spread of intellectual potential. She needs help. I'm sorry to say that my colleagues in general are often not supportive of her concerns or at least not sympathetic to her needs.

Few parents know that they can educate their children at home, although school administrators are not too happy about this alternative. Teachers are finding that parental involvement is one of the quickest ways to motivate a nonacademic child. Parents—yes, fathers too—interacting with their child in the classroom find that they are having fun because they have learned that they are important. Many dyslectic fathers have even learned to read for the first time.

Other pupils are quick and bright, but finish their work in a slapdash way, feeling the need to be first, as if they would get extra points. I had a medical school partner who had to get his exam papers in first although we were graded on accuracy, not speed. When he saw the number-one man about to turn his papers in, he would scribble anything down for the last answer just to be first, even though we had another thirty minutes to go. He now tries to do a twenty-minute appendectomy even though the O.R. has allowed him a full hour. These people are their own worst enemies. They *have* to win, *have* to achieve, *have* to be doing something; if they write a book, they write four. "Bill is a very conscientious ten-year-old. He is always having headaches and now gets his own aspirin. We compliment him for his academic achievements, but we don't push him. How do we get him to relax and have a little fun in life?"

Some teachers are able to keep these children busy with special projects—erasing boards, counting lunch money, anything. Don't fight them; join them. A wise teacher gets the hyperactive boy to take messages to the office, or feed the gerbils. But they all have some strengths. The trick the schools are learning is that they must not be all treated the same. Lise Liepmann in her classic book* tells all of us how to recognize each child's strong point and help develop it into a marketable skill or into a trait that allows the child to feel good about *something* he has going for him. If his life has enough compensatory wins, he may be able to stand the academic put-downs. If he is adroit, good in sports, he may be able to tolerate the boring classroom while awaiting the phys ed class.

We have a fair idea of what to do with the restless, adroit, bright, talkative, cheerful approacher. What can a school do with the child who doesn't seem to be all there?

And what do we do with the children who are bored, afraid of failure, and resentful of the inability to learn in their own individual style?

Your Child's Sensory World, Dial Press, New York, 1973.

Educators tell us that school is a microcosm of the real world, and that children have to learn how to handle stresses while young. They are *not* to get the message that they can get out of every tough situation because of anxiety or depression. Deviant behavior is usually the result of anxiety felt by a child in a stressful environment; if deviant behavior occurs in school, we must assume that the school is at least a partial factor. Adults have a few options in work choice, but most children don't. It is really up to parents and doctors and educators to make school as meaningful and individualized as possible. I'm sure we would need less medicine to make the children fit in.

The school is not expected to do everything. The parents are ultimately responsible for the job of acceptance, and must find activities that allow the feeling of success. Parents with a child who seems a little slow to reach the developmental levels, who seems a little more accident prone than others and who seems just a little maladroit are usually aware that something is amiss but don't know how to communicate this to the doctor or teacher. Medical and educational diagnosticians are loath to label them borderline cases because it tends to fix them into categories that reinforce the diagnosis. If one is placed in a class for retardates, he may become pseudo-retarded, acting the way he is treated.

Euphemisms like "special" or "exceptional" children may preclude this labeling, but the basic attitude of the teacher plus the encouragement of the principal make the difference with the child, his enthusiasm, his motivation, his sense that he is "OK." Even though it is only a small step at a time, he has to feel that he is accomplishing something and that he is accepted; don't make the rabbit swim.

The clumsy, accident-prone, hates-sports child must not be pushed into activities which will embarrass him, or he will hate himself more than he does already. He is strung too loosely, he is afraid to trust his body to try new things, and he refuses to get involved with sports as he knows he will be hurt or at least embarrassed. The very ones who need the practice and experience are the ones who are the least willing to try. Taunting, laughing, teasing only make them more morose and withdrawn.

School phobia, stealing, headaches, irritability, and other behavior and somatic clues indicate stress that is never resolved by slappings, scoldings, or deprivations. These measures only serve to deepen the self-hate and worthlessness that these children have already sensed about their sloppy bodies. We must be able to read and interpret the clues the child is waving at us.

He needs some exercise, but it must be noncompetitive. Nature-study walks, tree planting, rock gathering, butterfly collecting, etc. could get him moving. When he is ready then he might be willing, but it has to be on his schedule.

One of our daughters was a little floppy when she was a child, so we naturally thought that ballet would be the answer. After one lesson she threw her leotards in the corner, vowing, "That's the last of that damn ballet." It was. She swims, drives a car, rides a bike, bowls, skied twice; she can make parts of her body do some coordinated things, but getting it all together is impossible. She is a delightful, beautiful, intelligent woman; had we pushed too hard, we could have destroyed her sense of humor and would still not have made her a skilled ballerina.

The parents and the teachers of these losers must first identify them and then allow them to believe they are winners by getting them into some noncompetitive activity. I'm right-handed and left-eyed. I assume this is the reason why I'm not a national baseball hero or a famous pianist. The well-put-together boys in my neighborhood allowed me to play left field. "You're left out, Smith," was their sarcastic cry, and when a high fly would come my way it became patently obvious that I didn't have it. I would be right under it, but to my exquisite embarrassment the ball would land three feet behind me. This would begin a chain reaction: "Aw, come on Smith," then tears, then trouble finding the ball. "Throw it to first," interspersed with, "Throw it to second"; confusion; ball thrown between first and second. Batter makes home run. "I think my mother wants me." When I was twelve my mother thought I could get the "cobwebs out of my head" by enrolling at the Y. I took one look at those guys swimming, diving, and shooting baskets and walked right out. I knew I couldn't handle that.

My helpful parents got me into stamp collecting. I'd put a

stamp in the album, show it to mother, and she was good enough to say, "That's nice." I'd put another stamp in. "Wonderful." I was even into cross-stitching and knitting, if not in public. Somehow these held me together.

I was just bright enough to do well academically, so in spite of athletic klutziness and doing stupid things, I had enough good things going for me that I developed a fairly good self-image. Maybe my mother figured that since this was all she was going to get, I was worth paying attention to. Maybe my frequent colds and ear infections made her pay enough attention to me that I felt just worthwhile enough to compensate. Maybe the hot oatmeal and egg every morning helped.

But there is a thread of consistency that runs through all these disciplines. If the child develops a good self-image from birth on, he will mature into a worthwhile social human.

I hope to stir up in you—if you have a little energy left—the will to agitate for children. I am appalled that we can let our government spend fifty billion dollars in two decades on a space program, but do so little to encourage and fund meaningful educational, social, nutritional, and work programs.

18 · Unlucky Thirteen

I enjoy being—or perhaps more accurately, I *need* to be —successful as a pediatrician. I make mistakes, but what errors I make in diagnosis and treatment I make up in being conscientious. I am pretty good with colic, colds, strep throat, and the hyperactive six- to ten-year-old, but my downfall is the thirteen-year-old boy with an "emotional problem" who comes to me for the first time. If I have seen him since birth, I have a hook in his psyche. But if we don't know each other, I might as well turn him out and not waste his family's money or my time. He ruins my statistics as well as my composure.

I recall seeing a failure-oriented, distrustful, thirteen-year-old boy whose mother dragged him to the office to be influenced by my magic. He had a few of the symptoms mentioned elsewhere in this book. I turned on all my charm and persuasion, but he just sat there like a paranoid rock—no expression except distrust. He had his arms folded as he slowly shook his head from side to side while maintaining a sardonic curl to his lips. This age young person knows he has been brought to get "straightened out." He feels that although I am safer than a shrink, I am still an adult, perhaps a threat, and will undoubtedly end up on the parents' side in the domestic battle for power.

The visit has usually been triggered by some school action (expelled), some social problem (ran away), some police response (stole a car), or domestic violence (pulled a knife when asked to take the garbage out). It is frequently difficult to know if some rule was broken because it was too strict or whether the miscreant is asking for rules because he does not think the existing ones are helpful or consistent enough to control his own self-recognized, frightening impulsiveness. ("Stealing" candy and money is OK in the five-year-old who is testing limits, but in the eleven- to fifteen-year-old it is a sign of school failure, non-functioning conscience, peer-group pressure, or bad self-image.) Occasionally he was just experimenting and went too far: He was going to have a couple of glasses of wine and drank the whole bottle, or he was going to skip school to test the school's bureaucracy—would they notice?

The thirteen-year-old who pushes for more freedom at the first urgings of pubescent hormones is usually the least mature. The parents feel that if anything, *more* restrictions are the answer because this child seems to be so impulsive and childish. These young people see five years of pure hell facing them before they become liberated at about eighteen, when society by some magical fiat has ordained that they are reasonable adults.

In talking to the youth alone, hostile feelings roll out, all seemingly justified. "I can't do anything. They watch me like a hawk. They treat me like a two-year-old," is usually blurted out through the tears. Is he really angry or bitter and depressed?

In talking to the parents alone, exasperation seems to be the mood. "We can't trust him at all. We told him if he brought his grades up, he could have a minicycle. He didn't, so we said no. Now he's furious. He says he will get even. He periodically tears up his room. The door is scarred from knife jabs. We try to ignore it. My husband here says he needs a good thrashing, but he tried it and although his outward behavior becomes better temporarily, I can sense the anger seething underneath. He's either going to kill us or run away. We love him, but don't like what he does. He has to learn better self-control if we are to give him privileges, but he doesn't see it that way."

The background history usually reveals the life style of the approacher. It is not difficult to see how he would have easily developed the bad self-image or felt "What's the point; everything I do is a disaster." The story that usually unfolds is that of years of noncompliance, school failure, not working up to his own potential, goofing off, skipping out at night, petty theft, lying, and no response to the usual forms of discipline —grounding and deprivation had no effect.

Remember now the depressing statistics that Dr. Lee Robins has given us: Fifty percent of those involved with truancy and stealing end up as criminals. If the father is a criminal and/or an alcoholic, eighty percent of these, usually boys, turn to crime.

So how do we change the odds so the child I see before me does not have to end of as another gloomy statistic?

I have been in pediatrics long enough to become aware that the doctor's chief job is to accept the patient as he comes in the door no matter how odious, gross, stupid, or odd he may appear to family, friends, peer group, or teachers—or even to the doctor. My chief job is to give both sides some options to which all parties can adhere. A truce, albeit armed, seems to be all we can hope for. Somehow, accepting this human being as a potentially worthwhile person will ignite a spark of hopefulness in this loser, and maybe he can be salvaged from his destructive, negative self-image.

Surely he was not born this way. Did his caretakers or parents sabotage his psyche? Or was he put down by the environment because he was a misfit? Was he on a twenty-one-hour day when the household was on a twenty-four-hour day, and did he sense by the hostile faces that he was bad because he wanted to start the day at four A.M. and not at seven?

How much of the child's problem can be blamed on environmental factors (home, school, society), and how much is related to diet, heredity, biochemistry, odd brain waves, and other subtle hurts we are unable to measure yet?

Usually we can turn these people around at age six to ten years, but the psychological overlay is so heavy and compelling at age thirteen years that the task is almost too formidable. By age thirteen he could have lost his reversibility because his brain and body may be unable to manufacture the "nice" chemicals, or these chemicals are stimulating the wrong nuclei in the limbic system. But we always try.

Psychiatric literature gives two sides to childhood depression. Some Freudian psychoanalysts believe that the condition does not exist until a superego or conscience has developed because this psychic structure is essential to the guilt formation which is the sine qua non of depression. Others feel that impulsive acting-out is the hallmark of childhood depression. The child has lost a loved one—really or symbolically (death of mother, no acceptance, and/or cold parents)—and he feels cheated. He was denied his birthright of love and acceptance, and he will fight if need be to get it back. He lives in a chronic state of feeling that he never gets his due. All his life he must *get*; he has no *give*. He is a narcissist.

The early "object loss" may be the inciting event. We see the occasional child in the hospital at age one year who has been deprived, neglected, or battered; he is suspicious, apathetic, follows the ward personnel with eyes only and does not reach out with the age-appropriate anticipatory gesture—crying, arms extended, asking to be picked up. It is easy to read depression, distrust, and some anger in his body language. It takes months or years of intensive love, cuddling, warmth, acceptance, and feeding to turn this child back into a friendly, open, trusting, human being. I would call this a primary depression, and it could happen to any child whose parents turned him off because they were unable to feed him love and acceptance.

Our experience has been that these children so psychically deprived are in a minority, although a hyperactive child may be his own worst enemy and sow the seeds of parental rejection. His colic, vomiting, constant sickness, overresponse to family fun or tickling, and night wakefulness may force the parents to play a hands-off role, which this sensitive child may interpret as rejection. If every cuddle, rock, kiss, or hug produces crying or emesis for two hours, parents of such a responsive child may tend to stop the gestures, pats, and other expressions of love that indicate to all infants that they are wanted and worthwhile, or at least accepted. Without help he might grow up a bitter, antisocial criminal ("I'll show you"), or an unsatisfied alcoholic ("They drove me to it"), or a constantly striving underachiever ("I'm no good").

Many hyperactive children I see are cheerful and outgoing, talkative clowns or successful athletes. They are so obviously disruptive that they are brought to our attention early and we are able to interrupt the march to nonacceptance with medicine, diet, counseling, and scholastic manipulation. It is axiomatic that if they are successful in some area of their daily activities, they have few somatic complaints.

But the unsocialized, aggressive disruptors are more likely to be saddled with headaches, stomachaches, withdrawn behavior, tiredness despite adequate sleep, and neurasthenia, an all-encompassing term for a lack of enthusiasm for life. When psychiatrists write for the pediatrician, they frequently list these symptoms so we will more promptly refer these depressed children to them. The flattened affect (lack of facial, emotional expression) and/or the turned-down mouth further confirm the diagnosis. When they are prodded to perform, they usually respond with a violent act. All this is to be interpreted as depression and the somatic complaints are the patient's cry for help. Stomach acids are the tears of the subconscious.

"This morning Charley's work was messy, so I told him to do it over again. As his teacher I have a minimal standard of neatness; I thought it a reasonable request. He scowled, leaped out of his seat, and tried to choke me. I screamed, and the principal came and pulled him off. His eyes rolled up and then he giggled for an hour."

This unsocialized aggressive child is by far the toughest problem faced by parents, teachers, society, and doctors. Hyperactivity and impulsive acting-out are the observable clues; the somatic complaints are confirmatory evidence.

Usually if the child is suffering only from the secondary type of depression (due to school failure), then the academic help from school (reading therapy) and the disappearance of the impulsive behavior will allow a normally supportive home to do its own therapy. Because he feels better about himself, he is happier and his parents can say, "You're a nice person. We're so proud of you."

But back to our primary depressive—is he lost forever? Does he have to see the psychiatrist? Is that the only option? Because impulsive acting-out, hyperactivity, and school failure *can* have their roots in this early childhood rejection and "object loss" (usually the mother), many critics of neurochemical hyperactivity treatment feel that only a psychiatrist should be allowed to treat these wild, uncontrolled, sometimes sullen and depressed children. What right does a pediatrician or family-practice physician have to treat what appears to be a psychological problem?

For one thing the family doctor's suggestions about environmental changes might be more easily accepted than recommendations from a stranger. Young people may feel as if labeled crazy if dumped cold onto a psychiatrist; the primary physician is safer. The biochemical approach would seem to me to be a better and cheaper way to begin therapy.

Assuming someone brings him into the office so we can get our hands on him early enough, we have a few other things we might try first. Vision and hearing malfunction could cause perception disorders; anemia and infections can make anyone feel surly. A high carbohydrate diet might be causing low blood sugar response, and allergies are debilitating.

"Our fourteen-year-old is grumpy, laconic, uncommunicative, and bursts into tears if we say 'good morning.' She sleeps twelve hours at night but seems exhausted. She is pale, picks at her food, and has blue half-moons under her eyes. Is she on drugs, pregnant, anemic, or does she have low thyroid or mono? If there is nothing wrong, I'm going to strangle her."

The adolescent who is growing fast seems tired all the time and on the verge of tears, may be suffering from the low blood sugar syndrome. It is worthwhile to change the diet—a boy might be motivated by the prospect of having more sustained energy for sports, and the girl might stop sugar because she wants a better figure or to lose weight.

Because of the interest in reactive hypoglycemia, many families are pleading to have the five-hour glucose-tolerance test done. I see little need to have this done in most cases. It involves seven separate venous blood withdrawals via the needle and syringe, and the child is usually out the laboratory door after the second venipuncture. I have ordered this test for the negative teenager who needs some "science" to convince him to change his diet. It is amazing how sugar and junk-food eating becomes a way of life or close to an addiction in these people despite the fact that they know it leads to sickness, allergy, obesity, tiredness, headaches, and stomachaches. One further problem: Because doctors believe that the condition is a fad, and they were taught in school that it is rare, they tend to read abnormal glucose-tolerance-test curves as normal. They discount the rapid rise and fall, for they feel that if the individual sugar determinations are somewhere in the normal range, then the patient cannot be labeled as a sugar hyperreactor.

My next job, and the toughest, is to talk this surly, slouching, arms-folded, negative, and jacketed (ready to go) young man to believe me and try medicine, vitamins, and diet. Predictably, he again says, "No way, man." (If he agreed, it would be an admission that he is to blame or at least partially responsible for the family mess, and he already feels the world is sitting pretty heavily on him now.) When I ask the youth if he would try my suggestions, and he says, "No way, man," I frequently find myself getting angry—and trying not to show it. Of course my anger would reinforce his feeling that everyone is against him and would again justify his antisocial life style.

Undaunted and scarcely loath, I try again. "How about the whole family trying the protein-nibbling diet and no sugar, white flour, ice cream, and milk for a month? Then if you're all living more peacefully, we can talk about some other options," I say, hoping I'll think of some when the time comes. "At least cut out the desserts at night and try some peanuts at bedtime and see if you can get out of bed more easily in the morning. Remember, no dry cereal for breakfast. Try eggs, meat, or at least old-fashioned peanut butter on whole-wheat toast for breakfast." Sometimes, if he is interested in sports, I try, "You need sugar for energy, but white sugar is deceptive. It helps for maybe ten to twenty minutes, and then you are gone. Take a piece of cheese or some nuts for the next athletic endeavor and see if you don't last longer."

The more reluctant the family is to get out of the sugar bowl, the more likely are they all to have reactive hypoglycemia *en famille* and the more likely are the intramural battles related to low blood sugar and, consequently, the more important is it to get them all to nibble on protein. I am flattered how often the mother will say how sensible it all seems, but am dismayed when she says how impossible it will be for her to get her husband off his three meals a day and pie a la mode. (There are, however, sneaky things she can do with honey and sugar substitutes.)

Maybe I just relieve some guilt feelings, or maybe the ventilation of family problems has reduced some pressure, like confession. I try to call back in a week or so to evaluate the domestic stress. For some reason the mother is the best communicator of feeling tones. About sixty percent of the time she will say, "Everything was fine for five days. Our son thinks you're OK because you didn't put him down. But yesterday I asked him nicely to take the garbage out; it's his job. He gave me the finger and said he was no slave. I got mad and hit him. My husband grounded him again for three months. I've *had* it with that kid. What's next?"

"Are you really off the sugar?"

"Yes and no. We've cut down and feel better, but I know he steals money and buys his own candy. I find wrappers under his bed."

"Let me talk to him again. If he doesn't think I'm a villain, maybe I can get him to try some things. I've got to find something in his life that is fun to balance what are to him unrewarding drags. He must have a win to stand out against the losses. These people have a low tolerance for just ordinary living. Just going to the bathroom is a bore; it's no fun." Approaching types of people at this age especially feel if life is not fun, what's the point? They don't seem to have the capacity to endure present hardships so some future joy can become that much more exciting. Most things have to be fun *right now*.

If the history of the hereditary traits related to abnormal sugar metabolism is elicited, and he has been an approacher with ticklishness and sleep problems, my next question is, "Has he been better with schoolwork on a one-to-one basis and worse in a classroom?" If the answer is yes, I can't help but ask, "Why didn't he get some help or medicine early that might have helped his academic performance?"

The parents may give two answers: "We didn't want to push drugs and let him think he could rely on medicine all his life to solve problems," and, "We knew he had to learn self-control sooner or later." Waiting is an unfortunate choice of options, since the self-image and the superego are still fairly malleable from age five to ten years of age. Someone should have educated the parents in the knowledge that a child doesn't get hooked on these stimulants because for him they act as downers. Also, self-control is a chemical phenomenon at this early age: no chemical, no self-control.

After a couple of conferences in which the youth seems to find new and clever ways to con me into thinking he is doing well and his life is OK, the mother again reports some violent flare-up. "My sixteen-year-old is so awful when he gets home from school—kicking the door and biting my head off if I try to be nice with, 'How was school dear'? If I'm not right there with a medium-done T-bone steak, he makes a plate of fudge, eats the whole gooey mess, and in two hours is in a coma on the floor—all to get even." Now my reputation as a healer is at stake, and I grope about for something.

"Let's get a five-hour glucose-tolerance test."

The test does show a rise and fall compatible with his Jekyll-and-Hyde personality. Occasionally the graph will convince the boy that he does have a problem and he would at least feel better if he followed the diet. He gets the message that he may not be such a bad person after all. School intervention may have to be undertaken by the doctor to get something done to allow him some measure of success at school so he won't have to quit in a rage. If he has the family stigmata of diabetes, obesity, alcoholism, migraine, and/or allergies and he is ticklish, with nocturnal restlessness or bed-wetting, then we know he is sensitive at least, and our basic treatment program should allow him ten to eighty percent relief from his symptoms. Then, depending upon his response in a week or so, a decision would be made about the next step. If that test doesn't show that he is being made evil by carbohydrate, I've got a few more things to try.

If improvement on the above is minimal, a decision is next made about further testing; things get more expensive from now on. A complete blood count (hemoglobin, hematocrit, white blood cell count and differential) and sedimentation rate (elevated result suggests a chronic infection somewhere), a T_3 and

T₄ (thyroid tests may pick up a borderline thyroid malfunction), a TSH (thyroid-stimulating hormone from the pituitary may indicate some dysfunction either in the feedback control or in the hypothalamic activity), urinalysis, and a blood-chemical screening test may be helpful in ruling out rare chemical, hormone, and enzyme disorders. Don't forget to treat for pinworms whether they are suspected or not. An EEG occasionally (infrequently, really) is a help if temper flare-ups are not related to diet or significant stress. Hair analysis is proving valuable in diagnosing mineral disorders.

The EEG or brain-wave test would be worthwhile but not absolutely essential if one has arrived at this point with no improvement from the diet change and no clue from previous tests. It is a thirty to fifty dollar test including interpretation from a skilled neurologist. A positive test does *not* have to mean brain damage, which is a rather pejorative label. A normal EEG may mean that the cortex shows no dysrhythmia but some unmeasurable dysfunction may still be present farther down or deep inside the brain. Only now is a trial of amphetamines, Ritalin®, or the new Cylert® suggested. Dilantin® can be an outstanding therapeutic triumph if he is really suffering from some dysrhythmia that may be making him act violently.

Many doctors use these psychostimulants to make the diagnosis of hyperactivity and, if the child is calmed or shows some self-control, it is supposed to mean he has the biochemical problem: not enough norepinephrine in his limbic system. Because of the stimulating effects of thyroid, it might be best to try one to four grains of this hormone for a while on the assumptions that (a) it is a stimulant and (b) it "opens up" cell walls and allows the nutriments and vitamins inside where the enzymatic work of the cells is being done. It just may be possible that one of the chief effects of amphetamines is to mobilize sugar from the liver. Dilantin (Phenotoin) may have a similar effect on sugar metabolism.

Every now and then I send the child and parents home with the forecast that he will end up in jail, or a juvenile court judge will assign him to a psychiatrist. I can do nothing. A work program or some forced therapy could help, but the control rate is low. Many of these parents have had psychotherapy and parent effectiveness training plus behavior modification involvement. No doubt these methods work, but because these people are in my office, I assume that the results have been less than perfect. The psychiatric treatment of hyperactive children has been found to be almost worthless.

Because of the negative results of these programs on certain children, the therapists indicate to these distraught parents that maybe they did not try hard enough. Guilt and anger may be the result. Getting them to understand that the child's behavior may *not* be the direct result of poor parenting seems to help initiate a renewed enthusiasm for treatment.

The chemical imbalances are still present in the older age groups, but the secondary psychiatric problems may have become more obvious (suicide, depression, guilt, divorce, alcoholism). Thus psychiatric techniques are valuable in adolescents and adults to help with self-image, life styles, and peer relations.

Even enjoying violence on TV may be a clue to some odd personality growth; parents might be able to learn how their child's mind works by standing *behind* the set and observing the reactions to violence.

But psychotherapy and environmental manipulation still go hand in hand with the nutritional treatment. The psychologist, school counselor, reading therapist, or psychiatrist should be reassured that the child has all his enzymes and chemicals operating at an optimum level; no therapist can modify any behavior that is largely initiated at the lower, animal brain. The cortex is necessary; an inconsistently functioning cortex cannot learn or remember socially acceptable responses. Behavior modification, alpha awareness, modified education techniques, and psychotherapy are always important but must await the full function of the cortex. There is no point to or lasting benefit from these treatments if the cortex of the brain is not nourished properly.

Foster home placement, small classrooms, carpeting on the floor, incandescent lights (not fluorescent), and reading therapy are all helpful but are only a part of the total program. We know that love and acceptance are essential first requirements. But many overly active, snarly children don't seem to be very acceptable or conform to the parent's concept of what a normal child is supposed to be or do. They don't fit in.

When asked to analyze their communications with the child, the parents may find they are asking questions and giving commands more than rewarding socially acceptable behavior. The child learns that bad behavior gets attention so he continues this. All he hears is bad news so he begins to believe he is unwanted and unacceptable. The bad self-image becomes established. Thus without some sympathetic support from relatives, the doctor, the school, and friends, the parents may be forced to apply more disciplinary pressure to get the "deviant" child to conform to the rules of living.

It's a high-wire balancing act: Teach self-control without destroying the self-worth concept.

We have to have rules, but we must allow for some options within those general rules. The parents or caretakers have to develop in the child a conscience which will serve him all his life but at the same time build a good self-image. If his conscience is overwhelming, he may not be able to sense he is worthwhile and will remain guilty, depressed, and withdrawn all of his life. Everything is aimed at getting him to see that he has a friend, that he isn't a bad person (although that is all he has heard all his life), that he can do something well, that there is hope ahead, that we are all in this together, that we all had significant problems at that age, and that the world is not that close or threatening.

19 · Alcoholism

I have often wondered why the divorce rate is so high in families where hyperactivity is a life style. For a while I had thought that because of the short attention span, poor impulse control, explosive violence, and feelings of dissatisfaction, a restless hyperactive would make a poor marriage partner. He would be unable to nest. "Is this all there is?" is his philosophy.

In dealing with families who have brought me their unable-to-achieve-in-school child, a high percentage of the mothers have divorced the fathers, and/or have many complaints referable to the father as a parent. He is usually described as impulsive, dissatisfied with his job, nervous, restless, stays up late at night, blows his top too easily, is loud, embarrasses everyone at parties, and drinks too much. He may come home, have a few drinks, take a nap, and become verbally or physically abusive, especially directed against the hyperactive child who is formed in his own image. He constantly complains about his wife's ineffective discipline; he assumes their child is an irritating pest because his wife is not forceful enough in her discipline. *He* was beaten and put down by his parents, so the same should be done for his child. After all, he turned out all right, didn't he?

The following is from Monte's story. He is a self-admitted alcoholic.

The life of a wino and a fool: "This is a true story of what can conceivably happen to others as it happened to me. At home Mom and Dad would fight and argue, and if I took either side the other would be mad at me. Dad drank heavy and worked during WPA days on the green chain in the sawmills. If I did something that angered him, he would knock me down and then kick me around like a football. Many a time I'd go to school with a black eye and had to lie to the teacher how it happened. If I didn't and Dad found out, I'd get another whipping.

"Mom threatened to commit suicide and even had Dad put in jail for assault. I begged Mom to let him stay in, but he promised he'd never mistreat us if she would just not press charges. Well, they let him go and a week or so later on payday with a quart of rock and rye, a quart of whiskey, and a gallon of wine, he blew his cool. For some reason I can't recall now, he started beating on Mom and me. Well, I told Mom she could go with me and I'd try to make it for us both, but she wouldn't leave Dad."

Why not divorce such a mean, unpredictable jerk? Sometimes the wife feels that the vow of "for better or for worse" puts her in the position of a therapist and she must try more love and understanding—trying to ignore the bad behavior, hoping it will go away. Usually she ends up on Valium® for her stress headaches because she is getting a double dose; she is surrounded with oddballs.

She has seen, however, the potential for humaneness, love, and sensitivity in this man who seems to be overwhelmed by forces he and she cannot understand, much less counteract. He is frequently gentle, loving, exciting, funny, and touched with that free spirit—a soul trapped in a clay body. He's like a broken thermostat, too hot or too cold; if she could just stabilize him in the middle between his highs and lows. Something's wrong with his feedback circuit. He gets the wrong message from his environment.

The condition we are talking about is five times more frequent and certainly more obvious in the male, but all the above could fit the female just as well. Just substitute "she" for "he" if you like.

Is this why wives of alcoholics stick with them in spite of the despicable treatment they receive? Is this why the child of an alcoholic father may not get all the love he deserves? Are the wife's emotions so truncated by her marriage problems that she cannot pour out some love onto her child? Or, because she cannot freely love her inconsistent husband, she overdoes her devotion to her child, thus stunting his psychosexual development. The possibilities are almost endless. She may find that the child of their union is so sensitive that any overtures of love and cuddling, which she needs from someone, are rewarded by colic and/or vomiting.

But still another problem has surfaced that I hadn't considered until I received a letter from the young wife of a self-admitted hyperactive medical student. She describes him as loving, kind, and thoughtful, but restless, touchy, unable to sleep or eat when under stress, and constantly concerned about his ability to function as a student and, if he graduates, as a doctor. Her immediate concern is their sex life; he is so ticklish and goosy that any foreplay rapidly terminates in a premature ejaculation. Even if his tumescence survives these preliminaries, he is gone a couple of seconds after intromission. He figures it is so unsatisfactory to both of them that he might as well relieve himself by masturbation, which obviously leaves her a bit up in the air.

Many married men find masturbation a necessity because it deadens some sort of feedback control. Is the sexual fun center exhausted of enzymes and chemicals after self-stimulation so that heterosexual excitement is not so overwhelming? Is this why one cannot tickle oneself? Is an unstimulating prostitute the best sexual outlet for some men? Are Latins better lovers because they have brown eyes? Can an Oriental really delay his orgasm for hours, lingering on the brink?

Inadequate or unfulfilled sexual contact must be one more item on the list of failures for these people who already feel cheated and put down. Maybe if he took a Ritalin® or a Dexedrine® tablet about an hour before attempting sexual activity, his limbic system might allow him a modicum of self-control. Hypnotherapy (or acupuncture?) should be useful if he could find the time. Biofeedback control and/or the new sex therapies must be dealing with this problem all the time.

The low man on the academic, athletic, sickness, and now the sexual totem pole. A real loser. Alcohol ingestion is helpful but unreliable. Still, he'll probably drink to that. Alcohol should be the "perfect" drug for those who have difficulties with their limbic system (too many messages are getting through) and their cortex (it overresponds once the stimuli get through). Alcohol in small amounts can enhance the inhibitory effects of the limbic system and reticular activating system and also dull the cortex so the messages, once they get through, are not so painful. However, not only does alcohol wreck the liver, but when it wears off, the environment seems more uncomfortable or threatening than before. The victim has little recourse but to drink again to ease the pain of that trapped feeling. It is no surprise that about one third of alcoholics are schizophrenic when sober; alcohol must screen out a hostile world.

A boy who feels the stress of school might become hyperactive, fight back, or throw a rock through the school window. An overly constricted child might become depressed or withdrawn. Some would find marijuana the answer.

We all have our defenses against anxiety. Some drink Coke; others eat sweets and get fat. I drink coffee without sugar to hold myself together. Many doctors suffer stress to the point of slipping into alcoholism or drug addiction themselves; they know they have a problem, but will not admit to it as that would put them in the embarrassing position of being a weak, can't-take-it neurasthenic. So they may be able to judge but not help you.

It is quite obvious that Monte's father was an alcoholic—it runs in families. Alcoholics have a low frustration tolerance, so I am impressed that Monte stayed home so long with all the beatings. But he did have strong dependency needs (attempts to contact his mother), but tried to overcome them.

"I was gone about six months and hiked back to see Mom. I stayed too late and in came Dad from work. In so many words I was asked what I was doing back, and I said I just came home to see Mom. He said for me to get going as I wasn't welcome. I bid Mom a tearful goodbye and off I went again. I was on my own at fifteen years.

"I kept on wandering around the country and got into almost every crime in the book. I always thought about what Dad had said to me, 'You're no good; you're a tramp. You'll never amount to anything.'

"I was lonely and seeking companionship. I often went back and joined the folks who befriended me before."

Alcoholics are very social, convivial, charming, and good storytellers. They try to impress others with their adventures. But they are usually unable to have any deep satisfying relationship with relatives or friends (one new drinking companion after another). Their feelings of inferiority alternate with feelings of superiority, especially when drinking; these ideas of superiority are considered a defense against the feelings of worthlessness. Monte's low self-esteem ("Wino and a Fool") is the theme of his essay; it is as if he had to drink so he wouldn't have to dwell on his shortcomings.

"I drank till I was past sixteen and wrote and received a letter of consent from Mom to join the Navy. Well, I passed the physical, and to celebrate I got a pint of whiskey (bootleg in those days) and landed in jail. The next morning the shore patrol took me to the recruiting officer. He took one look at me and said, 'We don't need your kind in our Navy.' Well, that ended my career there. Next I worked on bay barges unloading sacks of rice, cement, wheat, or anything else I could get. When I had a few dollars I'd always find someone who could buy me drinks and I even got a bum ID, so I can safely say I was an alcoholic at age seventeen. I got in and out of jails and detention homes only to wind up back in the only environment I knew and felt I could be really wanted.

"Later in life I got on pills and shooting opium and dissolving codeine and took benzedrine, red birds, yellow jackets, you name it. Canned heat, rubbing alcohol, the works. Good whiskey when I could afford it, then to beer, ale, then wine and then pink lady (canned heat), green lizard (shaving lotion), rubby dub (rubbing alcohol), paint thinner, the works.

"Something took place and I tried studying for the ministry, but I couldn't be a fence straddler. When I went back to drinking I quit the church, choir and all.

"I rode freight trains, hitchhiked, and walked from coast to coast, caught side-door Pullmans (boxcars) on the move. Flat cars, oil tankers, and once rode atop a cattle car in August across the Mojave Desert. I walked from downtown Las Vegas to the city limits of Bakersfield, California. Why? Because I couldn't keep a job and stay sober."

Drinkers have good reasons for their failures. They interpret ordinary frustrations as personal rejections (this probably accounts for short-term employment). They are never satisfied, they need to win but can never quit drinking and pull it off.

"I kept writing letters to my mother. I got to feeling uneasy as I always would hear from her once a week at least. I finally found out why I had not received a letter from her. She had passed on.

"Naturally it hit hard, but I thought maybe I could be man enough to forgive Dad. So I called long distance and asked him if I could do anything to help. He said yes, and wished I'd come home to help him as he was so lonesome. I rode by bus and freight to Wilmot. I worked there to get road and drinking money. I really needed it after being shut out of a home life for over twenty-three years.

"I met a fellow almost dead from the cold, so I said join me and we'll mix some pink ladies. I bought a case and we left Wilmot.

"We both got well. I had plenty of cans of kipper crackers, sardines, and candy bars so we wouldn't get hungry. We had a good supply of tobacco so we made it fine. When it got too cold we'd just dip into our pink lady and were numbed to where we didn't feel the cold. In a town about five miles from where Dad was we stopped and shaved, cleaned up, and got a cab to Dad's place. It was sure changed. And so had Dad. Mom said in one of her letters that Dad had quit drinking and had thrown his pipe away. He had quit altogether.

"My dad greeted me and my friend warmly. I hid what little pink lady (about half a gallon) I had left as I was afraid my dad would blow up if he knew I drank. He made a call and ordered a cab to bring two fifths of wine. After about two days and nights of this, my buddy and I started to clean up the dirty dishes and the upstairs bedrooms. We carried out five washtubs of bottles. There were empty bottles all along behind his bed and all over the downstairs. He had dug a hole out behind the house about five feet wide and six feet deep; it was full of wine, whiskey, and gin bottles of all descriptions. He owned another acre next to this land which was overgrown with weeds and alder trees, so it is hard to say how many bottles had been thrown over there.

"The last straw came when he said he wished he could find some woman to stay and cook for him and keep him company. I said, 'Is that all you ever wanted of Mom? Someone who would just be your servant at your beck and call?' I knocked him down—the only time I ever hit Dad—took my suitcase and left. He asked me what I wanted to do with all my kid books and souvenirs. I told him to just burn them for all I cared; I didn't want anything from the past.

"All my past troubles and over eleven years in jails and penitentiaries were basically due to drinking. I got to where I could get more money in a few minutes than I could make in a month, but my methods were crude and senseless, for when I got false courage through drinking and dope, I thought I was smarter than anyone with a college degree. That's what it will do to you. Then you get to where you lose all self-respect, and mistrust your friends and turn to strangers and find they only care for what you have or can do for them. It's a miserable life that only those who lived it can understand."

Alcoholics are fearful people; anyone who challenges their abilities is a threat. (Of course these snarly people usually blame the world for the trouble and fights they are constantly in. The world is where the stimuli come from.) They frequently feel gypped and cannot trust the world. Drinking allows an escape. Restlessness, impulsiveness, short attention span, and feelings of frustration because of parental and peer-group nonacceptance are all easily controlled with alcohol. The drinking allays the anxiety, but because society labels drinkers as "bad," it reconfirms their own feelings of worthlessness.

"That's my past. But I finally figured out that drinking was not the answer to any of my problems. So now I have a new life to start from scratch. Now I have a decent future ahead, with still a chance to help others to not make the mistakes I brought on myself. With God's help, I'll still make it, I know."

Monte still has problems. He is easily frustrated, has disappointments and painful arthritis, but he has finally been able to accept the respect of others with whom he works. He writes poetry and feels needed.

It is easy to see similarities between the approacher and the alcoholic. Monte does not mention an attack of meningitis at age six years and rheumatic fever at age ten years; these could have left his body drained.

Genetic factors, hurts to the nervous system, and unaccepting family all contrived to force Monte to feel unacceptable, then when he began to drink he couldn't quit. But vitamins, protein nibbling, and encouragement have kept him from slipping into his old habits.

I am a pediatrician and devote much of my time to the care and feeding of hyperactive children, but because of the known family relationship with alcoholism, I have worked in a peripheral way with alcohol programs. A thirty-year-old alcoholic woman came to my office a few months ago seeking my help. She had heard that there were alternate treatments to AA, Antabuse®, group therapy, tranquilizers, and alcoholic abstinence.

She was bright and motivated, saying she was bored and disgusted with her craving. Her onset was fifteen years ago (age fifteen) when she had a bottle of beer; she has been drinking ever since. The few times she was able to quit were associated with such nervousness, insomnia, and depression that the sobriety was hardly worth it.

She distinctly recalls the effect of those first few ounces. Two things happened almost simultaneously: "I felt right away as if I had more energy; I was awake and alert."

Since then we have discovered she has reactive hypoglycemia. She must have been suffering all her life from low blood sugar. The quick pickup one gets from a drink is the energy from alcohol turning to sugar in the liver, plus the potentiating effect alcohol has on norepinephrine in the reticular activating system. Alertness and even memory *are* enhanced—for a while.

The second feeling was even more rewarding. "I felt good about myself. All my life I have hated my looks: my big nose and my crummy figure. For once I didn't mind. I held up my head proudly and laughed." She was rewarded for drinking and wondered why she hadn't done this before.

I'm sure you've already guessed what happened next. She

couldn't quit. She was doubly rewarded; inadvertently she found her "fun button." But her entrapment was her inability to recognize the reason for her continued craving.

In no other psychopathological condition is the interaction of individual biochemistry and environmental forces so clearly expressed than in alcoholism. This girl inherited the potential for developing reactive low blood sugar, but it only became manifest when she ate sweets or drank alcohol. (She also admitted to a childhood craving for sugar and junk food.) This potential coupled with the environmental or parental influence that suggested to her that she was not completely acceptable, virtually forced her into chronic alcoholism.

Psychiatry has long toyed with a variety of theories of the causation of this wasteful disease. Unrequited or at least a disturbed early mother-infant relationship; nipple holes too big (so unfilled sucking pleasure); fixation at this early level of development due to these frustrations; absence of a warm, giving relationship with some human; early loss of a loved caretaker with subsequent feelings of rejection and depression; high degree of anxiety; feelings of inadequacy and inability to do anything well; inability to accept stress or tolerate painful stimuli; immaturity and a disruptive, non-nurturing, broken family are but a few of the antecedents found in the life stories of the chronic, unable-to-abstain alcoholics.

I'm sure the reader will recognize a few of the same family and individual characteristics in the section on the approachers. Indeed, in a questionnaire we used in our own local alcohol study, the personality traits most consistently checked were (1) never satisfied, and (2) approach rather than withdraw.

The psychiatric literature about alcoholism gives a few helpful clues, but these are interspersed with inconsistencies. The conclusion one draws is that alcoholism is multifactoral in origin, which brings us to a nice global statement: In the many efforts to describe the alcoholic personality, nothing is as universally applicable as the observation that the alcoholic drinks too much. This one common characteristic is so destructive and the craving is so forceful that the basic personality fault that led to the first drink may be too deeply buried for analysis.

So with this difficulty confronting us, perhaps we should attempt to find out why the chronic alcohol user cannot quit. Many children, adolescents, and adults experiment with alcohol ingestion, but not all continue for years. The need to return again and again to alcohol would suggest some reward process. The discomfiture of low blood sugar and the relief of the associated anxiety feelings when alcohol immediately elevates the sugar level has been demonstrated. There is some evidence that in some people, alcohol is converted to acetaldehyde, which may combine with some of the brain chemicals to create a new chemical with addictive powers. So the drinking behavior is forced to be maintained by its own consequences, a vicious cycle of entrapment.

One could move down to the cellular level and hypothesize that, alcoholics being notorious noneaters, the brain and liver cells become starved for protein and enzymes. Without these nutriments the cells would not make the chemicals essential to brain and body functions. So when a drunk attempts to sober up, his increased awareness of incoming stimuli and his own bad self-image would be even more acutely painful than before he had the first drink. The filtering mechanism in his limbic system is now almost nonoperative; another drink is the answer. Why do you drink? "It feels good."

Our thirty-year-old drinker also remembered feeling better after a doctor gave her a vitamin B shot. It sounded safe and, to me, fit in with the idea that her enzyme systems were poisoned or asleep. She had been off sugar, was nibbling on protein and taking big vitamin B and C doses, but could not find comfort. It took all her energy to fight the craving for alcohol.

I gave her a combination shot of vitamins B and C, and wished her luck. She returned the next day saying she had never felt better—and she looked it. She had slept well, had energy, and her skin looked pink and healthy in contrast to the puffy pallor of the day before. She now continues the shots from her own doctor twice a week. She has noticed also that if she receives the B complex without the B_{12}, she is not as buoyant. (A recent report suggested that if vitamin C is ingested in large amounts simultaneously with B_{12}, it tends to destroy the latter in the stomach, obviously reducing its effectiveness.) I assume her intestinal tract cells have inadequate enzymes, which all her life have failed to pick up the proper nutriments from her food. The nutriments must be absorbed into the circulatory system so they may be distributed to the cells that make the enzymes that make the chemicals that digest and absorb the nutriments that get into the system to feed the cells that make the enzymes that . . .

She hasn't had a drink in months, claims she no longer has the craving for alcohol, has found a job, and feels better about herself. Half of her recovery may be that she believes she has a chemical problem and not a moral one. She is not a bad person. She can handle ordinary stress now because she can read her own body. She nibbles on protein whenever she gets that "all-gone" feeling in the late afternoon and the boss gives her one more thing to do. She hasn't had a stressful situation yet that she can't handle. When it comes, she may seek comfort in alcohol, but we have at least shown her an alternate way to push her "fun botton." In her intoxicated state she might have just enough cortical brain cells left working to make her remember what to do.

20 · Addicts and Geniuses

The same approaching type of behavior underlies the personalities of the great as well as the alcoholic, the obese, the migraine sufferer, the dyslectic, and the criminal.

Thomas De Quincey was a brilliant nineteenth-century classical scholar, able to converse in fluent Greek and write Latin verses, but most of his life he suffered from headaches and had "hideous sensations" as he fell asleep. Anxiety, exhaustion, periods of lucidity and intellectual brilliance alternated with spells of thought vacuums. These debilitating symptoms were relieved by opium, occasionally over three hundred grains a day. This allowed him to function, use his great intellect, and maintain his sanity and charm. He died at age seventy-five. Could we have helped him in some way today?

Compare this with the following story of a forty-three-year-old man who stopped in my office a couple of times two years ago wondering if I could help him with his craving for anything he could shoot in his veins. He figured that he had spent twenty-one wasted years in prisons and "therapeutic settings"; he was bitter, hostile, paranoid, and a little too old and set in his ways for me to tackle. But I did promise to use his following story, which is interesting in that it raises some questions about a segment of our population that we call weak, immoral, constitutionally inadequate, and inferior.

My Views on Addiction
Written by an Opiate Addict

"Over the years I have been transformed by authority and society from an exclusively opiate (opium, heroin, morphine, codeine) addict to a take-anything, get-high-on-anything addict.

"My character and personality have already been molded, and I don't see much chance for change. But everything that led up to my addictive personality is important to parents, because this is where the problem begins.

"I can look back now and see this problem starting in my first seven or eight years. It probably started long before that, but that is as far back as I can remember. I am not laying the blame on any individual. I am what I am through the combination of all the personalities in my family.

"I can remember my father was a hard worker, but that is about all he was. We probably haven't said two hundred words to one another in my forty-three years. He never took me fishing, hunting, camping, to ball games, fights—nothing. He didn't present a poor example for me to mold myself into—he presented none at all.

"My mother was a surgical nurse. In the late twenties and early thirties (Depression time) she worked twelve to fifteen hours every day. When my mother was at home with my brother and me, she sensed my father's lack of enthusiasm, so she tried to compensate by becoming both father and mother.

"Wanting to be a man, naturally, I rebelled against her leadership. As far back as I can recall, I was trying to do things that my pea brain imagined manly—petty thievery, cutting school, fighting, and, believe it or not, at the age of six, seven, and eight years old, lining up every night with seven or eight other kids to make it with two neighborhood girls.

"Even though my mother was just trying to do what she thought right, it was destroying me even then. That's why, when I give talks on addiction, I always stress the importance of a happy, balanced relationship between mother, father, and child. Not at a certain age, but from birth. This way the child learns who to identify with and how to go about it. He won't have the frustration that could lead to addiction. You have to prevent this from ever coming about, because once a child or person gets a taste of Lady Morphia real good, the damage has been done, and believe me, there is no turning back.

"By the time I was twelve I had made such a bad name for myself in this little town in Pennsylvania that my people thought we should move. This was 1942. Jobs were plentiful. Southern California seemed attractive, and I suppose they thought the change would do me good. We moved to East Los Angeles, then and now the heart of heroin country."

His early childhood and school history suggest hyperactivity. Did his mother hurt the developing brain because she ate only doughnuts and coffee between surgical cases at the hospital? Was this boy so obnoxious that his father would have nothing to do with him and would take him nowhere, thus initiating the bad self-concept? Did he have colic at a time when the mother was under stress because of a nonsupportive husband, and her blood sugar happened to be at such a low point that she became surly and punitive, thus transmitting vibrations of nonacceptance to the sensitive brain? Did a bright child, eager for school and education, suddenly find his enthusiasm and ebullience for learning squashed by a teacher who felt that compliant passivity was the only way to be successful in school?

"With my knack of picking friends already on their way to trouble, it didn't take long until I started using—at about the age of fourteen—heroin. I was a proud, even vain person. I kept myself neat and clean and was proud of my profession (barbering and trucking).

"From fourteen to sixteen I shot heroin, smoked weed, dropped reds and yellows, dropped Dexedrine, and ate the old Benzedrine inhalers.

"When I was sixteen I went into the Army—as I can see now, another attempt to become a man and escape that female influence. Almost immediately I ended up in Japan. I spent a year over there shooting some of the best white dope I guess I'll ever see."

Was this restless youth only trying to become comfortable? He found the drug to do it but, of course, became addicted. Are his feelings of restless anxiety due to the same inadequate limbic screening device, but now exaggerated because the addiction has produced a more permanent enzyme defect inside the cell?

"I had drive and ambition; I was through the service by the time I was seventeen, and almost immediately married. I had a daughter and was extremely proud of her and my wife. This marriage was the first thing I loved and lost, not because of what the drug was doing to me—it gave me a better disposition, more drive and ease in and comfort with communicating—but because I was a 'dope fiend.'

"This term is the one society has put on me. As I said, I was proud and happy and content until that title was put on me. At first I was viewed as a good father, a hard worker, a good citizen, etc., which I was as far as I can see. But because people heard I was a terrible narcotic user, their views reversed.

"Everything started to crumble, and I was transformed into the thing they said I was—a fiend. After things had deteriorated to a point, I could see the futility of trying to hang on or rebuild. I just went on down to the level they said I would. I don't think I can stress too much that people's views and ignorance have caused the addict to be in the miserable shape he is in.

"Our leaders have tried to quell society into thinking that addicts are insane or bordering on insanity. Out of ignorance I went along with this view. I allowed the state of California to place me in institution after institution, group after group, session after session with head doctors. They did nothing except convince me they were wrong.

"I just read a book on drug addiction written by a group of preachers, scientists, philosophers, etc. It made me so mad I forgot the title. Who gave these people the authority to write on such a subject? I realize that they are entitled to their views, but the book was written as if their word was the last. Society has told us hypes that this terrible drug has made them emotionally imbalanced, or they were that way in front and that is why they take this terrible poppy. If they would take as much time and effort as I have in investigating addiction, I am sure eighty percent would come to the conclusion that they don't want to give up opiates at all, just the scuffle.´

"Except for *The Confessions of an Opium Eater* by Thomas De Quincey, all the books that I have read have been misleading. They are dramatic and exaggerated in the direction that sells books, but don't get to the real meat of the problem. If the horrible side issues—the stealing, pimping, whoring, conning—were removed, the addict would be happier, and so would society. And to remove them would be simple. Give us fifty cents to one dollar per day worth of heroin or morphine, and none of these things would be necessary. We could be productive, useful citizens.

"You, society, and your ignorance on this subject is what destroys an addict—not the drug. I actually owe my sanity to heroin. When I was young I was terribly oversexed and terribly violent. Heroin made me almost passive in my temper, and more normal in my sex life. (Again, most people think that when you take heroin you become a sex fiend and extremely violent.) However, for a person with my previous temperament, it was the ideal drug. It seems that its effects are lasting, also, because without the drug I am still reasonably normal now. I still crave heroin, but not for those reasons.

"I, along with some doctors, believe that there is a chemical imbalance in the systems of most addicts and some other drug users, including alcoholics. Through my years of doing time and sitting in on therapy sessions, I started to notice that opiate users cannot tolerate alcohol. Alcoholics cannot tolerate opiates. Neither one seems to be able to tolerate speed or barbiturates. Each one seems to have his own favorite poison. We try them all until we find the one that makes us comfortable and seems to satisfy, or rather balance, some chemical imbalance. Everyone overdoes it, true, but I believe you could find a good stable dose, one that doesn't overload us but still makes us comfortable, and keep us on that dose. If our tolerance starts to rise, put us back, but gradually.

"I experimented with this system when I lived in California. Over almost a five-year period, I kept myself down to no more than five caps a day (equal to approximately two or three grains of morphine, depending on the connection). I supplemented this with a grain or so of codeine. Codeine isn't my favorite drug, but it helped tide me over. As long as things were emotionally stable with me, I was comfortable with that little taste of stuff. But when my social or family life started to disintegrate, I gave up hope and I went 'hully gully' or whatever you want to call it. I went over the hill into Los Angeles each night and scored. Before too many weeks I was shooting five or six grams—a hell of an increase.

"I suppose you are all thinking, 'Give him methadone.' It blocks the effects of heroin, true. But it doesn't give the true addict what he is looking for. At least it didn't satisfy my craving for heroin, and others have had my same experience. I can say that the majority of people on methadone are not or were not addicts to begin with. Fifteen to twenty-five percent never had a shot of heroin in their life. They get on it through the courts. They commit crimes and get caught. Their defense is, 'I'm an addict.' So the judge has compassion and puts them on probation with methadone. That's fine; they don't have to go to the penitentiary—which is why so many are so content with that drug.

"That last paragraph and all that will follow tonight (3 A.M. Monday morning) will probably be a bit strange. The last four or five days I've been off and running, shooting stuff (heroin, Ritalin, Benzedrine) and drinking to boot. I don't know why I got on this trip. I've got a beautiful legitimate thing going for me and a nice lady who is extremely interested in me. I'm managing a combination boarding-halfway house, and I have a chance to get somewhere. Now I am jeopardizing all of this to get off, but this is a good example of what a hype goes through.

"If heroin or morphine were legal I could go two blocks down the street and for no more than a dollar, get all I need for twenty-four hours. I could be back in five minutes and be comfortable and functional. I could take care of the lawn, do a few repairs, write a little on this article—in other words, put in a nice productive day. As it is, I wake up feeling uneasy for one reason or another. I would like to have some stuff, but it's too expensive, too risky, and too much hassle to get. I drink a small jug of wine, thinking this will calm me down, but I can't stand what it does to me, so I say 'I'll get a couple of Ritalins.' Well, that is almost more expensive than stuff, sometimes harder to find. So I waste two, three, or four hours. I come home and fix the Ritalin. I'll be fine until I start to come down off them and I get the jitters, headaches, etc. So I always end up getting at least a ten-dollar paper of heroin. I've become stuck between a rock and a hard spot, to use an old Okie saying.

"Everyone who hasn't had any experience in the life of an opiate addict is under the false illusion that the way I'm living now is typical of an addict. Everyone thinks I am getting hooked again. I am falling apart! I have lost forty pounds. I've lost almost all of my muscle tone. I feel weak. In other words, I am shot. Not because I'm hooked, but because I'm trying every other substitute known to man.

"Most uninformed people would say, 'That guy must be crazy to continue with that horrible drug. He will kill himself.' Believe me—and I have proof if necessary—the alcoholic will die much sooner from your legal drug than I would if mine were legal. I have reversed my exclusive habit of heroin and now drink wine, shoot Ritalin, shoot Desoxyn—taking anything, which is harmful physically and mentally. It has been proven that these drugs destroy cells and tissues. Heroin, on the other hand, has been proven harmless to both cells and tissue structure. My reason for switching is not out of preference, but to keep the man off my back. In his eyes these are more or less harmless habits. He is wrong, but who am I to argue? Now I have spent time in the Oregon mental institutions and prisons, and have tried methadone—not out of my own need, but because they thought I needed it.

"Although I am now beginning to deteriorate again after two months out of the joint, I am still extremely healthy, mentally and physically. If I have slipped, it is because society, the parole board, etc., etc., say I shouldn't use heroin.

"I am not bitter or sorry that my addiction came about—only that it cannot continue legally. It's a ridiculous circle, I know, seeking satisfaction I could get in five minutes for ten cents if it were legal. I always end my day frustrated, not satisfied, just as uneasy as when I woke that morning. But this is probably going to continue with me and many, many others, no matter what the expense or the consequence. When a hype gets that thought in that little center, he ignores everything and everyone. Until it is somewhat satisfied. Then he'll sit back and say, 'Well, I lost my children, my wife, my business, my home, the love of everyone.' By mouth he tells everyone, 'It ain't no big thing,' but believe me, it is. Addicts have emotions, feelings of love, and a great desire to make it. But when everything is gone and all the pins have been pulled, what else is there to say except, 'To hell with it!' You keep on saying it until you become so calloused you mean it. Then you have a lost soul.

"All this could be avoided and a few lives salvaged by the simple act of legalizing true opiates of some kind for those of us who have tried cure after so-called cure to no avail. I know the United States doesn't agree with the English system, but I do. One of their requisites is: 'An addict who with a stable dose can function in society, but who cannot without this dose, should be allowed to have a minimum dose daily, legally, if all attempts at cure have become futile.'

"That fits me to a tee. What has this country got to lose? Addiction is not going to get any less if this country continues on its course. Sure, they can put addicts behind those gray walls forever or shoot them in the head. But believe me, everyone in this country would lose someone close to them. I'll bet everyone, rich or poor, white or black, knows someone or has someone in their immediate family who is involved with opiates. That is a pretty strong statement, but I believe it will prove out.

"I don't want to turn back. I want to continue to pioneer this legal addict thing. I hope it can come about so I can achieve some comfort in the years I have left, but if it hasn't happened by the time I die, maybe it will be well on its way for future addicts. This will give me some satisfaction to go to the grave with. But until I achieve my goal, legal addiction, I guess I'll just have to damned near destroy myself. A damned few know or are at least trying to understand the problem and are aiming for the only logical answer, but their voices are drowned out by a nation, so what the hell is the use?"

Are we contemptuous of these addicts because we see in them something of ourselves? If they could work, pay taxes, and not bother us with crimes to support their expensive habits, would we be willing to supply them with the drugs they need? Will we ever be willing to accept them like we do the diabetic who needs insulin? If the man who wrote the above had been as brilliant as De Quincey, could we ignore this silly little habit?

Jean Cocteau was a poet, painter, novelist, filmmaker, play-

wright, actor, scene designer, and social gadfly. After his second
cure for opium smoking (ten pipes a day), he wrote the following:

> Certain organisms are born to become the prey of drugs.
> They require a corrective without which they cannot
> make contact with the outside world. . . .
> Living is a horizontal fall.
> Without some fixative, a life perfectly and continually
> conscious of its speed would become intolerable.
> With it, a man condemned to death can sleep. This fixative
> is what I lack. Some gland, I suppose, is sick. . . .
> Without opium, projects—marriages, for example, or
> trips—seemed to me as insane as someone who has
> fallen out the window trying to make friends with people in
> the rooms past which he is falling.
> We are no longer, unfortunately, a nation of farmers
> and shepherds. That we require another therapeutic
> method for the defense of our overworked nervous system
> cannot be doubted.
> I remain convinced, despite my own failures, that opium
> can be beneficial and that it is our duty to make it so.
> We must learn how to handle it.

Reading the detailed lives of the great and near great makes
me wonder if physical and psychological suffering must accom-
pany fame. Mozart thought that God was acting through his
brain, and he had little recourse but to write down what his mind
was telling his hands. Does pain and misery push these people
into activity that, coupled with a genius IQ, makes us all notice
them? Or does the genius mind encourage activity which is too
much of a stress for the inadequately endowed body that cannot
possibly respond to all the demands of the nervous system?
    How would you react if you were the mother of Thomas Car-
lyle, reputed to be the smartest man in history? When he was two
years old, he was supposed to have turned to her and said,
"Mother, what do you think of the transmigration of the soul?"
    Carlyle was plagued with a variety of somatic aches and pains,

but managed to live until his eighty-fifth year. His moods would swing from miserable gloom to delirious joy. He felt as if "a rat was gnawing at his stomach." He might read for a time only to discover he could remember nothing. He was occasionally irritable and violent; social affairs shattered his nerves for hours afterwards. He had severe insomnia. Despite great success, he was miserable.

How about all those symptoms adding up to a diagnosis of a bright approacher who suffered from the effects of low blood sugar, mood swings, tension in crowds, distractibility, and that never-satisfied feeling, "Is that all there is?" He was helped temporarily by exercise, walking or horseback riding. Is that because he was hyperactive and restless, or do these people discover that exercise releases glucose from glycogen stores and feeds the starving brain? I would like to know if he drank alcohol or put a lot of sugar in his tea.

Richard Wagner had a chronic skin condition (eczema or neurodermatitis) which required him to wear special silk underwear as he was constantly overstimulated by itching, burning sensations. He was irritable, short-tempered, and had fits of depression. Stomachaches and nervous exhaustion restricted him to two hours of work a day, but he lived until age seventy years. Could he have been more productive if he had felt better? Did he suffer because he was a victim of a sloppy filtering device in his limbic system, plus an overreaction to a carbohydrate diet?

Winston Churchill was thrown out of almost every school he attended as an incorrigible mischief-maker. We know what happened to Tom Edison. Albert Einstein had a reading problem, as did Nelson Rockefeller.

We have seen that these people accomplished great things in their lives. Did they need psychosomatic symptoms to goad them into performance? Or are many of the symptoms secondary to the fact that their type of personality made them approach situations that became stressful and symptom-provoking once they became involved?

Our world, and most parents, don't really know what to do with geniuses; they are freaks and we treat them as such. The artistic child is told to stay within the lines; creativity is stifled. Is this attitude another source of stress which might be responsible for some of their many symptoms?

If our children are restless, have insomnia, headaches, stomachaches, depression, fears, bed-wetting, ticklishness, allergies, sugar craving, dyslexia, and seem sensitive and do odd impulsive things, it does not *have* to mean that they are of genius potential. It implies that they are at least sensitive and they may perceive the world as being too close. They may sense their environment as a threat and withdraw; we must find ways to make them feel more comfortable before they find an easing of their anxiety in drugs or alcohol. If they have already found their way into these addictions, we must never label them as bad or immoral. Our program of psychological support, coupled with nutritional fortification, may just give them the strengths they need before we accept the morphine-for-all-addicts policy.

It is hoped that more of these bright children may find the world an exciting challenge. We can help them find fullfillment with as few debilitating symptoms as possible as they approach the world.

BIBLIOGRAPHY

E. Cheraskin, M.D., D.M.D., William Ringsdorf, D.M.D., M.S., J. W. Clark, D.D.S. *Diet and Disease* (Emmaus, Pa.: Rodale Books, 1968)

Adelle Davis. *Let's Cook It Right* (New York: Harcourt, Brace and World, Rev. ed. 1962)

Francyne Davis. *Low Blood Sugar Cookbook* (New York: Grosset and Dunlap, 1973)

Carlton Fredericks, Ph.D., and Herman Goodman, M.D. *Low Blood Sugar and You,* 27th printing, 1975 (New York: Constellation International, 1969)

Beatrice Trum Hunter. *Natural Foods Cookbook* (New York: Simon and Schuster, 1961)

Barbara Kraus. *The Barbara Kraus Dictionary of Protein* (New York: Harper's Magazine Press, 1975)

Lise Liepmann. *Your Child's Sensory World* (New York: Dial Press, 1973)

Richard Passwater. *Supernutrition* (New York: Dial Press, 1975)

Lee Robins, Ph.D. *Deviant Children Grow Up* (Baltimore: Williams and Wilkins, 1966)

Dr. Harold Rosenberg, D. N. Feldzamen, Ph.D. *The Doctor's Book of Vitamin Therapy* (New York: G. P. Putnam's Sons, 1974)

Steven Ross. *The Conscious Brain* (New York: Alfred A. Knopf, 1973)

Geo. Watson, Ph.D. *Nutrition and Your Mind* (New York: Harper and Row, 1972) *also available in paperback.*

PAPERBACK

Ellen B. Ewald. *Recipes for a Small Planet*
Barbara Kraus. *The Barbara Kraus Guide to Fiber in Foods*
——————. *Calories and Carbohydrates*

Index

Dyslexia, 7, 12, 37, 143, 159, 173, 220
  approaching behavior and, 210
  reading and, 153
  school and, 182
Dysrhythmia, 147, 173, 196
Dysperception, 14, 115, 181

E globulin, 72, 73
Eating problems, *see* Allergy; Colic; Food-
    related problems; Vomiting
Eczema, 60, 61, 71, 73, 78, 86, 219
Edison, Thomas, 219
EEG (electroencephalogram), 11, 55, 58,
    168-74
  diagnosing aggression and, 11, 195, 196
  minimal cerebral dysfunction and, 155
  when called for, 29, 65, 68, 112, 115,
    141, 167
Einstein, Albert, 219
Electroencephalogram, *see* EEG
Emesis, *see* Vomiting
Encopresis, 53, 56, 130
Enuresis, *see* Bed-wetting
Enzymes, 3, 40-42, 44-48, 73-76, 85, 98,
    133-35, 140, 162, 196, 201
  alcohol and, 208
  calcium and, 109
  composition of, 45-46
  cortex and, 16, 123
  diarrhea and, 90
  digestion and, 47
  disorders of, 174, 179, 208
  genetic factors and, 38
  liver and, 49
  milk and, 74, 78
  obesity and, 92
  precursors of, 81, 94
  stress and, 25, 89
Epilepsy, 5, 11, 113, 148, 168, 170
Erythroblastosis, 28
Ethnic background, hyperactivity and,
    35-37
Eye color, hyperactivity and, 33, 35-38

Farmer, Jean, 100
Finger agnosia, 65
Flattened affect, 191
Flour, white, *see* White flour
Fluorescent lighting, 152
Food-related problems, 82-94
  See also Allergy; Colic; Vomiting
Freud, Sigmund, 3, 114
Fructose, 89

Gas, intestinal, 5, 12, 55, 87-88
  as symptom, 61, 71, 72

Genetic factors, 12, 25, 32-38, 58, 72, 76,
    177, 195
Gilman, Ray, 45
Globulin E, 72, 73
Glucose, 40, 43, 74, 89, 101, 123, 174
  brain and, 14, 41, 44-45
  exercise and, 49
Glucose-tolerance test, 41, 49, 192-93, 195
Glutamic acid, 57
Glycogen, 93, 101, 114, 219
  stores of, 41
Glycerin suppositories, 88
Goat milk, 79, 90

Hair analysis, 195
Hair color, hyperactivity and, 33, 35-38
Hand dominance, 57-59, 183
Headaches, 4, 65, 79, 83, 96, 191, 210
  in family, 43, 195
  sugar and, 99
  vascular, 161
  See also Migraine headache
Hearing loss, 62, 64, 72
Hemoglobin level, 65, 195
Heredity, *see* Genetic factors
Heroin, 157, 210, 212, 214-17
  See also Drug abuse
Holdman, Mrs., 100
Hormones, 14, 40, 41, 74, 75
  disorders of, testing for, 196
  pubertal, 176, 188
Hyperactivity, 16-17, 20-21, 41-43, 130,
    141, 191, 196-97
  alcoholism and, 199, 201-2
  diagnosis of, 7, 20, 21, 130, 131, 146,
    147
  genetic factors and, 32-38, 120
  hypoactivity and, 149-50
  norepinephrine and, 46, 48, 161, 163,
    164
  ticklishness and, 20, 29, 38, 67, 162, 174,
    194-95
  vitamin B complex and, 38, 162, 174
  vitamin C and, 38, 48, 141, 162, 174
Hypertension, 27, 72, 97
Hypnosis, 73, 144, 201
Hypothalamus, 10, 40, 196
Hypoglycemia, 37, 41, 161, 193, 206
Impetigo, 71
Insomnia, 41, 56, 106, 111, 219, 220
  genetic factors and, 37
  migraine and, 43
  vitamin B6 and, 48
  See also Night wakefulness; Sleep resis-
    tance
Insulin, 40, 49, 94, 108
  sugar and, 41, 45, 92, 97, 98

228   INDEX

Vitamin B6, 48, 86-87, 108, 112, 115, 137,
    174
Vitamin B12, 86, 87, 208
Vitamin C, 80, 208
    food problems and, 86-89, 94, 98, 99,
        107-8, 135
    hyperactivity and, 38, 48, 141, 162, 174
Vitamin D, 48, 49
Vitamin E, 48-49
Vitamins, 47, 134-35, 156, 161, 173, 193
    early use of, 16
    thyroid and, 196
Vomiting, 82-83, 95-103, 158, 190, 201
    allergy and, 27, 72, 78
    cyclic, 43, 100-3

Vomiting *(con't.)*
    as symptom, 60, 63, 72
Wagner, Richard, 219
Wheat, 77, 79, 162
White flour, 30, 46, 97, 99, 132, 174
    allergy and, 49, 79
    obesity and, 93-94
Withdrawers, 16, 17, 21, 150-51
    See also Hypoactivity
Working (Terkel), 35
Worms, 2, 5, 112-13, 157, 159, 162, 196

Your Child's Sensory World (Liepmann), 185n

Zinc, 47-48